THE ORIGINS OF MODERN ARCHITECTURE

Selected Essays from "Architectural Record"

Edited and with an Introduction by

Eric Uhlfelder

DOVER PUBLICATIONS, INC.
Mineola, New York

Copyright

Introduction Copyright © 1998 by Eric Uhlfelder
All rights reserved under Pan American and International Copyright Conventions.

Published in Canada by General Publishing Company, Ltd., 30 Lesmill Road, Don Mills, Toronto, Ontario.
Published in the United Kingdom by Constable and Company, Ltd., 3 The Lanchesters, 162–164 Fulham Palace Road, London W6 9ER.

Bibliographical Note

The Origins of Modern Architecture is a new anthology of articles that originally appeared in "Architectural Record," 1891–1913. The Introduction has been specially prepared for this edition.

Library of Congress Cataloging-in-Publication Data

The origins of modern architecture : selected essays from "architectural record" / edited and with an introduction by Eric Uhlfelder.
    p.   cm.
  Includes bibliographical references.
  ISBN 0-486-40145-6 (pbk.)
  1. Architecture—United States. 2. Architecture, Modern—19th century—United States. 3. Architecture, Modern—20th century—United States. 4. Architecture—Europe. 5. Architecture, Modern—19th century—Europe. 6. Architecture, Modern—20th century—Europe. I. Uhlfelder, Eric. II. Architectural record.
NA710.O74   1998
724'.6—dc21   98-38522
                                                     CIP

Manufactured in the United States of America
Dover Publications, Inc., 31 East 2nd Street, Mineola, N.Y. 11501

Table of Contents

Building Critique

Architects

General Interest

Bibliography   284

The Eiffel Tower as pictured in *The Illustrated London News,* May, 1889.

INTRODUCTION

Architectural Record and the Coming of the Modern Age: 1891–1914

Eric Uhlfelder

Imagine what it was like in Paris a century ago, to step out of your home in Montparnasse or Belleville or around the Parc Monceau and see rising off the neighborhood's curved masonry walls a metallic skeletal construction nearly a thousand feet tall, as unknown in form and character as anything imaginable, dominating the horizon that had belonged to Notre Dame and Sacré Coeur.

In 1889, if you were architecturally inclined, you might have heard of a new American construction technique that allowed buildings to rise higher and faster than ever before. Yet, the structures supported by this new frame were sheathed with facades that recalled traditional design, keeping things more or less familiar.

But the bizarre shape rising here in the world's most beautiful city was left naked without any finish at all. And while there were bets within the engineering community as to how long the Eiffel Tower could indeed stand before collapsing under its own arrogant mass, Parisians eventually realized that what they were looking at was not an architectural aberration, but the future: an innovation in construction so revolutionary that it would change forever the look and function of our cities, how we would work and how we would live. In abstract form that served no essential purpose, the Eiffel Tower made this point about the coming century more clearly than any other structure of its time.[1]

Experiencing this change in architecture through the words of those who reported it at the turn of the century is the purpose of this book. The articles reprinted here provide a contemporaneous look at the collision of tradition and technology in architecture and at some of the major figures who were redefining design in America and Europe. Historical styles were still dominant. This factor tempered evolving architecture, restraining and shaping the effect that structural developments were having on design. The result was a new, disciplined look, far richer than much of what has been built since. And this look is most evident in the Eiffel Tower.

Unlike the architecture that was to characterize modernism, the Eiffel Tower was a reflection of culture and place. Foremost a statement of French imagination—which was breaking new ground in painting, design, and technology—Gustave Eiffel's design was also an essay of the motif that best characterizes Paris. The curve is evident in the contours of the city's streets, the stairs that wind up nearly every residence, the flow of the Seine, and in the lines of Art Nouveau, a style that was becoming an integral part of the city's architectural heritage. The tower's four corners curved gracefully to a point higher off the earth than had ever been achieved. Its base was reinforced by tracery so delicate and intricate that it was easy to see the structure as more than just an engineering triumph. It was an expression of the Fin de Siècle and time that was to come. But what could be heard reverberating in the future it articulated was uncertainty about where architecture, design, and society as a whole were heading.

Technological and scientific innovations affecting nearly every aspect of life were inspiring the most adventurous architects and artists to create expressions of this metamorphic time. Yet, critics and much of the public often turned away from any alteration of the familiar. Art Nouveau, Post-Impressionism, Fauvism were soundly attacked from all sides. The old order was threatened, even by time itself, as the numerical familiarity of the 19th century was forced to give way. Across society here and abroad echoed the sentiment of Marcel Proust, the remembrance of things past.

What you see in the articles that follow are glimpses into this cultural struggle—in Guimard's and Wright's essays on design, in descriptions of a revolutionary structural system that generated an entirely new building type, in monumental architecture that married technology and classicism, and in the work of a new generation of artists known as *The Wild Men of Paris*.

FIN DE SIÈCLE

Today, with events from around the world reported nearly instantaneously, it seems that change is occurring more rapidly than ever before. Most people find it difficult to remember how life was lived just a generation ago. This collapse of collective memory makes us believe that history tended to progress more slowly in times past.

---

[1]While one of the first Modern structures, the Eiffel Tower ironically reflected a paradox of modernist thinking. Effective design reveals the essence of structure, of purpose. But what was the point of this seemingly senseless landmark that shattered the continuity of the city's overall design?

But the score of years that this book covers were so rich in events and discoveries that they were to lay the foundation of modern life. A brief chronology of the late 19th and early 20th centuries provides a context for the articles that follow, helping readers to sense what it might have been like to live at the turn of the century.

Business and Society

Between 1889 and 1890, Congress admitted six western states to the Union. Soon after, the Alaskan Frontier was opened by the Gold Rush. The American population boomed from 63 million in 1890 to 106 million in 1920, assisted by the influx of 18 million immigrants.[2]

Fortunes were being made at a record pace. J. P. Morgan organized U.S. Steel in 1901, and Henry Ford founded his automobile company two years later. Expanding businesses helped forge a new middle class. Though tremendous numbers of rural and urban poor continued to live in wretched conditions, a real sense of hope and destiny colored the American psyche. The nation was literally on the move, pushing westward toward the coast, building up towns all over. Opportunity abounded.

Europe and America were becoming continents of cities. By 1906, 2 million people lived in Berlin, 2.7 million in Paris, 4 million in New York, and 4.5 million in London.[3] The shift from a rural to an urban-oriented society triggered major changes in how people earned a living, the kind of home they kept, their social relations, and access to the latest news and information.

In Panama, during the early years of the new century, work began on a canal that would physically cut the American landmass in two, linking the Atlantic and Pacific Oceans. In major U.S. cities, buildings grew wider, taller and more luxurious. Woolworth built a *cathedral of commerce* soaring 750 feet, the tallest structure in the world, save for the tower in the Champs des Mars. New civic monuments—libraries, city halls, and bridges—were demonstrations of municipal pride. But perhaps the most renowned architectural expressions of the time were the monumental railroad stations that celebrated both place and the wealth of the companies that owned the lines. New York's Grand Central Terminal and Pennsylvania Station—perhaps the two most magnificent buildings of the era—were completed just a few years apart.

Intense economic growth, however, stalled twice. The Panic of 1893 saw 4,000 American banks and 14,000 businesses fail. There was widespread unemployment, strikes met by violence, and marches on Washington. The economic depression lasted until 1897. Ten years later, the Panic of 1907 again showed the fragility of U.S. financial markets, which had been collapsing with frightening regularity—every 20 years or so since the country was founded.[4]

Politics and War

Today, our political tastes swing metronomically between the right and left. But our mercurial sentiment seems downright stable compared with the 23 years between 1891 and 1914. Six presidents served in office, one was assassinated—and only Teddy Roosevelt was reelected to consecutive terms.

[2]*Statistical Abstract of the U.S.—1993,* U.S. Department of Commerce: Washington, D.C., 1993.
[3]Bernard Grum, *The Timetables of History,* Touch Stone Books: New York, 3rd Edition, 1991, p. 459.
[4]*Dictionary of American History—Volume V,* Charles Scribner's Sons: New York, 1984, pp. 207–208.

The United States fought the Spanish-American War in 1898. Less than a score of years later, the nation entered World War I. The armed collision of nearly all of Europe in the Great War of 1914–1918 was foreshadowed in the preceding years, characterized more by mutual hostility than by peace. In 1895, the Turkish-Armenian conflict boiled over in a bloodbath of Armenians. The Boer War in South Africa erupted in 1899, the Russo-Japanese War in 1904. Italians and Turks fought each other in 1911, while revolution struck Central China. Then, in 1912, half a dozen nations went to war in the Balkans. This conflict was precariously settled in an array of treaties and misalliances that collapsed two years later.

Art

While imperial and regional powers were locked in struggles that were redefining spheres of influence and control, the turn of the century was a watershed in art defined by the emergence of Modernism. The first years of the 20th century witnessed the development of Art Nouveau and Cubism. Kandinsky began his exploration into abstract painting, Matisse finished *The Dance,* Picasso progressed from his Blue to his Pink period, and Gauguin discovered Tahiti.

Between 1910 and 1913, Stravinsky composed *The Firebird, Petrouchka,* and *The Rite of Spring.* Catcalls and demonstrations that greeted *The Rite* at its 1913 premiere in Paris were echoed across the Atlantic in the Armory Show in New York—the first retrospective of European contemporary art, which included works of Matisse, Picasso, Kandinsky, Braque, Cezanne, Van Gogh, and Gauguin. *The New York Times* described the show as "nothing else than the total destruction of art."[5] Threats of physical violence followed the exhibition as it toured across the country.

Around the same time, the Ashcan School was also breaking away from traditional painting. The *Eight,* as the school's prime practitioners were known, led by Robert Henri, were part of the larger movement in Social Realism that avoided things elite, instead looking at common subjects more characteristic of society. In literature, Zola, Dreiser, and Hardy were similarly focused.

Evolution of photography as art, the marriage of technology and culture, further contributed to the Realist movement. The first important group exhibition of this time was held in Vienna in 1891. Professional organizations sprang up three years later in Paris, and in New York in 1902 Alfred Stieglitz founded the Photo-Secession. As its name suggests, this movement redefined photography away from being a support tool for other art mediums to being a legitimate, original fine-art form in and of itself.

Science and Technology

Scientific discoveries made around the turn of the century form the bases of much of today's technology. X-rays were discovered in 1895, radioactivity in 1896, the electron in 1897. Electricity was generated and distributed in 1901. Four years later, Einstein published his *Special Theory of Relativity.*

In transportation, Diesel patented his internal combustion engine in 1892; Karl Benz and Henry Ford built their first four-wheel cars the following year. The Paris Métro opened in 1898, and in 1904 a subway began rumbling below Broadway in New York.

---

[5]Milton W. Brown et al., *American Art,* Prentice Hall: Englewood Cliffs, N.J., 1979, p. 382.

Wilbur Wright flew thirty miles in 1908. Five years later, René Lorin discovered jet propulsion.

Innovations in communication included the first automatic telephone switchboard in 1892 and Marconi's radio telegraphy in 1895. The Lumière brothers demonstrated the first motion picture camera in 1895 and then pushed photography into the realm of color in 1907.

With his *Interpretation of Dreams* and other writings, Freud advanced psychotherapy into the public mind with theories that challenged the faith in man's ultimate rationality by focusing on the unconscience as a strong determinant of behavior. He made many people wonder for the first time how much control they really had over their own destinies.

At the turn of the century, man's imagination and ingenuity seemed to have kicked into overdrive, with each discovery feeding realization of new things previously unimagined. This chain reaction was not without paradoxical effect, for everything that was learned often challenged what was thought to have been known.

With a Dickensian air, historian David Thomson observed that,

> Thought by 1914 revealed the most astonishing contrasts and conflicts. In one sense, a keynote of the new trends was precision and refinement. The precision of modern science made possible not only construction of new giants in oceanliners, skyscrapers, and bridges, but also the investigation of the most minute objects in the universe . . . In another sense, the keynote of the period was just the opposite. There was a crudity of conflict between religious faith and materialism, between nations competing in wealth and armed might, . . . attack on the old human values of personal freedom and rationality, even upon the human intellect itself; a profound disorientation of established beliefs and habits of mind which led to mental and moral bewilderment.[6]

How then to go forward, holding onto the past while also attempting to assimilate all that was being discovered and challenged? This was task confronting Western man. And once reckoned, how then to deal with the catastrophic failures that were to become an indelible part of the new world? This was perhaps the most profound realization when the *Titanic* sank in 1912 and when a new kind of warfare ripped Europe apart just two years later.

MAJOR ARCHITECTURAL EVENTS: 1891–1914

Like the attempt to select a dozen articles to reflect 23 years of a magazine's work, the following description presents but an impression of the time by focusing on key architectural events, movements, and individuals around the turn of the century.

SKELETAL CONSTRUCTION

One of the seminal developments in Modern architecture was the creation of the steel frame, or skeletal-type construction. First utilized in William Le Baron Jenney's Home Insurance Building in Chicago in 1885, the steel frame soon was recognized as the fourth

[6]Daid Thomson, *Europe Since Napoleon,* Knopf: New York, 1977, p. 409.

great structural advance in the history of architecture (following the Roman vault, the Gothic ribbed vault and buttress, and the metallic truss) So obvious was the impact of this innovation that *Architectural Record* was quick to describe the steel frame in its second issue:

> A new process of constructing very high buildings . . . has come into vogue . . .[It] uses iron or steel columns, with thin curtain walls between, in place of solid thick brick walls. The curtain walls themselves are carried on wrought iron or rolled steel girders spanning the distance between the columns which is usually 15 feet. In addition, the weight of the floors is also transmitted to the columns so that the latter support the entire building. The columns are encased with brick-work, and when the building is plastered and finished in the inside there is no visible evidence of novelty.[7]

In 1892, a year after the article appeared, French engineer François Hennebique strengthened the frame by reinforcing steel columns and beams with concrete.[8]

Coupled with the development of electricity, the elevator, and the telephone, the steel frame supported the skyscraper's rise and thus made possible the development of rentable space 10, 15, 20 times a property's size. Land that formerly could accommodate four or five businesses could now house dozens more. Property values, assessments, and real estate taxes soared, giving rise to the wealth of cities.

All this affected every physical aspect of urban form, from the amount of light and air that reached the street to the contours of the skyline. In contrast with the anonymous high-rise designs of the mid-20th-century, many of the skyscrapers built between 1891 and 1914 were the most distinctive ever conceived, helping to give cities their own visual identity.

1893 COLUMBIAN EXHIBITION IN CHICAGO

The World's Columbian Exhibition was the first international fair held in the United States, marking the 400th anniversary of the discovery of America. Chief designer Daniel Burnham gave Americans their first glimpse at a classical ensemble of architecture, sculpture, and gardens executed on a grand scale. According to architectural historian James Marston Fitch, the "White City," as the fair was known, "left Americans dazzled by a totally new concept of urban order," familiar only to the "few who had visited Haussmann's Paris or Franz Joseph's Vienna."[9]

Simply put, the exhibition was a celebration of the country's international standing by the end of the 19th century. Its power and grandeur were symbols of how Americans saw themselves. In realizing that the influence of architecture could go well beyond individual design, the fair's designers gave birth to the City Beautiful movement. In the early decades of the 20th century, this movement was to produce the most important civic improvements we would ever see in cities across the country. And this would subsequently bolster the profession of city planning.

It was ironic, however, that at the time the United States was recalling the glory of Rome, architecture was struggling to rid itself of traditional facades that were no longer

[7]William J. Fryer, Jr., "Skeletal Construction," *Architectural Record,* Oct.–Dec. 1891, p. 228.
[8]Patrick Nuttgens, *The Story of Architecture,* Prentice-Hall, Inc.: Englewood Cliffs, N.J., 1983, p. 249.
[9]James Marston Fitch, *American Building,* Schocken Books: New Jersey, 1977, p. 210.

Palace of Mechanic Arts at the 1893 Columbian Exhibition in Chicago.

considered relevant or appropriate. Foreshadowing the coming Modern movement, architectural critic Montgomery Schuyler concluded his prophetic review of the fair by observing that while it excelled in "unity and magnitude," its greatest accomplishment was in theater and deception.

> To reproduce or to imitate the buildings [in real life] would be an impossible task, and if it were possible, it would not be desirable. The art of architecture is not to produce illusions or imitations, but reality, organisms like those of nature.[10]

French critics said the fair smacked of *Projet Architecture* derived directly from the studios of the École des Beaux Arts. The architecture was disconnected from the internal functions of each pavilion and therefore from the real issues American architects were grappling with—the effects that new technology was having on design, both inside a building and without.

BUILDING STYLES AND ART NOUVEAU

The early articles in *Record* show a preoccupation with what one author called the battle of architectural styles in America. One could gather from the essays that there were three camps debating the matter: the historicists, who were relying on various precedents and or eclectic variations; the Modernists, calling for a new American style that would give the country a look of its own; and (with hindsight we could call) proto-Modernists, who wanted to move architecture completely away from the past because the structural and functional foundations of contemporary building were demanding a different kind of design.[11]

---

[10]Montgomery Schuyler, "Last Words About the World's Fair," *Architectural Record,* Vol. III, No. 1, Jan.–March 1894, p. 301.

[11]Ironically, a building approach that was "American," functional, and naturalistic—the latter element having been the basis of the most influential design in the 20th century—was basically ignored: Pueblo architecture. See, Vere O. Wallingford, "A Type of Original American Architecture," *Architectural Record,* Vol. XIX, No. 5, June 1906, pp. 467–469, reprinted in this book.

Ralph Adams Cram (1863–1942), a leading practitioner of American Gothic architecture, provided his own particular overview of the stylistic state of building in the U.S. By 1890, he observed two "tendencies" that roughly paralleled the character of architecture predominating in Western Europe around the same time. One was a "new and revivified Classicism with McKim as its protagonist," the other, a new Gothic.[12]

The classical trend, he went on to say, was composed of three distinct movements: "pure Classic, Beaux Arts, and Colonial, each vital, brilliant, and beautiful in varying degrees." The Gothic was less splintered, derived largely from the "late Gothic of England."

> [By 1900,] pure Classic has won new laurels for its clean and scholarly beauty, the Beaux Arts following has abandoned most of its banality of French bad taste and has become better than the best contemporary work in France, while the neo-Classical has developed into a living thing of exquisite charm ... Gothic's advance has been no less than that of its Classical revival.[13]

By the turn of the century, Cram observed two movements which, by the way he referenced them, reflected his intuitive understanding of their importance. The first he referred to as steel-frame construction; the other, Secessionist. Labeling the former as "the *enfant terrible* of architecture," Cram was not alone in his fear of the steel frame's impact on design and on communities, having seen it as an uncontrollable beast that must somehow be tamed. Secessionism was a term used vaguely to describe a number of architects (predominantly European) who were anti-Academy, wanting to break from the Classical movement in an effort to reduce architecture to more articulate volumes with cleaner lines and surfaces. Intrigued by Secessionism's link to Post-Impressionism and Cubism, Cram, however, questioned the viability of a movement that "severs oneself from the past—its forms and expression."[14]

If there was a movement in architecture that most characterized the Fin de Siècle, it was Art Nouveau. A decorative style that influenced illustration, textiles, glassware, jewelry, and furniture, Art Nouveau shook up the design world. Like Secessionism, it broke from the circles of historicist design. Yet, ironically, Art Nouveau was "backward looking," according to architectural historian Doreen Yarwood. "It shied away from the current trend towards industrialization. It was an extension of the ideas of Ruskin and Morris, based upon a return to the craftsmanship of a smaller population in a pre-industrial age; it could not last."[15]

Victor Horta, a Belgian designer, was the first architectural practitioner of Art Nouveau. In his Tassel House [1893] in Brussels,

> the organic, swaying, and interweaving lines of the metalwork, both structural and decorative, were originally ... echoed in purely ornamental curvilinear decoration painted on the walls, and ... in the pattern of the floor mosaic.[16]

[12]Ralph Adams Cram, "Style in American Architecture," *Architectural Record,* Vol. XXXIV, No. 11, September 1913, p. 236.
[13]*Ibid.*
[14]*Ibid.*
[15]Doreen Yarwood, *A Chronology of Western Architecture,* B. T. Batsford Ltd.: London, 1987, p. 191.
[16]Henry Russell Hitchcock, *Architecture: 19th–20th Centuries,* Penguin Books: London, 1958, p. 391.

But it was the work of Hector Guimard, particularly his Parisian subway kiosks, that brought Art Nouveau to public notice. In his article reproduced in this collection, Guimard explained his source material. "Nature is a big book from which we can draw inspiration."[17] And its transposition into architecture must be tempered by a "logic, harmony and sentiment" in application. In this way, Guimard was hoping Nouveau—wherever it reached—would take on an individualistic, nationalistic character.

However, the reach of the style proved to be geographically limited, especially in architecture. In the United States, Art Nouveau was known primarily from the detailing of Louis Sullivan's skyscrapers. The movement was also short-lived, falling quickly from favor by the second decade of the 20th century because of its costs and its moot relationship with building functions. But architect/historian Henry Russell Hitchcock argued, contrary to Yarwood, that Art Nouveau could be seen as the first stage of modernism: in its application of new metal technology, its use of structure as design, and in its "total rejection of historicism."[18]

ARCHITECTS AND FRANK LLOYD WRIGHT

The turn of the century was a time that held no shortage of influential architects. While Victor Horta was introducing the world to the ways in which Art Nouveau could be applied to every facet of a building's design, Antonio Gaudí was transforming the style

Frank Lloyd Wright's Fallingwater.

[17]Hector Guimard, "An Architect's Opinion of L'Art Nouveau," *Architectural Record,* Vol. XII, No. 2, June 1902, p. 127.
[18]Hitchcock, p. 416.

into the most sculptural architecture Europe had ever seen. With far less exuberance, Auguste Perret was designing apartment and government buildings in Paris with cleaner lines and massing that clearly delineated the future of architecture. The same could be said about the work of Scottish architect Charles Rennie Mackintosh, whose innovative work remains remarkably contemporary.

Unaffected by Art Nouveau, Austrian architect Adolf Loos (1870–1933), who proclaimed "ornament is crime," was to "renew the art of building [with an approach] that was as revolutionary as Wright's, if less positively creative."[19] German architect Peter Behrens' first generation of 20th-century industrial buildings showed that architecture could break from the past and express the new activities going on within its walls.

Meanwhile, in Chicago, architects Burnham and Root, Holabird and Roche, and Adler and Sullivan were developing the art of high building. And along the East Coast, the firm of McKim, Mead and White was crafting the legacy of the American neo-Classical tradition in civic monuments and mansions. But without qualification, Frank Lloyd Wright was the most important force in modern architecture, both in the States and in many countries abroad.

Following Art Nouveau's penchant for natural form, Wright embraced an organic architecture characterized by integration of setting and plan, form and material. As opposed to facade architecture, his conceptions were three-dimensional, with as much movement outside as there was within. In his article reproduced here, Wright describes a basic design principle:

> We will do well to distrust [the craving for ornament and] . . . look to the simple line . . . [for] the old structural forms which up to the present have spelled "architecture" are decayed. Their life went from them long ago and new conditions industrially, steel and concrete and terra cotta in particular, are prophesying a more plastic art wherein as the flesh is to our bones so will the covering be to the structure, but more truly and beautifully expressive than ever.[20]

*

The architecture produced in the United States between 1891 and the beginning of the Second World War was some of the most intriguing work the country has ever known. Why? While architects were exploring new ideas and directions, they still held to many basic principles of the past and thus preserved most of our urban fabric. Art Nouveau was largely a surface change, and its sinuous lines imbued architecture with artistic energy that gave it prominence without ignoring adjacent architecture of different periods.

Art Nouveau and, subsequently, Art Deco did not attempt to abstract and reduce buildings to a base simplistic form—these styles celebrated detail and complexity. Even the most adventurous architect of the time embraced continuity, texture, fenestration, and form that linked new buildings with the old. It was only when the next generation of architects started to declare these connections irrelevant and nocuous, and when technology provided them the means to physically abandon the past, that architecture

[19]Hitchcock, p. 470.
[20]Frank Lloyd Wright, "In the Cause of Architecture," *Architectural Record,* Vol. XXIII, No. 3, March 1908, p. 163.

evolved into what so many designers over the last decade or two have been trying to escape from.

*

The articles that follow enable us to transcend time. If you can shut down the neurons that secure your consciousness in the 1990s just for a moment, you can begin to imagine through the facts, descriptions, and voice of each article what it might have been like to live a century ago, sensing what was valued and what was cajoled, but foremost, what it was like to live in a time of unbridled optimism—when we didn't know too much. The outstanding architecture of the day reflected this reality.

> The turn of the century was an exciting, frenetic time. In both Europe and America, cities and technology developed at amazing speed. Music and the visual arts were as lively as at any time in history . . . And it produced an architecture international in its conception, but highly personal and idiosyncratic in its national manifestation. It was the last time that architects would have the opportunity of expressing such individuality in their work. [After] World War I, Europe, the Americas and the East were entering a new phase of internationalism, which suggested not so much variation as much as uniformity . . . represented by the International Style.[21]

ARCHITECTURAL RECORD
CONTENT & THEMES

Between 1891 and 1914, *Record* reveals an architectural panorama of remarkable breadth, especially when considering the limited nature of communications and travel at the time. The articles fall into 15 categories. The major topics: Building Reviews, Types and Styles, Architects, Cities, Allied Arts, and General Interest.[22]

While the magazine's primary focus was the United States, more than a third of its articles on cities were about foreign places, from the 19th-century redevelopment of Paris to the new Australian capital of Canberra. Most building reviews discussed American development. Nevertheless, you could easily find pieces on the Uffizi art galleries, Westminster Cathedral, and the reconstruction of the *Campanile* in San Marco, Venice.

The study of architects was one category that dealt nearly exclusively with Americans. Here, *Record* provided extended descriptions of the most successful and influential practitioners of the time: Daniel Burnham, Cram Goodhue and Ferguson, Frank Lloyd Wright, and McKim Mead and White.

Record also discussed nearly every conceivable building type—172 entries in all. One moment you could be reading about the "Last Dutch Farmhouse in New York," the next, about "Modern French Chateaux" and "Parisian Shop Fronts." *Record* took its readers from bridges in Germany to monasteries in Russia. In its early years, the magazine was as much travelogue as it was architectural narrative.

Debate over architectural aesthetics was especially popular. Perhaps no other time in history has witnessed such diversity in styles. In over 50 articles, *Record* covered the

---

[21]Patrick Nuttgens, p. 258.
[22]See Bibliography for a complete listing of categories.

range from Art Nouveau to Romanesque Revival. It also revealed how the execution of styles varied by nation and city: Early Renaissance in France and Georgian in Charleston. Interviews with leading practitioners of different movements offered an intriguing, if not always informative, look into their evolution.

The most unexpected articles focused on the allied arts. Literature, jewelry, painting, tapestries, furniture, and sculpture were written about with remarkable frequency—over 90 stories in all. You could as easily be reading about Chippendale as about Rembrandt and Whistler, Saint-Gaudens and stage sets for *Romeo and Juliet*.

While general-interest stories were more architecturally related, they too offered unique perspectives, from that of socialism and music to civic life and the meaning of metropolis. But this architectural potpourri also offered insight into the profession, describing the practice, what (if anything) architects were reading, the evolving relationships between architect and client and between architect and the general public. Articles also offered theories on beauty and bad design and on principles of architectural criticism.

Record also reported regularly on a variety of related matters. The magazine covered over a dozen major art and architectural exhibitions, not only the large fairs in Chicago, Paris and Brussels, but also the more specialized exhibits, including the display of German Arts and Crafts in the 1904 World's Fair and the New York Architectural League exhibition in 1911.

The curriculum and influence of leading architectural schools were studied, with particular attention paid to the institutions of the Northeast and the École des Beaux Arts in Paris. While many of these schools today teach city planning, the limited number of articles on the subject reflected both the infancy of this field and the haphazard nature in which towns were evolving in the U.S. around the turn of the century.

Record recognized from the beginning of its publication the importance of technology and engineering in the evolution of design. Indeed, it was sometimes difficult to separate the roles of these disciplines in the bridges, skyscrapers, and infrastructure improvements of the day.

SELECTED ARTICLES

If a dozen different editors were to compile this collection, they would likely produce a dozen different books. Most would agree that some articles are required inclusions because of their sheer importance to architecture at the turn of the century: Fryer's discussion of skeletal construction, Guimard's introduction to Art Nouveau, and Wright's essay "In the Cause of Architecture." The magazine's 25th-anniversary article, which surveyed American architecture between 1891 and 1916, would likely make every editor's list as well. But beyond these pieces, the selection reflects my own interests and, in particular, my judgment as to what were the most important events.

For instance, I found the inclusion of New York's Pennsylvania Station to be essential; others could argue that the Union Station in Washington, D.C., or the Gare de Lyon in Paris would make for better reading. Because we can no longer see Penn Station, because its destruction mythified the building beyond its own spectacular reality—jump-starting the preservation movement in New York—the article was uniquely important.

Overall, my primary concern was to capture the spirit of the times and to choose the best-written articles, a match that sometimes involved compromise. In addition, I sought a balance of stories in order to reflect the variety of buildings and story-types that appeared in the magazine. The articles reproduced here fall into five broad categories: Design Commentary, on traditional and evolving architecture; Building Reviews, which surveyed the range of developments reported on (with a disposition for the unusual as well as for the landmark); specific City surveys; several unusual short pieces on architects (because the standard descriptions of these firms ran very long); and a potpourri of stories that bring the reader into a Parisian charette, the atèliers of Dérain, Braque, and Picasso, and even a novel by Edith Wharton.

Design Commentary. Two themes run loosely through these articles. The first focuses on history and change. The authors of the three architectural chronologies reproduced here were keenly aware of the division between 19th- and 20th-century design. Something new was happening in both the United States and Europe. Stanley D. Adshead's piece on modern American architecture and European cities provides a broad background. Claude Bragdon's study of the birth of American design observed that it was evolving as rapidly as the national character, often reflecting that character as well. In his analysis of American architecture since *Record* was first published, A.D.F. Hamlin found that,

> Only when we consider concretely what was in existence in 1891 and compare it with what is in existence today, do we begin to grasp the extent and signficance of this marvelous activity.[23]

The second theme that runs through much of the design commentary is response to the new century. The skyscraper was the ultimate manifestation of technology's influence on architecture. With church towers having been the only precedent, designing taller and taller buildings was a formidable task. William Fryer's piece, "Skeleton Construction," outlines the technology that made the skyscraper possible. Barr Ferree's "Art of High Building" and Arthur C. David's "The New Architecture" then put us right in the middle of the debate, which was not only over how to dress 40 stories, but whether or not architects were creating what many were claiming was the first American style of building.

While this was happening, there were movements that railed against the increasingly manufactured quality of architecture. While not rejecting technology's advances, Wright and Guimard describe in their essays the value of design founded on principles of nature. H. A. Caparn, in responding to orthogonal restraints of grid cities, looks at the "Value of the Curve in Street Architecture" and development that responds to the natural character of a place. Vere Wallingford then gives a perfect example of this approach in the architecture of the Pueblo Indians.

City Critique. Brief tours of Paris and Budapest offer barely a glimpse of where *Record* took its readers. A book could be filled by these stories, which carry the reader from an old New England whaling village to the French Quarter in New Orleans and out west to San Francisco after the 1906 earthquake. Paris was the foreign city written about most frequently, but *Record* also traveled throughout Spain and Italy, north to Otto Wagner's Vienna, and east into Russia, China, and Japan.

[23]A.D.F. Hamlin, "Twenty-Five Years of American Architecture," *Architectural Record,* Vol. XL, No. 1, July 1916, p. 1.

Building Critique. With an extraordinary assortment of articles from which to choose—183 major reviews in all—it is impossible to convey the universe of buildings critiqued in 23 years of *Record*. Instead, I selected concise, sometimes quirky, sometimes obscure pieces that speak of the range of subjects and writing styles that appeared in the magazine.

Several "Architectural Aberrations"—the title of a department that appeared regularly and anonymously during the magazine's early years—were included. These pieces could be likened to an op-ed page in a 19th-century *National Inquirer*, except that they are much more literate and often (though not always) have a point. For examples, see the reproduced stories on the Dorilton apartment house and the Fagin Building.

Another series of commentaries, "Architectural Appreciations," included a review of New York's fabled Flatiron Building. The unknown critic skewered both building and architect, mocking Daniel Burnham for his unmitigated gall for having configured a triangular building in a triangular lot. Calling it "the most notorious thing in New York," the writer clamored that "it is not [Burnham's] solution which we have to discuss, but his failure to offer any solution to the site."[24]

Not many know that the *Campanile* in Venice's Piazza San Marco is not the original clock tower. That structure collapsed in 1902, killing no one, remarkably, but setting off building inspections and rehabilitations citywide. The article on the *Campanile* provides an account of why time momentarily stopped in San Marco.

How much we don't know about plans that were never realized could fill volumes. In the "Notes and Comments" department found in the back pages of the magazine were briefs about projects in the making. Two articles here tell of a Lincoln Memorial different from the one we know and of a street that would run counter to New York's Broadway. The "Crossway," as it was known, was to link Penn Station with Grand Central Terminal. Had the cut been made, West 37th Street—where Broadway and the Crossway would have crossed—would likely have become New York's *Etoile* and Times Square just another interesting intersection.

The only formal building review included in this collection is of a wonderfully eccentric 65-room residence designed by its owner, Henry C. Mercer. The house is a mixture of what at best could be referred to as suggested styles, making it appear as a conglomeration of meandering additions inspired by old European castles. Embracing traditional building and modern construction, this "personal architecture . . . flies defiantly in the face of all precedent, but in an equal number of points its growth is from stronger and better based convictions than [those which] govern the greater part of our more widely accepted American architecture."[25] The review is one of the most fascinating published in *Record*—and one of the best written.

Architects. *Record* provides extensive descriptions of contemporary architects, along with essays on some well-known designers of earlier times, including Palladio and Michelangelo. The two pieces reproduced here were anomalies, unlike the typical firm descriptions that ran long and were full of illustrations. One would imagine the architect of New York's Dakota Apartments and Plaza Hotel to have been a rather celebrated fig-

---

[24]"The Flatiron Building," *Architectural Record,* Vol. XII, No. 5, October 1902, pp. 528–536.
[25]W. T. Taylor, "Personal Architecture," *Architectural Record,* Vol. XXXIII, No. 3, March 1913, p. 243.

ure. Yet, most would not know who Henry Janeway Hardenberg was. The conversation with him allows us to hear in contemporaneous words and thoughts the salient issues with which architects were struggling.[26]

While implying gossipy content, the "Intimate Letters of Stanford White" provides a personal look into the thoughts of one of the most celebrated architects of the day, his friendship with Augustus Saint-Gaudens, and the events that were to lead to his untimely death. The article containing these letters, edited by Saint-Gaudens' son, was the last of a series of three installments that appeared in consecutive issues in 1911.

General Interest. When first published, *Record* sought a wide audience. It was not exclusively for the profession. Its agenda was to tell about the state of the fine arts as they related to architecture. As a result, we find a wonderful collection of stories. And those farthest removed from architecture were often the most delightful to read.

The "Wild Men of Paris," by Gelett Burgess, takes us into the *Salon des Independents* in Paris, where Burgess realizes that he has "entered a new universe of ugliness. And, ever since, [he has] been mentally standing on [his] head" to figure out what in the world the *Fauves* were up to. By the end of his journey through cafés, exhibitions, and ateliers, Burgess finds that the renegades were indeed not so mad. With remarkable parallel to Art Nouveau, the *Fauves*' art,

> is the product of an overplus [sic] of life and energy, not of the degeneration of stagnant emotions . . . an attempt at expression, rather than satisfaction; it is alive and kicking, not a dead thing, frozen into a convention. And, as such, it challenges the academicians to show a similar fervor . . . to set one thinking. And anything that does that surely has its place in civilization.[27]

The École des Beaux Arts in Paris was the most influential design school of its day, attracting students from around the world, including many who were to become some of America's best-known architects. The École gave shape to American Classicism. In contrast with the series of articles that documented the institution's status, George Chappel's charming tale brings us into the studio life of the École, where we learn how architects are made. More brutal than the "comps" for medicine or law, the charette is the sleepless, nerve-wrecking process that burns both midnight oil and students' psyches, proving that architecture, above all other professions, is a labor of love and lunacy. And any recent graduate will verify that training for this seemingly genteel profession has not changed much since Chappel's days at the École.

We end with Herbert Croly's look at architecture in contemporary fiction, finding that at least in America, the architect had finally gained sufficient status as to merit literary consideration. Debate over good versus expedient design, of responsibility versus the unconscionable, was the way architects were often depicted. This suggested that the profession's most challenging issues were those linked to morality, as though the architect was the protector of our lost innocence. Perhaps then it was no surprise that the most celebrated novel about an architect, Ayn Rand's *The Fountainhead*, was a tale of principles preserved.

[26]A more extensive look at Hardenberg's work is found in Montgomery Schuyler's monograph [January–March 1897, pp. 335–375.]
[27]Gelett Burgess, "The Wild Men of Paris," *Architectural Record,* Vol. XXVII, No. 5, May 1910, p. 414.

The Architect and the Critic

I have been troubled always by the utter lack of rational explanation as to why, to-day, so great a distance separates the artist from the critic in matters architectural. Certainly we expect difference wherever, taste is concerned. Who is not ready to meet, even to welcome, in all artistical discussions the charming obliquities of the Personal Equation and the infinite variety of the kalidescopic Point of View? But the "artistic variable" in any one of its multitudinous manifestations should not legitimately account in our judgments for more than for distinctions, discriminations, modifications — divergencies which, no matter how extreme they may be, still stop this side of fundamental differences. All that falls further over, as it were, on the other side of this line, and therefore really is contradictory or antithetical surely should not be regarded as coming fairly within the operation of the rule of De Gustibus or anything of the kind. Rather should too wide a divergence of opinion create instantly a fair presumption that all parties to the difference stand in immediate need, not of further argumentation, but of a searching examination of their fundamental principles. So I take it, there must be somewhere a false element or (to switch the simile) an undigested particle in the complete opposition that exists between contemporary architectural practice and contemporary architectural criticism.

"Architecture," the critic pronounces, "is dead. It is not any more a living art. It is a sort of man millinery—little better. The Ladies' Home Journal' tells my women-folk that skirts will be cut full this spring, or after the pompadour manner, and can I not see by the common practice that cornices are heavier this year and worn lower; the colossal order is in vogue and so forth. Do not tell me that the modiste and the architect do not meet on a common ground. Architecture is defunct." This may be so. On consideration, however, I ask how can I be sure of it, for the practice of architecture or the attempt to practice it continues. Indeed, with the critic's speech, and the tone of it ringing in my ears, I can almost with greater certainty bring myself to the belief that the defunct one is criticism. Yet, I know that conclusion is not true either. The very bitterness of the reproach against modern architecture indicates reaction. The dead do not indict the dead. But the phenomena remains—the architects on one side, the critics on the other. And the separation itself is not the deplorable aspect of the situation. The dark side of the opposition is the indifference, the real indifference, of the critic to all the architect does, or tries to do. And, on the other hand, we have to lament the complete apathy of the architect towards wellnigh everything the critic can conceivably say—except praise, and that he may lay on with a trowel. Apparently the architect has completely departed from the intellectual highway whereon (to transmute old Hooker's phrase) "the general and perpetual voice of man is as the sentence of God Himself," and the critic has retired from the Present and cloistered himself somewhere in the Past, making of architecture wholly a spectacle, an historical panorama, not (be the result artistically excellent or otherwise) a real and continuing element of social and æsthetic evolution.

Of course, the present condition of the architect's mind is disclosed best by his buildings. Very few members of the profession are at all able to "explain themselves." If any individual succeeds in formulating himself, or even some of his factors, and understanding his own practice, the resultant theory, description or explanation is wonderfully vague, and usually is so tenuous that it cannot be resolved into useful concrete

1

terms that may be passed, like a working tool, from hand to hand. Yes! If we would know the architect we must confine ourselves strictly to the building. But the critic! He is harder to get at. He may be "a terror for his size," but the race is not numerous. Are there a score of competent exponents of the theoretical side of architecture in the country? I don't know why I put the number at a "score" instead of a dozen or less, unless it be that one would be careful to eject the element of the ungracious from even a rough calculation. But, really, apart from a few names that we all know, who are our critics? No doubt much writing is done for architectural journals. There are also "papers" delivered before Society meetings. But, I think, we all agree these utterances are, in the mass, pretty poor stuff—straw with little grain. Perhaps we find an explanation for this barren state of affairs in the statement recently made to the head of a publishing firm by one of our busiest (should I not say, therefore, one of our greatest?) architects: "We've no time to read. All we need is pictures just to see what the 'other fellow' is up to." The man who spoke thus was not entirely fair, even to himself, but the fact remains that the critical body with us is so small, so withdrawn, so utterly "in opposition," it is impossible to produce sufficient testimony from American sources to establish indubitably the exact whereabouts of the "critical position" in regard to the mass of contemporary architecture. Lacking "domestic" evidence, no good American will object if we invite witnesses from France. It is somewhat of a boast with us to-day that we are near neighbors artistically to Paris. Even those who deplore the fundamental folly of the Greek Revival, the Gothic Revival, the revivals Romanesque, Queen Anne, and Classical, assure us that there is a special virtue in going to France for our Architecture, for they say Modern Architecture is really to be found there as a living thing. In that happy capital the art is taught and practised. To this belief is due the fact that after many "revivals" we have

now instead an "importation," which is not only supposed to be a very vital addition to our artistical possessions, but something so essentially different from our attempted rifacimenti of the past that the claims made for the Gothic acquisition pass over, in a sense, into the critical field itself. The critic who said there was nothing fundamental in the Gothic or any other of our "revivals" that would be permanent was scorned of the passionate revivalist, and then justified by the fate of the revival. When he speaks likewise now regarding the French importation he is supposed to be dumbfounded by the appeal to Cæsar. It is French! And the French, you know, is the living modern form of architecture.

In order, therefore, to reform, assert and establish the "Critical Position" upon a broader basis than the United States alone affords, let us call in some alien witnesses. There is much discussion of architcceture in French literature to-day, and let it be said at once, much of current French criticism has the same antagonism to current architecture, possesses the same pessimistic note that one observes in American criticism. De Baudot says: "Architecture is dead; our architects have killed it." H. Fierens-Gevaert applauds and adds: "We know passably how to compose a Roman palace, but we do not know how to create a house." Maquet, J. K. Huysmans and others express the same opinion. Henry Provensal assures the world that we can put in comparison with the great works of art only "pastiches médiocres." Pastiche! Banal! Mediocrity!—these are the words of judgment sown up and down the pages of current French criticism in regard to current French architecture. The critics across the water seem to be quite convinced that the modern architect proceeds in his work after the manner of the good stylist "who made a phrase and then sought something to put into it." The architect's case is diagnosed with painful unanimity to be one of brain atrophied by lack of effort, by a love for mere style devoted too exclusively to the work of past epochs. Victor Hugo said, but with another sense, "the book has killed the building." The Latin language is not a living speech, and we are told the architect, if he would work greatly must————. Well! Here is the quick of the subject, and it would be wiser for me to let the French authorities continue to speak themselves: "Architecture must discover the rational use of modern materials—iron, concrete, the glazed and enamelled brick, for example—and achieve a harmonious union of these new elements with the traditional elements—stone, brick, wood. This 'mis-en-œuvre' and these combinations will transform the repertoire of forms, lines, colors, and revivify the art of building. The Architect has before all to pre-occupy himself with the plastic qualities of his materials; he should feel, dominate those resources of construction and draw from them expressive results. It is by rebecoming constructor that the architect will rebecome artist." Undoubtedly this is the modern critical attitude towards modern architecture. Yet the architect is deaf. If he is artist at all he is repulsed by this wholesome, may I say? materialistic doctrine of progress. His attitude is rather that of Ingres toward music: "What seduces me is the design, the line." If he does not adopt quite so "intense" an incorporeal attitude he is likely to say with Taine: "Really to change any conception of a thing so general as form, what a change must be effected in the human brain." No doubt! And the critic would rejoin: "I am only pointing the direction that change must take if it is to be fruitful. Nature does not abandon Tradition or the Past;

nevertheless she does not reproduce the extinct Æpiornis. Some adhesion to precedent is necessary, and means no more than an assertion of the validity of some experience. Greek and Gothic may be the settled precedents of good architecture, but let them be no more to us than 'points de repère.' American architecture depends too much upon a factitious inspiration. There is no mordant in our designs which have not bitten into the material. What, indeed, shall we say of an architecture that has never been established or conditioned by necessity. In recognizing what it is we also recognize that it might have been almost anything else. Thus, I fancy, the critic would, if he could, bring the architect to the Vicar of Wakefield's frame of mind: "To say the truth, I was tired of being always wise," and to Goethe's notion that no artist should say that reality lacks poetical interest, for he proves his vocation by winning from a common subject an interesting side. And by winning this interesting side from modern materials and modern necessities, the modern architect will be working as artists in other great epochs have worked, and having by these means established modern architecture in a vital form, he will come by and by to laugh at the archæological-architect, the maker of pastiche, the copyist, and sing with Holmes:

I know it is a sin
For me to sit and grin
    At him here.
But the old three-cornered hat,
And the breeches and all that
    Are so queer.

H. W. Desmond.

THE
ARCHITECTVRAL
RECORD

VOLVME XL

NVMBER I

JVLY, 1916

TWENTY-FIVE YEARS OF
AMERICAN ARCHITECTVRE

By A. D. F. Hamlin

FIFTY years ago the close of our Civil War was but one year in the past. If we divide the half century since then in two, the year 1891 may be fitly taken as marking the close of the early renascence of American architecture and the beginning of a new period of activity and progress. If this period has been less remarkable than that which preceded, in the contrast between its earlier and later years, it has certainly been extraordinary in the extent and quality of the works it has seen rising from their foundations. Only when we consider concretely what was in existence in 1891 and compare it with what is in existence today, do we begin to grasp the extent and significance of this marvelous activity.

The first ten years of the half-century saw little or no emergence from the abysmal depths to which our architecture had sunk in the Civil War period. It was in 1876 that the awakening began. Trinity Church in Boston, the Philadelphia Centennial, the rise of H. H. Richardson, the maturing of the work of architects like R. M. Hunt, George B. Post, McKim, Mead and White, Peabody and Stearns, Ware, Van Brunt and Howe, Burnham and Root and others; the entrance on the stage of architectural practice of scores of trained young men newly from Paris; the establishment of the Columbia and other schools of architecture, the opening of new art museums and schools and the expansion of old ones, all these imparted to the architecture of 1876-1891 an exhilaration, an enthusiasm as of a host winning new conquests, which the older men of the profession can recall, but of which the younger men can have little conception. That period was marked by the imma-

THE CONGRESSIONAL LIBRARY, WASHING-
TON, D. C. SMITHMEYER & PELZ AND
EDWARD PEARCE CASEY, ARCHITECTS.

turity, the enthusiastic confidence of youth, less conscious of its deficiencies than of its opportunities.

The profession has in these last twenty-five years grown more mature, and also more sophisticated, more self-conscious. There are a hundred capable architects now where there were ten in 1891—and the ranks are beginning to be over-crowded. The actual achievement has been vastly greater than in the preceding quarter-century; its average performance is vastly superior, its greater master-pieces undoubtedly surpass those of that earlier time; the general public taste has notably risen to a higher level. But the earlier enthusiasm has largely evaporated. The requirements laid upon the architect have enormously increased the complexity of his task, and the struggle of competition has become intense beyond the limits of a generous and enthusiastic emulation. The commercializing of large building operations has raised new and often embarrassing problems of professional ethics and practice.

Moreover, the most pressing needs of the nation have been measurably supplied. In the earlier period, the extraordinary awakening of the country to its artistic destitution gave occasion for an equally extraordinary demand for new and better buildings for existing needs. A relatively small body of trained architects had all they could do to supply at the same time this new provision for existing needs, and also that for the constantly increasing new needs of growing communities and freshly-created institutions. The country was prosperous. The "New West" and "New South" were rapidly developing, and in spite of the activities of the Knights of Labor, building operations were not greatly disturbed.

All these conditions have changed in the last quarter-century. The "panics" of 1893 and 1907 sadly checked the tide of architectural activity. Strikes and lockouts on a colossal scale, and during the last two sad years the frightful war in Europe, have again and again thrown the financial and the architectural world into confusion. The tremendous tide of western development reached its flood years ago, and if it has not begun to ebb,

it is at least quiescent. The country has been fairly well supplied with buildings; overbuilding is complained of in some of the great centers. The relatively diminished demand for new buildings falls upon a greatly increased army of capable architects, among whom the prizes are very unequally distributed. It is much harder now than in 1891 for a young architect to start in independent practice, and his chances of securing important commissions are relatively smaller. There are more big firms to absorb these than there were then, and more young architects like himself to compete for what does not go to their big rivals. Undoubtedly the prospects are less certain, less alluring than they used to be.

On the other hand, the American architect of the last twenty-five years has enjoyed, and enjoys today in increasing measure, a host of advantages denied to the men of earlier days. The facilities for study, the educational resources, have been immensely increased. The volume of architectural literature available in libraries has grown tenfold. The Society of Beaux-Arts Architects has provided every section of the country with *ateliers* and stimulating opportunities for self-improvement in design and draftsmanship. A remarkable advance in the public taste and in standards of performance has made possible a quality of work which was out of the question twenty-five years ago except in a very few centers, and only in exceptional cases in these. The architect of today has at his disposal materials and resources both for construction and decoration, which have been created within the quarter-century. Competitions have been systematized under regulations which have greatly reduced the scandalous practices that used to be rife. The whole profession of architecture has been raised to a higher level in the public esteem as well as in the tone and standards of its own practice. The American Institute and other organized bodies of architects have developed, throughout the country, an *esprit du corps,* a solidarity, a community of interest, which have more than kept pace with the increasing intensity of competition.

II.

The most noticeable features of our architectural progress during the last twenty-five years have been the development of steel skeleton construction and the influence of several great exhibitions, especially of that at Chicago in 1893. The steel skeleton was born and first developed in Chicago. This statement is made despite the fact that in 1888 the late L. A. Buffington of Minneapolis patented a system of metallic skeleton construction which embodied many features of the present system. But most of these features were not new; each had been used in varying forms in earlier buildings, and the Buffington column was an unscientific laminated affair of flat plates, wastefully and inefficiently combined. Mr. Buffington failed to induce reputable lawyers to prosecute his suits for infringement against Chicago and New York architects. Whatever may have been the merit of his claims of priority in the conception of the steel skeleton, it was the Chicago architects Jenney and Mundie who first gave the conception practical form and carried it into successful execution: to them belongs the credit for its design in its essential features. Thus it is from the metropolis of the Middle West that the two most potent forces emanated that have transformed modern American architecture.

The steel skeleton was really born in 1889; but the year 1891 saw it accepted as more than a mere experiment, and we may say that from that year dates its definitive adoption in American architecture. It is fair to consider it as the fourth of the great structural advances which have given architecture really new resources. The Roman vault for the first time made vastness of unencumbered space attainable. The Gothic ribbed vault and flying arch and buttress created the masonry skeleton and made possible the majestic loftiness and airy lightness of the medieval cathedral: another new architecture was created. The metallic truss, developed towards the middle of the last century, permitted a wholly new spaciousness and lightness of construction: our vast exhibition halls,

train-houses and armories would have been impossible without it; again a new architecture came into existence, hardly recognized as a new architecture. The steel skeleton, the last of the four developments, has brought into being a new loftiness and lightness of construction; it has freed architecture from the limitations of massive walls which had for ages kept it from soaring otherwise than in the frail and beautiful but practically useless form of the spire. We have not yet solved the problem of the ideal artistic treatment of the sky-scraper, but we have gone a long way towards it; and meanwhile our architecture has been endowed with wholly new resources and possibilities.

If the influence of the Columbian Exhibition was less revolutionary than that of the invention of the steel skeleton, it was nevertheless very far-reaching. The ten architects who collaborated in that remarkable enterprise, in agreeing to adopt a uniform cornice line and a general neo-classic or Renaissance style for the exteriors of the chief buildings, signed the death-warrant of the still lingering Richardsonian Romanesque. The "White City" was scoffed at by many of our French visitors as nothing but "Ecole" *projet* architecture. In Europe the movement of protest against the academic and traditional had begun; the visitors were surprised and disappointed to find us still in the fetters of the bondage they were trying to throw off. They failed to appreciate the fact that we had never yet been under this bondage; that this was the first time in our history, at least since Thomas Jefferson's modest experiment at Charlottesville, that our architects had had an opportunity to design, or our people to see, a monumental group of buildings planned as an *ensemble;* the first time that they had seen such buildings set in an environment of gardens and architectural and sculptural adjuncts designed to enhance the total effect. The impression it produced was extraordinary. The grandeur of scale and the intrinsic beauty of the Fair alike elicited universal enthusiasm. There were some, it is true, who deplored the whole scheme and character of the display, as false in principle, un-American, meretricious, and they regretted the imposition upon our people of French ideas and of a "façade architecture" of Renaissance forms as a substitute for thoughtful, original design proceeding logically from American requirements to solutions specially fitted to them. The late Montgomery Schuyler expressed this regret forcefully in his article on "United States, Architecture of" in the Sturgis *Dictionary of Architecture*. We of today feel that, whatever the justice of this criticism, there was a countervailing benefit in the impression made by the White City that outweighed its drawbacks. It was an object lesson in the possibilities of group-planning, of monumental scale, of public decorative splendor and harmony, and of worthy landscape setting, that was of incalculable value. The detail was neo-classic, and much of it was, as we now recognize, deplorably poor; but the harmony, the general picturesque effect, the union of all the arts in producing it, were merits quite independent of the styles used. Moreover, not all the buildings were in neo-classic styles. Adler and Sullivan's Transportation Building and Beaman's Fisheries Building, though in totally diverse styles, somehow fell into place in the general harmony, while uttering their declarations of independence of formal compulsion.

Other exhibitions since—at Omaha, Buffalo, Jamestown, St. Louis, San Francisco, San Diego—have followed the general methods of the Chicago Fair, two of them on a vaster scale, the later ones revealing more knowledge, more skill, greater resource, greater freedom and richness of treatment than their prototype. But none has exerted so potent an influence upon the national architecture, for each has had behind it a better-trained, a more knowing public taste; it has lacked the sensational effect of a new discovery, of an utterly novel achievement.

III.

Next in importance to these two epochal events in our architectural history we must certainly count the educational activities of the past twenty-five years.

The growing influence of the French school, which had contributed powerfully to the architectural awakening of the eighties, reached its highest mark during the last decade of the last century. The number of Americans in the *Ecole* at Paris rapidly increased, and the leading offices depended upon their return for the recruiting of their draftsmen. With each year some among the older Paris-trained draftsmen emerged from these offices to practice independently. In 1894 the Society of Beaux-Arts Architects began its remarkable campaign of education by the establishment of "ateliers" and "concours" of "projets," which have since been extended into all parts of the United States. Their success has been prodigious; and despite their tendency to dwell unduly upon clever draftsmanship and "paper architecture," they have done a great service in training competent draftsmen, in instilling sound ideas of planning, and in fostering the artistic spirit. The general quality of American design and of American draftsmanship has certainly been greatly raised.*

But the credit for improved design and draftsmanship does not by any means all belong to the labors of the Beaux-Arts Society. Since 1891 important architectural schools have been founded or developed in the Universities of Harvard, Pennsylvania, Syracuse, Tulane, George Washington at Washington, Washington at St. Louis, Michigan, and Minnesota; in the Carnegie Technical Schools at Pittsburgh, the Armour Institute at Chicago, Rose Polytechnic at Terre Haute, Ohio State University, Alabama Technical Institute and many others; while the older schools have been greatly strengthened and developed. Many traveling fellowships have been founded, and the American Academy at Rome has been built up into a strong institution. Countless night classes and "extension" classes have been established, and Princeton and Yale have built up departments of architecture which are excellent feeders for the more advanced professional courses in other universities. The influence of all these schools, conservative and aca-

*See discussion of the "Influence of the Ecole des Beaux-Arts," in the *Architectural Record* for April, 1908.

THE BOSTON PUBLIC LIBRARY.
McKIM, MEAD & WHITE, ARCHITECTS,

demic in the main, but by no means narrow or superficial, has served to raise the standards of our architecture, and to bring it more and more into its proper place as a learned profession as well as an art; a profession in which science and general culture unite with imagination and trained taste to make it a worthy pursuit for men and women of high aspiration.

In this general raising of standards, the American Institute of Architects has played an important part. Through its conventions, the meetings of its chapters, its official representations and memorials to Congress and to other authorities on matters relating to public architecture, and its consistent efforts to improve the conduct of competitions and to systematize professional ethics and practice, it has rendered great services to American architecture. These activities have been prosecuted in no spirit of exclusiveness or trades-unionism, and the profession at large, both in and outside of the Institute, has profited by them.

IV.

It is not easy to characterize in any brief statement the architecture of the past twenty-five years. That it is extraordinarily varied, in subject, material and style, goes without saying. That it has made remarkable structural advances is evident to anyone who takes the trouble to examine many buildings erected before 1891. Taken as a whole, it is certainly more knowing, more competent than that of the preceding period, better in all four matters of planning, construction, composition and decorative detail. It could hardly be otherwise, given the vast increase in the number of architects and draftsmen trained in excellent schools in this country and abroad; and given, at the same time, the amazing increase in wealth, in general education, in resources of all kinds, of the nation at large during the same period.

Perhaps there is no better way of presenting the progress we have made than to call to mind what were some of the most noted buildings erected in the preceding quarter-century; and then to list a few of those of the later period. It is most instructive to read the late Montgomery Schuyler's *American Architecture,* published in 1892. The notable buildings described in this book were various works of Mr. Richardson, the three Vanderbilt houses in New York, insurance buildings in Minneapolis and St. Paul, a number of Romanesque houses in those cities and in Chicago: not much else. Mr. Richardson's death in 1886 was not yet so far in the past that his influence had wholly lost its power; but Mr. Schuyler notes how personal to him were the excellences of his work, and deplores the weakness and ineptness of most of his imitators, who copied his mannerisms without his largeness of conception, good taste and imagination. The tall buildings of that time were eight or ten stories high; collectively they were referred to as "elevator architecture"; the steel-frame building had appeared it is true, but it had as yet made no impression when Mr. Schuyler wrote his book—at least upon him. If one had been asked to name the finest of recent buildings in America at that time he might have enumerated Trinity Church and the near-by terra-cotta Fine Arts Museum at Boston (now demolished); the County Court House at Pittsburgh, the Albany City Hall, some of Richardson's libraries and his Harvard Law School, the Harvard Memorial Hall, the Connecticut Capitol at Hartford, the Chicago Auditorium, St. Patrick's Cathedral, the Madison Square Garden, the three Vanderbilt houses, the "Villard houses" and the Mills Building at New York, Link's St. Louis railway terminal, and the Ponce de Leon at St. Augustine. Not another church, railway terminal, or library (except Hunt's Lenox Library at New York), not a museum or theatre or town hall could be named of any importance, that rose above absolute mediocrity; while in general our civic, Federal and ecclesiastical architecture was beneath contempt, and our railway stations were a disgrace. A sarcastic survey of American architecture in the London *Saturday Review* of that period excited considerable indignation; reading it to-day we cannot help recognizing in it a large element of just

THE MASONIC TEMPLE, CHICAGO.
BURNHAM & ROOT, ARCHITECTS.

criticism, though expressed with that airy superiority which Lowell so deftly satirized in his famous essay on "A Certain Condescension in Foreigners."

In Mr. Birkmire's *Skeleton Construction in Buildings,* published in 1892 or '93 (Second Edition, 1894), the early triumphs of the new system are recorded: the W. C. T. U. Building, the Owings Building, the Masonic Temple, the Schiller Building and the Auditorium, in Chicago; the Havemeyer, Home Life, Jackson and World buildings and the New Netherlands and Waldorf hotels in New York. Bruce Price's scheme for a 34-story tower for the New York *Sun* had appeared and been laughed at; twenty years later the 46-story Metropolitan tower embodied his idea on a still loftier scale. In 1892 in New York the talk was of the new Madison Square Garden, "the most beautiful building in America"; of the World building, the loftiest of inhabited edifices; a little later, of the Park Row building, over 300 feet high; of the competition for the proposed Episcopal cathedral, of Grant's Tomb on the Riverside Drive. Boston had just begun the erection of her new Public Library, and Washington that of the Congressional Library, two edifices destined to exert a powerful influence on our public architecture in the direction of interior decorative painting of the highest character. Philadelphia had but just begun to feel the stirrings of a new architectural impulse, led by a group of young architects who are now the veterans of the profession in that city, with a long list of excellent buildings to their credit. The Pacific Coast had not yet begun the development of that interesting domestic architecture which distinguishes it today. The Ponce de Leon and Alcazar at St. Augustine had but recently made the reputation of their young architects—Carrère and Hastings; there was at that time hardly another recent building of artistic importance in the South. Turn the pages of the RECORD in its first year; look through the columns of the *American Architect* and *Architecture and Building* for 1891-2-3, and you will realize how meagre, in those days, was the list of American buildings

of really successful design, or of any lasting importance. Taken as a whole, our domestic architecture was the best product of our offices—but how inferior even the best of that to the best that is being built in the same class today! And how much more numerous were the freaks—the conspicuous failures and blunders; *vide* the quarterly *Architectural Aberrations* published in the RECORD, if you doubt it!

A full or even a fairly representative list of the great and worthy works of our architects of the past twenty-five years would be too long for the limits of this article. But a few may be mentioned by way of example. There have been seven important exhibitions of national or international scope since the Columbian at Chicago in 1893; the "Cotton States" Exhibition at New Orleans; the "Trans-Mississippi" at Omaha in 1898; the "Pan-American" at Buffalo in 1901; the "Louisiana Purchase" at St. Louis in 1904; the Jamestown in 1906; and the two in California, at San Francisco and San Diego, in 1915. Each of these, with the possible exception of those at New Orleans and Jamestown, was of first-rate architectural importance. They were all scenic displays of "staff" architecture, decorations rather than durable buildings, but they all stimulated the imagination and developed the decorative resource of our architects, and for the first time in our history exerted a reflex influence on European exhibition architecture. The Boston Public Library was completed in 1895; the Congressional at Washington in 1897; the Public Library of New York in 1912. With the accession of Wm. Martin Aiken to the office of Supervising Architect of the Treasury in 1893 there began a remarkable reform in our Federal architecture, which continued under his successor, J. Knox Taylor, and was further stimulated by the passing of the Tarsney Act, unhappily repealed in 1914. The Custom Houses, Court Houses and Post Offices of this régime, at New York, Indianapolis, San Francisco, Cleveland and other cities, the Senate and House offices at Washington, and a host of lesser Federal buildings, have lifted our National offi-

THE PENNSYLVANIA STATION, NEW YORK.
McKIM, MEAD & WHITE, ARCHITECTS.

cial architecture from pretentious infe-
riority to a level of high artistic merit.
The great railway terminals at Washington and New York and the Northwestern
at Chicago, and others of less magnitude
at Pittsburgh, Baltimore and other cities,
have redeemed us from the former disgrace of the old-time shabby and dis-
reputable makeshifts.   University and
collegiate groups have been created that
are the envy of foreign professors and
scholars: Palo Alto and Berkeley in California, the University of Pennsylvania,
Chicago, Columbia, Johns Hopkins,
Princeton, Washington at St. Louis, Bryn
Mawr, Vassar and Sweetbriar Colleges,
the College of the City of New York
and others, represent a branch of architecture which hardly had any existence
before 1891.   At the same time a new
architecture of public school buildings
has been developed, based on scientific
principles and the logical expression of
plan and structure; witness the modern
schools of New York, Boston, Chicago,
St. Louis and a dozen other cities.   Certain types of buildings have been subjected to a process of standardization,
within well defined limits, as the result
of prolonged and systematic study of
their requirements; for instance, public
libraries, hospitals, Y. M. C. A. buildings, office buildings, public schools.
That is to say, a general consensus has
been reached as to certain of their requirements and the best arrangements,
proportions and dimensions of their fundamental elements, so that all architects
have profited by the combined wisdom
of those who have worked out these
standards.   The librarians were the first
to attempt such a formulation of requirements, and American library architecture now leads the world, both in the
larger buildings like those already mentioned, and such other important examples as the libraries of Milwaukee, Detroit, Newark, Springfield, Providence
and Manchester (N. H.), and in the
smaller libraries and branch libraries. In
any American city the library is likely to
be one of the handsomest buildings in
town, and a creditable work intrinsically;
and in any college or university the same
is often true, as at Columbia (the Low

Library), Harvard (the Widener), Vassar (Thompson Memorial) and many
others.

Our skyscraper architecture hardly requires the mention or comment of my
pen.   It is omnipresent and insistent, the
most conspicuous, revolutionary and
American architectural product of the
last twenty-five years, from Jenney and
Mundie's Home Life Building in Chicago
and Bradford Gilbert's Tower Building
addition in New York to the 750-foot
Woolworth and the vast Equitable in New
York, and Boston's much-belauded Custom House.   It has been more "cussed
and discussed" than any other modern
type.   It has changed the skyline of New
York and of every large American city
from Seattle to Bangor, from Los An-
geles to Galveston.   It has produced a
new architectural style, irrespective of
that of its varied decorative trimmings;
and it speaks so loud for itself as to
make further words on this page unnecessary.

The past twenty-five years have given
us the fine State capitols of Rhode Island,
Minnesota, and Wisconsin among others,
and also, alas! the scandal of Harris-
burgh; the great Municipal Building of
New York; the choir and chapels and
attendant buildings of the Cathedral of
St. John the Divine; a large number of
fine churches and the beginnings of several cathedrals; the design for the greatest court house in the world, at New
York—but space forbids continuing the
list.

This remarkable development exhibits
an almost sudden substitution of Renaissance forms for the previously popular
Romanesque, in the years following the
Columbian Exhibition, and a rapid advance in the planning of buildings as
well as in the design of their decorative
details.   During the last fifteen years
there has been witnessed the growth of
a very interesting phase of eclecticism in
style, by which certain classes of buildings are habitually treated in various
phases of neo-classic design; others in
free versions of the Gothic.   The neo-
classic styles in use vary from the picturesque Francis I. Renaissance of the
Biltmore château to the severe Greco-

THE GRADUATE COLLEGE OF PRINCETON UNIVERSITY, PRINCETON, N. J. CRAM, GOODHUE & FERGUSON, ARCHITECTS.

Roman of the Senate offices at Washington and the Pennsylvania Terminal at New York; the Gothic from the very free treatment of the New York City College or the Woolworth Building to the ecclesiastic Gothic of St. Thomas' at New York and the scholastic Gothic of the Princeton Graduate School. Even the Greek Doric appears in porticoes and façades of banks, libraries and museums. But this use of historic styles is, after all, for the most part a matter of dress and apparel of architecture. Underneath the Gothic, Greek and Renaissance details and through them all, one may discern the real American architecture—American in planning, construction and material; in conception and in spirit American, and nothing else.

V.

This paper is already too long to permit of doing justice to five other features of the architectural history of the period, which deserve several pages apiece. These are: (a) the various phases of the movement for civic improvement, in city planning, garden cities, civic centres and municipal art generally; (b) the great advances in mechanical equipment of buildings, with the attendant increase in the complexities of architectural design and practice; (c) the progress of domestic architecture and especially the Colonial revival in rural and suburban architecture; (d) the emergence of an American school of landscape design; and (e) the extraordinary increase in the variety and improvement in the quality of building materials. The temptation is strong to list the most important of the events in the nation-wide campaigns for better city plans, for improved tenement housing, for the artistic rebuilding of wrecked and burned cities, for reclaiming waterfronts, for grouping public buildings; but we must refrain. It is hard to have to omit all account of the new uses of concrete, hollow-tile, Guastavino vaulting, and new kinds and forms of brick, tile, glass and what not; of the development of the "bungalow" and "mission" types, and the influence of English rural architecture, and so on, and so on! The reader's patience and the

writer's time allowance and paper have limits.

VI.

A page or two on architectural literature must close this inadequate attempt to sketch the architectural achievements of the past twenty-five years.

In 1891 there were published in the United States, disregarding minor and ephemeral periodicals, two architectural journals: the weekly *American Architect and Building News* in Boston, and the monthly *Architecture and Building* in New York. In that year the ARCHITECTURAL RECORD first made its appearance, as a quarterly, hailed from the outset as a much-needed addition to our periodical literature, and marked by a seriousness of artistic and literary purpose which has ever since characterized it. Its change in 1903 to monthly issues was a natural result of its high quality, and it has constantly maintained that quality ever since. Meanwhile the *Technology Review* of Boston has entered the field, and that has developed into the excellent *Architectural Review*, filling a field midway between that of the RECORD and the other periodicals mentioned. The *Inland Architect* of Chicago long served the interests of the Middle West; the *Western Architect* came later, and in 1903 first appeared *Architecture*, another New York monthly, making a specialty of photographic illustrations. Occupying a field of its own, and standing at a very high level of scholarly, literary and artistic excellence, is the *Journal* of the American Institute of Architects, now in its third year; the latest comer in the field of American periodical literature on architecture. Other additional periodicals there is not now space to mention; they are many, and there are still others which, though not primarily architectural, devote a part of their space to architecture or issue special architectural numbers. All this has served to diffuse an interest in architecture among the public, and to provide the architect with information, instruction and suggestion. This periodical literature, much of it excellent, some of it commonplace, some distinctly inferior, is both a cause and a result of

THE WOOLWORTH BUILDING, NEW
YORK CITY. CASS GILBERT, ARCHITECT.

the increased general interest in architecture.

Quite as significant is the increase in books on architecture, of which the output has been enormous of late years. These fall into three classes: technical-scientific books, among which the successive editions of Kidder's "Pocketbook" have been conspicuous; popular handbooks on house-design, stable-design, bungalows, house-furnishing, etc.; and books of scholarship, history and criticism, among which Sturgis's *Dictionary,* and *European Architecture,* Cummings' *History of Architecture in Italy,* Moore's *The Character of Renaissance Architecture* and *The Mediaeval Church Architecture of England,* Porter's *Mediaeval Architecture* and *Lombard and Gothic Vaults,* the Sturgis-Frothingham *History of Architecture,* Wallis' *How to Know Architecture,* my *History of Architecture,* Ware's *American Vignola,* Frothingham's *Christian Architecture of Rome,* Adam's *Mont Saint Michel and Chartres,* and several books by R. A. Cram may be mentioned among many others, as examples of the wide reach, variety and quality of American scholarship, research and literary skill in this field. They witness to the new position which architecture has reached in the public estimation since 1891. Such books could perhaps have been written before that date; surely but a fraction of them could have been published or could have had

any wide sale. Prof. Moore's epoch-making *Development of Gothic Architecture* appeared, it is true, in 1889, but that and W. P. P. Longfellow's *The Arch and Column* were almost the only serious books on architecture by American authors previous to 1891. It augurs hopefully for the future progress of our art that its literature is now firmly established in public favor, and that it has been of such generally high quality.

This brief and hurried survey of a vast subject leaves unsaid much that the writer would have gladly discussed had time and space permitted. The question of style has been left almost untouched. The monuments must speak for themselves; the subject is too big for mere passing mention. The writer hopes that even so inadequate a sketch may inspire its readers with a new respect for the work of our American architects, the veterans and the young men alike; and with a new hope and confidence in the future. Looking back to the architecture of 1865-91, and noting the progress made since then, we have good reason to hope that 1941 will see, throughout our great Republic, an architecture far nobler, purer, more serious and more beautiful than that of to-day, offering to the whole world models of good taste and sound construction, and making our cities and villages fairer and happier places to live in than they are in this year of grace 1916.

THE ART OF THE HIGH BUILDING.

FEW phrases have included such a miscellaneous collection of facts and statements as this—the art of the high building. For much of the phenomena to be classed and discussed under this head has no artistic quality or value whatever. It is sheer ugliness, uncouthness, misunderstanding and absurdity, if judged by artistic standards; and the true artistic elements—so far as they exist—are often of a singularly undeveloped nature. One has but to mentally compare the great high building of to-day—the typical and most noteworthy architectural creation of our time—with the great typical building of the Italian Renaissance or of the French mediaeval period to realize how very different modern standards of art in things architectural are compared with those of more genuinely artistic epochs.

The erection of the high building has been a recognized branch of our architectural industry for some time. For nearly a quarter of a century it has occupied the minds of our architects, given them their most important monuments, on the whole, and lined their pockets with the largest fees ever obtained in general practice. The participants and contemporaries in a movement are not apt to be competent judges of its tendencies and results, and yet so much thought and treasure have been poured out on the high building, it has become such an intimate part of the commercial life of our time, that it is by no means impertinent to ask, even at this early day, if some definite steps have been reached in the solution of the artistic problems involved in its construction, or if—and perhaps this is the more rational question—if tendencies have been shown which look anywhere, and whither is the direction towards which they tend.

It is more than right to insist on the artistic conception of the high building. Engineers will doubtless maintain that the chief problem is that of engineering. I am not in the least disposed to discount the importance of the engineering problems in buildings of this description; but I respectfully submit that in a building that covers a considerable area, that raises its head as high into the upper strata of the air as the engineers will carry it, which cries aloud for attention and consideration, which invites criticism because of its vast cost, and in which, moreover, the engineering part is carefully hidden and covered up from view—in such a building, surely, the artistic expression, the form, the covering, the outer aspects, are of supreme public importance.

One of the most interesting views in New York may be had from the junction of Liberty street and Maiden lane. Standing there

THE JUNCTION OF LIBERTY STREET AND MAIDEN LANE.

LOOKING UP BROADWAY FROM BOWLING GREEN.

THE BUILDING OF THE METROPOLITAN LIFE INSURANCE CO.
Madison Square, New York City.   N. Le Brun & Son, Architects.
This building will eventually occupy the whole block and will contain more floor space than any office building in the United States.

the spectator sees before him a little old brick building, five stories in height, placed at the intersection of Maiden lane and Liberty street. It is a simple little structure, absolutely devoid of ornament and detail, but with a flat, rounded end, a recognition of the site that was as much as its builder cared to consider. The windows are plain, flat-topped openings of the old style; the fifth floor is manifestly an attic floor since it contains fewer windows than the lower stories, and the roof is slightly pointed. How much of this structure may be modern or restored I do not know; but it is distinctly of the old type, and it bears the date "1823."

Here, then, is a fair starting point, a building eighty years old, standing in a district long since given up to commercial purposes, and itself used in the same way. And what strange things this little old house has seen grow up around and behind it! The buildings in the foreground are of a later date, but still entirely antiquated as commercial buildings go to-day. But behind it, what marvels and miracles of contrast! Directly at the back is the sheer solid brick wall of the John Wolfe Building, a structure moderate enough in height, as high buildings are built to-day, but colossal compared with the little old house of 1823. To the left, on Liberty street, is the generous facade of the Bishop Building—twelve stories, tier upon tier of windows—a building wholly different in material, in design, in expression, in use, from the old structure with which the neighborhood, as we now know it, started. Here is effort at architectural treatment, a great building, with a basement in design, a superstructure and a narrow attic, a building so different that the barest analysis of its parts shows how tremendously we have moved in eighty years.

But there is more than this; for still further off, and so huge as to almost overwhelm our little brick building, is the mighty tower of the new part of the Mutual Life Building, a building with piers and columns and cornices lifted so high in the air that, we may be very sure, the builders of 1823 could never have conceived of such things or of such possibilities. The entire progress of commercial architecture in seventy-five years is here brought into one view, and one may note the change and advance without moving a step from one's original standpoint.

There is another panorama in New York which is almost as instructive in illustrating progress—not perhaps so picturesque, yet better known—and that is the spectacle that may be viewed from the lower end of Broadway, looking up from Bowling Green. It is a wonderful sight, one of the most astonishing views in the metropolis. Starting with the vast facade of the Produce Exchange, the eye meets just beyond it, looking up the street, with an old brick building, five stories in height—the single antiquated note in this array of splendor as it is understood in commercial New York—then the Wells Building, the Standard Oil Building, with the later addition Mr. Kimball has so cleverly added to it, the Hudson Building, No. 42 Broadway—the newest of the series— No. 46 Broadway, a brick building of later type than the one at Beaver street, but already so out of date as to be quite comparable to a wedding guest without the wedding clothes in the sumptuous company in which it now finds itself; then an old type four-story building, brick—a veritable derelict—then the Tower Building— the first structure in this country, so an inscription tells us, in which the steel cage construction was used—Exchange Court; the Consolidated Exchange, and the vast bulk and height of the Manhattan Life Insurance Company's Building. There is more beyond, but surely there is more than enough here for the philosophic observer, more than even the casual critic can well digest and ponder over on a winter's day.

Surely, then, with these contrasts and this great activity in building, it is time to ask if anything has been accomplished towards the solution of the artistic expression of the high building, or if tendencies have been started which would seem to indicate definite results. Let me frankly admit that I am entirely skeptical on both these points. Progress in architecture does not consist in the multiplication of buildings, but in real artistic achievement; and progress is not obtained by a hundred individual efforts, each originating separately, each overlooking what has been done by others, each failing to note where others have failed, each ignoring where others have succeeded. Yet a survey of the modern commercial buildings bring out no clearer fact than that this is just what has been done, and, more's the pity, it is just what is being done, and what would seem likely to be done for some time to come.

I am speaking generally, of course, and of high buildings as a whole; for in the case of individual architects very genuine steps of progress may be noted. The Blair Building, in Broad street, is a much franker and truer expression of the high building than the Mail and Express Building in Fulton street, both by Carrère & Hastings; the Empire Building, overlooking Trinity churchyard is a much more interesting building than the Manhattan Life across the street, on Broadway, both by Francis H. Kimball. But does the Park Row Building proclaim any note of progress over the building of the American Tract Society? Or do any of a score of buildings erected in the last two years indicate that their designers have profited by the experiments of other architects or taken the lessons of other buildings to heart? Is the Atlantic Building any more notable contribution to art than the building of the National Bank of Commerce? Does the Broad Street Exchange

BUILDING OF THE LAND TITLE AND TRUST CO.

Broad Street, Philadelphia, Pa.   D. H. Burnham & Co., Architects.

THE NORTH AMERICAN BUILDING.

Broad Street, Philadelphia, Pa.   James H. Windrim, Architect.

sum up any nobler thoughts in architecture than the St. Paul Building?

These are pertinent questions, for the gentlemen who have built these structures have thrust them upon us for all time, so far as living man can see; they have spent huge sums in their architectural doings, and they have given our city—for limits of space in this discussion restrain me to New York—a new and characteristic aspect. It is quite beyond the question to point out the beauty of Manhattan's skyline—that has nothing to do with the case—and a building whose chief merit is that it out-tops its neighbors is necessarily wanting in most of the characteristics we are accustomed to associate with good architecture.

That the commercial building is a commercial enterprise is well known; that it is an architectural enterprise is a circumstance all architects would have us believe. Architectural it is, of course, being concerned with iron and stone, brick and glass; but is it architectural in any other way? Even in its short life of twenty-five years several steps or periods may be noted.

First, the introductory period; the first steps, in which such buildings as the Tribune Building and the Western Union Building were erected. The possibilities of high building design as they were afterwards made known were not at all understood in this remote epoch; but these first efforts were manly and straightforward, and still command respect.

Second, the advertising period. It was suddenly realized that a showy building was a good advertisement for its chief occupant. It attracted attention, it drew tenants, it became a profitable venture. The Pulitzer Building is a fair type, the Broadway front of the Mail and Express an extreme instance; the Manhattan Building a third example. The chief aim of the buildings which may be classed under this head was to be impressive by sumptuousness of parts, by splendor of appointments, by richness of effect. A great financial corporation felt that it might stand better in the community if it had a fine house, and the greater the wealth the more splendid its abiding place—a natural proposition to which no dissent can be taken.

It was a type of building that gave architects their greatest opportunities, for they were not merely required to build, but they were commanded to build well and sumptuously, a certain artistic character was required of them; and if the architects failed to rise to their opportunities it was simply and solely because they failed to comprehend the problem presented to them. It is true they have endeavored to proclaim that the fault was not in them, but in the problem; but the bitter fact remains that they gladly accepted

THE FARMERS' DEPOSIT BANK BUILDING.

Pittsburgh, Pa.　　　　　　　　　Alden & Harlow, Architects.

these impossible problems, and gleefully signed their names to designs that proclaimed their own incompetency.

Third. Then came the third period, which I take to be the present. A change has certainly come over the designing methods of high buildings within a very few years. The buildings are bigger, higher, broader, more costly; but there is less external art, less visible splendor, less effort to create interesting structures; on the contrary, the high building as illustrated in many of its most recent examples in New York, is a frigidly severe edifice, a sheer brick wall, lit with numberless windows, and with the smallest possible efforts to give it architectural form or rhythm.

As an illustration, let me take a group of buildings in lower William street. The Woodbridge Building has a front filling an entire block. Its facade contains no ornamental detail, and yet it is a very excellent effort to treat a commercial front in a dignified and architectural manner. It starts out with a basement of two stories in stone; then an intermediate story, in which the windows are in pairs and round arched; then a superstructure of eight stories, in which the walls are treated as piers carrying round arches; finally an attic story; all above the basement is in warm, yellow brick. The structure, as will now be perceived, is not a "high" building, as such structures are understood; but it is notable for the fact that its architect undertook to treat his front in an architectural way; he discarded ornament, but retained form; and he produced a design of considerable interest and of much architectural merit.

Pass down the street and compare it with the Wyllis Building, the Bishop Building, and No. 68 William street; compare it again with the Kuhn, Loeb & Co. Building, with the Wall Street Exchange, with the new structures in the lower part of Wall street. A basement of one or two stories is still retained; but above there is nothing but wall and windows, windows and wall. There is no effort to group the openings, no wall treatment, no piers; even the attic story fails to emphasize itself, or is so far removed from the street as to be actually out of the design. If these latest buildings are the last word in high design, as it is understood in New York, it is obvious that the artistic architect is out of the effort altogether, and the high building has become a simple box, with openings in it to admit the light.

An economic restraint has, apparently, come over our high buildings which is most detrimental to them in an artistic manner. Whether the architects have given up the problem in despair, whether clients have despaired of the architects, whether there has come a realizing sense on all sides of the utter commercial character of these structures and therefore, of the apparent folly of

"THE WHITEHALL."

Battery Place, New York City.   H. J. Hardenbergh, Architect.

THE RAILWAY EXCHANGE BUILDING.

Chicago, Ill.   D. H. Burnham & Co., Architects.

THE FIRST NATIONAL BANK BUILDING.

Chicago, Ill.   D. H. Burnham & Co., Architects.

STORE AND OFFICE BUILDING.

Minneapolis, Minn.   F. B. & L. L. Long, Architects.

making them artistic, I do not know; but here are the results, and very unpleasant most of them are.

Yet rigidity of treatment is not incompatible with successful and interesting results; huge height is not inconsistent with interesting efforts; a barren wall, the piling of windows one on top of another is not necessarily devoid of merit; all of which is most pleasingly and successfully illustrated in the Whitehall Building. Simplicity of parts could hardly go further than here. The stone basement is as devoid of unconstructional parts as the plainest building in New York; the tremendous superstructure has not a single note of ornament, and the walls are sheer brick fronts. But success here has been obtained by a clever use of color; the central walls are red brick; the end pavilions of light colored brick, with thin lines of red; the stone of the base is gray; the attic is simple and re-strained. In plain words, this elevation was studied, and studied intelligently and well; no one would think, for a moment, that its parts were thrown hastily together and the topmost course of brick laid with the utmost haste, that an unpleasant task could be com-pleted as speedily as possible, and with the smallest effort. Yet New York has not a few such buildings, and some of the latest and biggest are distressful examples of such unarchitectural proceed-ings.

Are we getting anywhere? Apparently we have run the gamut of ornamental structures and settled down—or is it up?—to use-ful ones, in which there shall be plenty of utility and the smallest possible amount of art. The basic type of design is still adhered to—basement, superstructure and attic—but the basement is hardly more than the protrusion of the foundation above the soil; the superstructure is a shapeless tier of windows; the attic a mere finish. The latter has long been a favorite feature with New York architects. The logic of their proceedings is quite irresistible; the lightest parts cannot be below, and a building must come to an end; let us, they have cried with one voice, adorn our buildings at the top. By this time, apparently, they have awakened to the fact that the tops of their structures are so remote from the ground that no one can see them, and it has become absolutely true that the enriched attic story is becoming a feature of the past. But they still remain with us, and as one travels down Wall street quite a series presents itself; the Atlantic Building, the Sampson Build-ing, and the structures below Pearl street, all characterized by a lower severity and enriched crowning, much of which, owing to the low altitude of the adjoining structures, is still visible, but seem-ingly destined, in the near future, to be well hidden from the view of posterity.

The ornamental entrance story has disappeared even more quick-

THE CORN EXCHANGE BANK BUILDING.

William Street, New York City.   R. H. Robertson, Architect.

ly than the decorated attic. The Atlantic Building boasts a crowning member of considerable richness, but the basement story is
quite bare in its simplicity. The single feature is a heavy entrance
portico, which is in striking contrast with the delicate carving of
the United States Trust Company Building, immediately adjoining
it. The latter is not a high building, although the time is not far
past when it was proudly labelled a "modern office building." The
contrast is most impressive. The United States Trust is a building
of moderate height, treated in an architectural manner, and decorated with finely carved capitals and bands. The Atlantic Building
is several times its height; has the barest of porticos as its chief
lower ornament; has a featureless superstructure, and flares out
above with a crowning member of several stories quite elaborately
treated, a system of design that has become almost typical in New
York.

The change towards simplicity in design, it should be thoroughly
understood, is quite for the worst. Mr. Hardenbergh has shown,
in his Whitehall Building, that simplicity is not incompatible with
dignity, and that this dignity may have a decided quality of beauty;
but the lesson has not been generally learned, nor its possibility
appreciated. The featureless high building—the front that is merely, built up, story on story, tier upon tier—until the appropriation
gives out—is no embellishment to our thoroughfares. Wealth of
ornamentation is not embellishment; the prefixing of unnecessary
parts is perhaps needless; but lack of interest is altogether inex-
cusable, and of this there is still a plenty and to spare.

A plain wall, however, has merits which the variegated treatment
entirely fails in. Our architects are apparently moving away from
the repetition of motif illustrated in the American Tract Society
Building, the Park Row Building, the St. Paul Building, in each
of which a large feature of several stories is repeated several times.
It was an unfortunate system that should never have been tried
more than once, for it quite ignored the idea that the high building
was a unity, requiring to be designed as a whole, and not treated
as a series of buildings piled one on top of the other. Yet the horizontal line remains in high favor, buildings which are without any
other effort at architectural treatment, being erected with each
story carefully indicated by bands and string courses repeated
"ad infinitum."

It is strange, this cutting up of buildings into layers. There is
a new building going up at Pearl and Beaver streets, unfinished
when these words are written; but a building with a sharply
rounded end, as befits the site. Each floor of the otherwise unmarked superstructure is indicated by bands of darker brick, as
though the breadth was the element to be insisted on in a building

whose greatest distinction is its height. The attic member of this structure promises to be a brilliant piece of polychromatic work, one of the most striking novelties in high building design.

The most impressive element in the high building is its height; that is the single feature that distinguishes it from all other structures. Of all the architects who have essayed to solve the problem of high design, Mr. Louis H. Sullivan, of Chicago, has alone frankly expressed the vertical element and given the high building logical, as well as genuinely artistic expression. New York is fortunate in possessing in a building in Bleecker street, a fine example of Mr. Sullivan's work. It would be interesting to transplant it to Broad street, set it up before Carrère & Hastings's Blair Building, and ask them to exchange views on each other's aspect.

The architects of both structures studied at the Ecole des Beaux Arts in Paris; the Western architect has long been our most conspicuously individual practitioner; the New York firm is easily one of the most distinguished practitioners in the academic style. Their buildings are as far apart as the poles; both are fine examples of their kind; both well illustrate the characteristics of their designers. And both are vertical buildings. It is a triumph of principles over art; for Mr. Hastings has not previously given us a vertical high building, having contented himself with the repetitive method. Mr. Sullivan can not count Mr. Hastings as a disciple—they are much too far apart artistically for that—but at least he has pointed the way which Mr. Hastings has gladly taken in this most distinguished design. One has but to compare it with the immediately adjoining Cable Building, to become aware of how much better things can be done to-day than were done a few years since.

The Kean, Van Cortlandt & Co. Building in Cedar street is another structure whose chief interest is the frank way in which it displays its Beaux Artism. Here again a vertical design, in so far that the chief part, the superstructure, is treated in great bays of seven stories, that emerge from a base and intermediate story of three floors; the attic is a single story. It is an honest effort to apply Beaux Arts ideas to the high building, although lacking in interest. Like many other new high buildings the ornamental enrichment of the lower stories is heavy and large; more vigorous by far than that which any French architect would produce, and heavier than seems called for in a building of such moderate dimensions.

It is a difficult problem, this of the scale of ornament. The buildings are so huge, the basements necessarily so heavy to seem to carry the weight above them, that the architect who would seek

BUILDING OF KEAN, VAN CORTLANDT & CO.
Pine Street, New York City.   Warren & Wetmore, Architects.

to treat the question logically from the standpoint of the whole,
has a sorry task. And his difficulties are not lessened when classic
detail is employed, for his capitals and ornaments increase with
diameters, and the laws of Vignola were not drawn to solve such
problems as the modern Beaux Arts architects set out to illustrate
them with.

The sightseer very soon learns to realize that there is little within
the high building to see—the more reason, therefore, it would appear—to make the outside beautiful and impressive. The problem
of the interior is chiefly one of plan and of construction. Yet our
great commercial buildings are not entirely without interior interest. The entrance and lobby, the elevator hall and vestibule,
are legitimate spaces for the display of the architect's personal
taste. Make them as splendid as possible, was once the universal
rule; I doubt if this is quite so general now.

Take the Mutual Life Building as an example. The entrance
hall on Nassau street—the oldest part of the building—is quite
splendid with its columns and arches, its walls and ceiling, all of
polished and carved marble. The entrance is up a flight of steps
within an outer porch, and one enters a rectangular vestibule, large
enough to give a decided sense of space. The Metropolitan Life
has a larger and more sumptuous vestibule than this, but that of
the Mutual Life is comparatively large and is by no means recent.
It is in striking contrast to the entrance of the National Bank of
Commerce—a later building—just across the street. One stumbles
there almost into the elevators, so narrow is the space; but even
this shallow entrance is sumptuous with polished marble, as are
most of the hallways and corridors of the large buildings.

But the Mutual Life Building has received several successive additions, and it would seem entirely proper to utilize them as types of
progress. Around in Liberty street, the first entrance is No. 32. One
goes in almost directly from the street level. There is nothing of
the splendor of the entrance on Nassau street; only a small, com-
pact corridor; marble walls, it is true, but the slightest decoration.
Further down, No. 26, is another type. The elevators are in a
branch corridor to the right; directly in face is a partly hidden
stairway; rich marble again; but restrained. This, then, would
seem to be the type of the high building entrance way: rich materials. These materials in older buildings were richly treated; in
the newer they are still rich in surface treatment, but the architectural parts have almost completely disappeared. Apparently, no
more money is being lavished on these great buildings than can be
absolutely avoided.

The outlook is not cheering. There is no standard of artistic
excellence. There is no indication of general appreciation of the

real problem involved. There is plenty of haphazard effort, a good
deal of well meant effort, an occasional success. We had as much
ten years ago; and we have to-day a vast quantity of uninteresting
building which harms through its very negativeness. Surely every
possible expedient and experiment has been tried. The time for
such ventures has passed. The high building problem is not one that
will solve itself, but it can only be solved by the most painstaking
care, by the most thorough study of past efforts and failures, and
by a thoroughly artistic meeting of the conditions involved. There
never was a type of building evolved yet of which it can be better
said "the more haste the less speed."

Barr Ferree.

THE MAJESTIC BUILDING.

Detroit, Michigan.   D. H. Burnham & Co., Architects.

AN ARCHITECT'S OPINION OF "L'ART NOUVEAU."

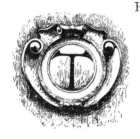

HE ARCHITECTURAL RECORD has done me the honor of asking me to define "l'Art Nouveau." It is difficult, at a time of transition—I might almost add, of trouble and commotion—to state exactly what would be the best solution of a given problem; but it may be said that the close of the nineteenth century witnessed the beginnings of a general evolution which is destined some day to give tangible and permanent results, and art has shared in this movement. During the past twenty years or so, various attempts at modern art have been made, in a more or less timid way; and these attempts have been based on the interpretation of the elements of the flower. I will cite, in this connection: in France, Rubrick Robert and the Union Centrale des Arts Décoratifs de Paris; in England, Ruskin, Walter Crane and Morris; and in Belgium, Victor Horta. In the last-named country the decorative base is no longer the leaf and the flower, but simply the stem.

Returning to a sound logical view of the matter, and abandoning the ostracism of all the classical schools, it is my belief that, by studying the principles of art which have guided artists from the very earliest period down to the present day, it is possible to make a selection, and that if we will take the trouble to find out how our predecessors managed to discover them, we can by applying the same method to the conditions prevailing in our own times, deduce therefrom the proper modern rules. In spite of the profusion of old examples, it cannot be denied that there exists something else, and this "something else" should be the main object of the researches of those who want to work for their epoch. It is upon us architects that falls more particularly the duty of determining, by our art, not only the artistic, but also the civilizing and scientific evolution of our time.

Nature is a big book from which we can draw inspiration, and it is in that book that we must look for principles, which, when found, have to be defined and applied by the human mind according to human needs. From this study I obtain three principles which should have a predominating influence in all architectural productions, viz.:

1. Logic, which consists in taking into account all the conditions of the case, and they are infinite in variety and number, which the architect has to deal with.

FIG. 4. HECTOR GUIMARD.

FIG. 5. MANTELPIECE AND WOODWORK DECORATION, BY ALEXANDRE CHARPENTIER.

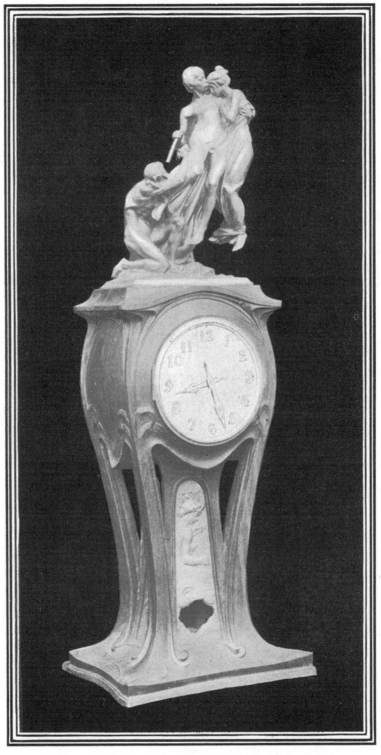

FIG. 6. CLOCK AND BRONZE. THE FLIGHT OF TIME, BY
ALEXANDRE CHARPENTIER.

FIG. 7. FOUNTAIN, BY ALEXANDRE CHARPENTIER; NOW IN MUSÉE
GALLIERA, PARIS.

2. Harmony, which means putting the constructions into full accord, not only with the requirements to be met and the funds available, but also with the surroundings.

3. Sentiment, which, partaking at the same time of logic and harmony, is the complement of both, and leads by emotion, to the highest expression of the art.

These are the principles which I have desired to exemplify in all my edifices, and particularly in the Castel Béranger, the Humbert de Romans Hall, and the stations of the Paris Metropolitan Railroad. It is these works, together with those of such men as Victor Horta and Van de Velde, which have inspired (chiefly in Germany, Austria and France) those productions described by the term "Art Nouveau." Un-

fortunately, I cannot say that all these productions illustrate the three principles which I have just laid down. For the most part they infringe them, for that undefinable thing called *taste*, which makes us like a chair, a clock, a vase or a jewel; taste, which is the embodiment of *esprit*, charm, emotion, life, whether in cloth or metal, an article for use or an ornament, is a quality which is lacking in the greater number of those who believe themselves to be modern creators, who in reality plagiarize more or less a motive made to ornament a necessary structure.

Fig. 8. Table, by Alexandre Charpentier.

Every great epoch has had a stylization of art. It is thus that all the styles which have preceded us came into existence, and it cannot be disputed that we are witnessing at present the creation of a style; but individual influences cannot have a universal effect. A style of architecture, in order to be true, must be the product of the soil where it exists and of the period which needs it. The principles of the middle ages and those of the nineteenth century, added to my doctrine, should supply us with a foundation for a French Renaissance and an entirely new style. Let the Belgians, the Germans and the English evolve for themselves a national art, and assuredly in so doing they will perform a true, sound and useful work.

Although it may be a daring thing for me to speak of the Ameri-

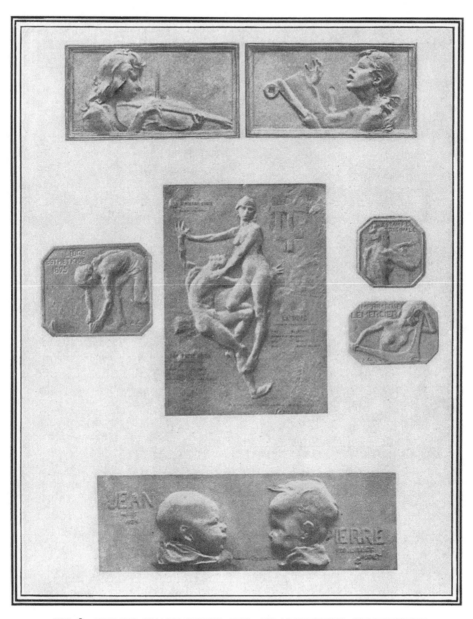

FIG. 9. MEDALS, TRADE MARKS, ETC., BY ALEXANDRE CHARPENTIER.

FIG. 11.   CUPBOARD FOR HOLDING A QUARTETTE OF STRINGED INSTRUMENTS, DESIGNED BY A. CHARPENTIER.
The body is of French yoke-elm, the paneling of Hungarian ash.   These woods are of a light, creamy color, and are well-grained.

cans, who are so gen-
erously extending to
me their hospitality
in your review, I will
venture to say that
my American con-
frères have been, and
are still, in the most
favorable position
for creating an "Art
Nouveau." I am
sorry that they have
not thought proper
to strive after a na-
tional art, evolved
from their own tem-
perament; that is, an
art produced on the
spot and instinct
with the life of that
spot. The artist does
not create his en-
vironment; he is the
product thereof.
When I see your
monuments and your
architecture, I think
I am again looking
at that of the houses

FIG. 10.   BRONZE CUP, BY VALLGREN.

and monuments of Paris, of Berlin, or of Italy, so utter is the lack
of all special mark of the soil.

Seeing that the "Art Nouveau" is now crossing the Atlantic
to your shores, I hope that my American confrères will not rest
content to be mere copyists, but will be creators, and it is my belief that the principles by which I am guided in producing French
architecture would enable them just as easily to create an American
art, a thing which your leading fellow-countrymen ardently wish
to see.

Hector Guimard.

The
Architectural Record

Vol. XXIII   **MARCH, 1908.**   **No. 3.**

In the Cause of Architecture

The reader of architectural discourses encounters with increasing frequency discussions on American Architecture, Indigenous Architecture. These are generally to the effect that in order to establish a vital architecture in the United States, it is necessary for the architect to sever his literal connection with past performances, to shape his forms to requirements and in a manner consistent with beauty of form as found in Nature, both animate and inanimate. Articles in this strain have appeared, from time to time, in this and in other architectural journals, and have been in most cases too vague in their diction to be well understood, either by the lay reader or the architect.

The sentiment for an American architecture first made itself felt in Chicago twenty years ago. Its earliest manifestation is the acknowledged solution of the tall office building problem. An original phase of that early movement is now presented, in the following article and illustrations, the work of Mr. Frank Lloyd Wright.

—Editors of THE ARCHITECTURAL RECORD.

Radical though it be, the work here illustrated is dedicated to a cause conservative in the best sense of the word. At no point does it involve denial of the elemental law and order inherent in all great architecture; rather, is it a declaration of love for the spirit of that law and order, and a reverential recognition of the elements that made its ancient letter in its time vital and beautiful.

Primarily, Nature furnished the materials for architectural motifs out of which the architectural forms as we know them to-day have been developed, and, although our practice for centuries has been for the most part to turn from her, seeking inspiration in books and adhering slavishly to dead formulae, her wealth of suggestion is inexhaustible; her riches greater than any man's desire. I know with what suspicion the man is regarded who refers matters of fine art back to Nature. I know that it is usually an ill-advised return that is attempted, for Nature in external, obvious aspect is the usually accepted sense of the term and the nature that is reached. But given inherent vision there is no source so fer-

tile, so suggestive, so helpful æsthetically for the architect as a comprehension of natural law. As Nature is never right for a picture so is she never right for the architect—that is, not ready-made. Nevertheless, she has a practical school beneath her more obvious forms in which a sense of proportion may be cultivated, when Vignola and Vitruvius fail as they must always fail. It is there that he may develop that sense of reality that translated to his own field in terms of his own work will lift him far above the realistic in his art; there he will be inspired by sentiment that will never degenerate to sentimentality and he will learn to draw with a surer hand the every-perplexing line between the curious and the beautiful.

A sense of the organic is indispensable to an architect; where can he develop it so surely as in this school? A knowledge of the relations of form and function lies at the root of his practice; where else can he find the pertinent object lessons Nature so readily furnishes? Where can he study the differentiations of form that go to determine character as he can

50

study them in the trees? Where can that sense of inevitableness characteristic of a work of art be quickened as it may be by intercourse with nature in this sense?

Japanese art knows this school more intimately than that of any people. In common use in their language there are many words like the word "edaburi," which, translated as near as may be, means the formative arrangement of the branches of a tree. We have no such word in English, we are not yet sufficiently civilized to think in such terms, but the architect must not only learn to think in such terms but he must learn in this school to fashion his vocabulary for himself and furnish it in a comprehensive way with useful words as significant as this one.

For seven years it was my good fortune to be the understudy of a great teacher and a great architect, to my mind the greatest of his time—Mr. Louis H. Sullivan.

Principles are not invented, they are not evolved by one man or one age, but Mr. Sullivan's perception and practice of them amounted to a revelation at a time when they were commercially inexpedient and all but lost to sight in current practice. The fine art sense of the profession was at that time practically dead; only glimmerings were perceptible in the work of Richardson and of Root.

Adler and Sullivan had little time to design residences. The few that were unavoidable fell to my lot outside of office hours. So largely, it remained for me to carry into the field of domestic architecture the battle they had begun in commercial building. During the early years of my own practice I found this lonesome work. Sympathizers of any kind were then few and they were not found among the architects. I well remember how "the message" burned within me, how I longed for comradeship until I began to know the younger men and how welcome was Robert Spencer, and then Myron Hunt, and Dwight Perkins, Arthur Heun, George Dean and Hugh Garden. Inspiring days they were, I am sure, for us all. Of late we have been too busy to see one another often, but the

"New School of the Middle West" is beginning to be talked about and perhaps some day it is to be. For why not the same "Life" and blood in architecture that is the essence of all true art?

In 1894, with this text from Carlyle at the top of the page—"The Ideal is within thyself, thy condition is but the stuff thou art to shape that same Ideal out of"—I formulated the following "propositions." I set them down here much as they were written then, although in the light of experience they might be stated more completely and succinctly.

I.—Simplicity and Repose are qualities that measure the true value of any work of art.

But simplicity is not in itself an end nor is it a matter of the side of a barn but rather an entity with a graceful beauty in its integrity from which discord, and all that is meaningless, has been eliminated. A wild flower is truly simple. Therefore:

1. A building should contain as few rooms as will meet the conditions which give it rise and under which we live, and which the architect should strive continually to simplify; then the ensemble of the rooms should be carefully considered that comfort and utility may go hand in hand with beauty. Beside the entry and necessary work rooms there need be but three rooms on the ground floor of any house, living room, dining room and kitchen, with the possible addition of a "social office"; really there need be but one room, the living room with requirements otherwise sequestered from it or screened within it by means of architectural contrivances.

2. Openings should occur as integral features of the structure and form, if possible, its natural ornamentation.

3. An excessive love of detail has ruined more fine things from the standpoint of fine art or fine living than any one human shortcoming—it is hopelessly vulgar. Too many houses, when they are not little stage settings or scene paintings, are mere notion stores, bazaars or junk-shops. Decoration is dangerous unless you understand it

thoroughly and are satisfied that it means something good in the scheme as a whole, for the present you are usually better off without it. Merely that it "looks rich" is no justification for the use of ornament.

4. Appliances or fixtures as such are undesirable. Assimilate them together with all appurtenances into the design of the structure.

5. Pictures deface walls oftener than they decorate them. Pictures should be decorative and incorporated in the general scheme as decoration.

6. The most truly satisfactory apartments are those in which most or all of the furniture is built in as a part of the original scheme considering the whole as an integral unit.

II.—There should be as many kinds (styles) of houses as there are kinds (styles) of people and as many differentiations as there are different individuals. A man who has individuality (and what man lacks it?) has a right to its expression in his own environment.

III.—A building should appear to grow easily from its site and be shaped to harmonize with its surroundings if Nature is manifest there, and if not try to make it as quiet, substantial and organic as She would have been were the opportunity Hers.*

We of the Middle West are living on the prairie. The prairie has a beauty of its own and we should recognize and accentuate this natural beauty, its quiet level. Hence, gently sloping roofs, low proportions, quiet sky lines, suppressed heavy-set chimneys and sheltering overhangs, low terraces and out-reaching walls sequestering private gardens.

IV.—Colors require the same conventionalizing process to make them fit to live with that natural forms do; so go to the woods and fields for color schemes. Use the soft, warm, optimistic tones of earths and autumn leaves in preference to the pessimistic blues, purples or cold greens and grays of the ribbon counter; they are more wholesome and better adapted in most cases to good decoration.

*In this I had in mind the barren town lots devoid of tree or natural incident, town houses and board walks only in evidence.

V.—Bring out the nature of the materials, let their nature intimately into your scheme. Strip the wood of varnish and let it alone—stain it. Develop the natural texture of the plastering and stain it. Reveal the nature of the wood, plaster, brick or stone in your designs; they are all by nature friendly and beautiful. No treatment can be really a matter of fine art when these natural characteristics are, or their nature is, outraged or neglected.

VI.—A house that has character stands a good chance of growing more valuable as it grows older while a house in the prevailing mode, whatever that mode may be, is soon out of fashion, stale and unprofitable.

Buildings like people must first be sincere, must be true and then withal as gracious and lovable as may be.

Above all, integrity. The machine is the normal tool of our civilization, give it work that it can do well—nothing is of greater importance. To do this will be to formulate new industrial ideals, sadly needed.

These propositions are chiefly interesting because for some strange reason they were novel when formulated in the face of conditions hostile to them and because the ideals they phrase have been practically embodied in the buildings that were built to live up to them. The buildings of recent years have not only been true to them, but are in many cases a further development of the simple propositions so positively stated then.

Happily, these ideals are more commonplace now. Then the sky lines of our domestic architecture were fantastic abortions, tortured by features that disrupted the distorted roof surfaces from which attenuated chimneys like lean fingers threatened the sky; the invariably tall interiors were cut up into box-like compartments, the more boxes the finer the house; and "Architecture" chiefly consisted in healing over the edges of the curious collection of holes that had to be cut in the walls for light and air and to permit the occupant to get in or out. These interiors were always slaughtered with the butt and slash of the old plinth and corner block trim, of dubious origin, and finally smothered with horrible millinery.

That individuality in a building was possible for each home maker, or desirable, seemed at that time to rise to the dignity of an idea. Even cultured men and women care so little for the spiritual integrity of their environment; except in rare cases they are not touched, they simply do not care for the matter so long as their dwellings are fashionable or as good as those of their neighbors and keep them dry and warm. A structure has no more meaning to them æsthetically than has the stable to the horse. And this came to me in the early years as a definite discouragement. There are exceptions, and I found them chiefly among American men of business with unspoiled instincts and untainted ideals. A man of this type usually has the faculty of judging for himself. He has rather liked the "idea" and much of the encouragement this work receives comes straight from him because the "common sense" of the thing appeals to him. While the "cultured" are still content with their small châteaux, Colonial wedding cakes, English affectations or French millinery, he prefers a poor thing but his own. He errs on the side of character, at least, and when the test of time has tried his country's development architecturally, he will have contributed his quota, small enough in the final outcome though it be; he will be regarded as a true conservator.

In the hope that some day America may live her own life in her own buildings, in her own way, that is, that we may make the best of what we have for what it honestly is or may become, I have endeavored in this work to establish a harmonious relationship between ground plan and elevation of these buildings, considering the one as a solution and the other an expression of the conditions of a problem of which the whole is a project. I have tried to establish an organic integrity to begin with, forming the basis for the subsequent working out of a significant grammatical expression and making the whole, as nearly as I could, consistent.

What quality of style the buildings may possess is due to the artistry with which the conventionalization as a solution and an artistic expression of a specific problem within these limitations has been handled. The types are largely a matter of personal taste and may have much or little to do with the American architecture for which we hope.

From the beginning of my practice the question uppermost in my mind has been not "what style" but "what is style?" and it is my belief that the chief value of the work illustrated here will be found in the fact that if in the face of our present day conditions any given type may be treated independently and imbued with the quality of style, then a truly noble architecture is a definite possibility, so soon as Americans really demand it of the architects of the rising generation.

I do not believe we will ever again have the uniformity of type which has characterized the so-called great "styles." Conditions have changed; our ideal is Democracy, the highest possible expression of the individual as a unit not inconsistent with a harmonious whole. The average of human intelligence rises steadily, and as the individual unit grows more and more to be trusted we will have an architecture with richer variety in unity than has ever arisen before; but the forms must be born out of our changed conditions, they must be *true* forms, otherwise the best that tradition has to offer is only an inglorious masquerade, devoid of vital significance or true spiritual value. . . .

The trials of the early days were many and at this distance picturesque. Workmen seldom like to think, especially if there is financial risk entailed; at your peril do you disturb their established processes mental or technical. To do anything in an unusual, even if in a better and simpler way, is to complicate the situation at once. Simple things at that time in any industrial field were nowhere at hand. A piece of wood without a moulding was an anomaly; a plain wooden slat instead of a turned baluster a joke; the omission of the merchantable "grille" a crime; plain fabrics for hangings or floor covering were nowhere to be found in stock.

To become the recognized enemy of

the established industrial order was no light matter, for soon whenever a set of my drawings was presented to a Chicago mill-man for figures he would willingly enough unroll it, read the architect's name, shake his head and return it with the remark that he was "not hunting for trouble"; sagacious owners and general contractors tried cutting out the name, but in vain, his perspicacity was rat-like, he had come to know "the look of the thing." So, in addition to the special preparation in any case necessary for every little matter of construction and finishing, special detail drawings were necessary merely to show the things to be left off or not done, and not only studied designs for every part had to be made but quantity surveys and schedules of mill work furnished the contractors beside. This, in a year or two, brought the architect face to face with the fact that the fee for his service "established" by the American Institute of Architects was intended for something stock and shop, for it would not even pay for the bare drawings necessary for conscientious work.

The relation of the architect to the economic and industrial movement of his time, in any fine art sense, is still an affair so sadly out of joint that no one may easily reconcile it. All agree that something has gone wrong and except the architect be a plain factory magnate, who has reduced his art to a philosophy of old clothes and sells misfit or made-over-ready-to-wear garments with commercial aplomb and social distinction, he cannot succeed on the present basis established by common practice. So, in addition to a situation already complicated for them, a necessarily increased fee stared in the face the clients who dared. But some did dare, as the illustrations prove.

The struggle then was and still is to make "good architecture," "good business." It is perhaps significant that in the beginning it was very difficult to secure a building loan on any terms upon one of these houses, now it is easy to secure a better loan than ordinary; but how far success has attended this ambition the owners of these buildings alone can testify. Their trials have been many, but each, I think, feels that he has as much

house for his money as any of his neighbors, with something in the home intrinsically valuable besides, which will not be out of fashion in one lifetime, and which contributes steadily to his dignity and his pleasure as an individual.

It would not be useful to dwell further upon difficulties encountered, for it is the common story of simple progression everywhere in any field; I merely wish to trace here the "motif" behind the types. A study of the illustrations will show that the buildings presented fall readily into three groups having a family resemblance; the low-pitched hip roofs, heaped together in pyramidal fashion, or presenting quiet, unbroken skylines; the low roofs with simple pediments countering on long ridges; and those topped with a simple slab. Of the first type, the Winslow, Henderson, Willits, Thomas, Heurtley, Heath, Cheney, Martin, Little, Gridley, Millard, Tomek, Coonley and Westcott houses, the Hillside Home School and the Pettit Memorial Chapel are typical. Of the second type the Bradley, Hickox, Davenport and Dana houses are typical. Of the third, Atelier for Richard Bock, Unity Church, the concrete house of the Ladies' Home Journal and other designs in process of execution. The Larkin Building is a simple, dignified utterance of a plain, utilitarian type with sheer brick walls and simple stone copings. The studio is merely an early experiment in "articulation."

Photographs do not adequately present these subjects. A building has a presence as has a person that defies the photographer, and the color so necessary to the complete expression of the form is necessarily lacking, but it will be noticed that all the structures stand upon their foundations to the eye as well as physically. There is good, substantial preparation at the ground for all the buildings and it is the first grammatical expression of all the types. This preparation, or watertable, is to these buildings what the stylobate was to the ancient Greek temple. To gain it, it was necessary to reverse the established practice of setting the supports of the building to the outside of the wall and to set them to the inside, so as to leave the necessary support for the outer base. This was natural enough and good enough construction but many an owner was disturbed by private information from the practical contractor to the effect that he would have his whole house in the cellar if he submitted to it. This was at the time a marked innovation though the most natural thing in the world and to me, to this day, indispensable.

With this innovation established, one horizontal stripe of raw material, the foundation wall above ground, was eliminated and the complete grammar of type one made possible. A simple, unbroken wall surface from foot to level of second story sill was thus secured, a change of material occuring at that point to form the simple frieze that characterizes the earlier buildings. Even this was frequently omitted as in the Francis apartments and many other buildings and the wall was let alone from base to cornice or eaves.

"Dress reform houses" they were called, I remember, by the charitably disposed. What others called them will hardly bear repetition.

As the wall surfaces were thus simplified and emphasized the matter of fenestration became exceedingly difficult and more than ever important, and often I used to gloat over the beautiful buildings I could build if only it were unnecessary to cut holes in them; but the holes were managed at first frankly as in the Winslow house and later as elementary constituents of the structure grouped in rhythmical fashion, so that all the light and air and prospect the most rabid clinet could wish would not be too much from an artistic standpoint; and of this achievement I am proud. The groups are managed, too, whenever required, so that overhanging eaves do not shade them, although the walls are still protected from the weather. Soon the poetry-crushing characteristics of the guillotine window, which was then firmly rooted, became apparent and, single-handed I waged a determined battle for casements swinging out, although it was necessary to have special hardware made for them as there was none to be had this side of England. Clients would come ready to accept any

innovation but "those swinging windows," and when told that they were in the nature of the proposition and that they must take them or leave the rest, they frequently employed "the other fellow" to give them something "near," with the "practical" windows dear to their hearts.

With the grammar so far established, came an expression pure and simple, even classic in atmosphere, using that much-abused word in its best sense; implying, that is, a certain sweet reasonableness of form and outline naturally dignified.

I have observed that Nature usually perfects her forms; the individuality of the attribute is seldom sacrified; that is, deformed or mutilated by co-operative parts. She rarely says a thing and tries to take it back at the same time. She would not sanction the "classic" proceeding of, say, establishing an "order," a colonnade, then building walls between the columns of the order reducing them to pilasters, thereafter cutting holes in the wall and pasting on cornices with more pilasters around them, with the result that every form is outraged, the whole an abominable mutilation, as is most of the the architecture of the Renaissance wherein style corrodes style and all the forms are stultified.

In laying out the ground plans for even the more insignificant of these buildings a simple axial law and order and the ordered spacing upon a system of certain structural units definitely established for each structure in accord with its scheme of practical construction and æsthetic proportion, is practiced as an expedient to simplify the technical difficulties of execution, and, although the symmetry may not be obvious always the balance is usually maintained. The plans are as a rule much more articulate than is the school product of the Beaux Arts. The individuality of the various functions of the various features is more highly developed; all the forms are complete in themselves and frequently do duty at the same time from within and without as decorative attributes of the whole. This tendency to greater individuality of the parts emphasized by more and more complete articulation will be seen in the plans for Unity Church, the cottage for Elizabeth Stone at Glencoe and the Avery Coonly house in process of construction at Riverside, Illinois. Moreover, these ground plans are merely the actual projection of a carefully considered whole. The "architecture" is not "thrown up" as an artistic exercise, a matter of elevation from a preconceived ground plan. The schemes are conceived in three dimensions as organic entities, let the picturesque perspective fall how it will. While a sense of the incidental perspectives the design will develop is always present, I have great faith that if the thing is rightly put together in true organic sense with proportions actually right the picturesque will take care of itself. No man ever built a building worthy the name of architecture who fashioned it in perspective sketch to his taste and then fudged the plan to suit. Such methods produce mere scene-painting. A perspective may be a proof but it is no nurture.

As to the mass values of the buildings the æsthetic principles outlined in proposition III will account in a measure for their character.

In the matter of decoration the tendency has been to indulge it less and less, in many cases merely providing certain architectural preparation for natural foliage or flowers, as it is managed in say, the entrance to the Lawrence house at Springfield. This use of natural foliage and flowers for decoration is carried to quite an extent in all the designs and, although the buildings are complete without this effloresence, they may be said to blossom with the season. What architectural decoration the buildings carry is not only conventionalized to the point where it is quiet and stays as a sure foil for the nature forms from which it is derived and with which it must intimately associate, but it is always *of* the surface, never *on* it.

The windows usually are provided with characteristic straight line patterns absolutely in the flat and usually severe. The nature of the glass is taken into account in these designs as is also the metal bar used in their construction, and most of them are treated as metal "grilles" with glass inserted forming a simple rhythmic arrangement of straight lines and squares made as cunning as possible so long as the result is quiet. The aim is that the designs shall make the best of the technical contrivances that produce them.

In the main the ornamentation is wrought in the warp and woof of the structure. It is constitutional in the best sense and is felt in the conception of the ground plan. To elucidate this element in composition would mean a long story and perhaps a tedious one though to me it is the most fascinating phase of the work, involving the true poetry of conception.

The differentiation of a single, certain simple form characterizes the expression of one building. Quite a different form may serve for another, but from one basic idea all the formal elements of design are in each case derived and held well together in scale and character. The form chosen may flare outward, opening flower-like to the sky as in the Thomas house; another, droop to accentuate artistically the weight of the masses; another be non-committal or abruptly emphatic, or its grammar may be deduced from some plant form that has appealed to me, as certain properties in line and form of the sumach were used in the Lawrence house at Springfield; but in every case the motif is adhered to throughout so that it is not too much to say that each building æsthetically is cut from one piece of goods and consistently hangs together with an integrity impossible otherwise.

In a fine art sense these designs have grown as natural plants grow, the individuality of each is integral and as complete as skill, time, strength and circumstances would permit.

The method in itself does not of necessity produce a beautiful building, but it does provide a framework as a basis which has an organic integrity, susceptible to the architect's imagination and at once opening to him Nature's wealth of artistic suggestion, ensuring him a guiding principle within which he can never be wholly false, out of tune, or lacking in rational motif. The subtleties, the shifting blending harmonies, the cadences, the nuances are a matter of his own nature, his own susceptibilities and faculties.

But self denial is imposed upon the architect to a far greater extent than upon any other member of the fine art family. The temptation to sweeten work, to make each detail in itself lovable and expressive is always great; but that the whole may be truly eloquent of its ultimate function restraint is imperative. To let individual elements arise and shine at the expense of final repose is for the architect, a betrayal of trust for buildings are the background or framework for the human life within their walls and a foil for the nature efflorescence without. So architecture is the most complete of conventionalizations and of all the arts the most subjective except music.

Music may be for the architect ever and always a sympathetic friend whose counsels, precepts and patterns even are available to him and from which he need not fear to draw. But the arts are to-day all cursed by literature; artists attempt to make literature even of music, usually of painting and sculpture and doubtless would of architecture also, were the art not moribund; but whenever it is done the soul of the thing dies and we have not art but something far less for which the true artist can have neither affection nor respect. . . .

Contrary to the usual supposition this manner of working out a theme is more flexible than any working out in a fixed, historic style can ever be, and the individuality of those concerned may receive more adequate treatment within legitimate limitations. This matter of individuality puzzles many; they suspect that the individuality of the owner and occupant of a building is sacrificed to that of the architect who imposes his own upon Jones, Brown and Smith alike. An architect worthy of the name has an individuality, it is true; his work will and should reflect it, and his buildings will all bear a family resemblance one to another. The individuality of an owner is first manifest in his choice of his architect, the individual to whom he entrusts his characterization. He sympathizes with his work; its expression suits him

and this furnishes the common ground upon which client and architect may come together. Then, if the architect is what he ought to be, with his ready technique he conscientiously works for the client, idealizes his client's character and his client's tastes and makes him feel that the building is his as it really is to such an extent that he can truly say that he would rather have his own house than any other he has ever seen. Is a portrait, say by Sargent, any less a revelation of the character of the subject because it bears his stamp and is easily recognized by any one as a Sargent? Does one lose his individuality when it is interpreted sympathetically by one of his own race and time who can know him and his needs intimately and idealize them; or does he gain it only by having adopted or adapted to his condition a ready-made historic style which is the fruit of a seed-time other than his, whatever that style may be?

The present industrial condition is constantly studied in the practical application of these architectural ideals and the treatment simplified and arranged to fit modern processes and to utilize to the best advantage the work of the machine. The furniture takes the clean cut, straight-line forms that the machine can render far better than would be possible by hand. Certain facilities, too, of the machine, which it would be interesting to enlarge upon, are taken advantage of and the nature of the materials is usually revealed in the process.

Nor is the atmosphere of the result in its completeness new and hard. In most of the interiors there will be found a quiet, a simple dignity that we imagine is only to be found in the "old" and it is due to the underlying organic harmony, to the each in all and the all in each throughout. This is the modern opportunity—to make of a building, together with its equipment, appurtenances and environment, an entity which shall constitute a complete work of art, and a work of art more valuable to society as a whole than has before existed because discordant conditions endured for centuries are smoothed away; everyday life here finds an expression germane to its daily existence; an idealization of the common need sure to be uplifting and helpful in the same sense that pure air to breathe is better than air poisoned with noxious gases.

An artist's limitations are his best friends. The machine is here to stay. It is the forerunner of the democracy that is our dearest hope. There is no more important work before the architect now that to use this normal tool of civilization to the best advantage instead of prostituting it as he has hitherto done in reproducing with murderous ubiquity forms born of other times and other conditions and which it can only serve to destroy.

*   *   *   *   *   *

The exteriors of these structures will receive less ready recognition perhaps than the interiors and because they are the result of a radically different conception as to what should constitute a building. We have formed a habit of mind concerning architecture to which the expression of most of these exteriors must be a shock, at first more or less disagreeable, and the more so as the habit of mind is more narrowly fixed by so called classic training. Simplicity is not in itself an end; it is a means to an end. Our æsthetics are dyspeptic from incontinent indulgence in "Frenchite" pastry. We crave ornament for the sake of ornament; cover up our faults of design with ornamental sensualities that were a long time ago sensuous ornament. We will do well to distrust this unwholesome and unholy craving and look to the simple line; to the clean though living form and quiet color for a time, until the true significance of these things has dawned for us once more. The old structural forms which up to the present time, have spelled "architecture" are decayed. Their life went from them long ago and new conditions industrially, steel and concrete and terra cotta in particular, are prophesying a more plastic art wherein as the flesh is to our bones so will the covering be to the structure, but more truly and beautifully expressive than ever. But that is a long story. This reticence in the matter of ornamentation is characteristic of these structures and for at least two reasons; first, they are the expression of

an idea that the ornamentation of a building should be constitutional, a matter of the nature of the structure beginning with the ground plan. In the buildings themselves, in the sense of the whole, there is lacking neither richness nor incident but their qualities are secured not by applied decoration, they are found in the fashioning of the whole, in which color, too, plays as significant a part as it does in an old Japanese wood block print. Second; because, as before stated, buildings perform their highest function in relation to human life within and the natural efflorescence without; and to develop and maintain the harmony of a true chord between them making of the building in this sense a sure foil for life, broad simple surfaces and highly conventionalized forms are inevitable. These ideals take the buildings out of school and marry them to the ground; make them intimate expressions or revelations of the exteriors; individualize them regardless of preconceived notions of style. I have tried to make their grammar perfect in its way and to give their forms and proportions an integrity that will bear study, although few of them can be intelligently studied apart from their environment. So, what might be termed the democratic character of the exteriors is their first undefined offence—the lack, wholly, of what the professional critic would deem architecture; in fact, most of the critic's architecture has been left out.

There is always a synthetic basis for the features of the various structures, and consequently a constantly accumulating residue of formulae, which becomes more and more useful; but I do not pretend to say that the perception or conception of them was not at first intuitive, or that those that lie yet beyond will not be grasped in the same intuitive way; but, after all, architecture is a scientific art, and the thinking basis will ever be for the architect his surety, the final court in which his imagination sifts his feelings. . . .

The few draughtsmen so far associated with this work have been taken into the draughting room, in every case almost wholly unformed, many of them with no particular previous training, and patiently nursed for years in the atmosphere of the work itself, until, saturated by intimate association, at an impressionable age, with its motifs and phases, they have become helpful. To develop the sympathetic grasp of detail that is necessary before this point is reached has proved usually a matter of years, with little advantage on the side of the college-trained understudy. These young people have found their way to me through natural sympathy with the work, and have become loyal assistants. The members, so far, all told here and elsewhere, of our little university of fourteen years' standing are: Marion Mahony, a capable assistant for eleven years; William Drummond, for seven years; Francis Byrne, five years; Isabel Roberts, five years; George Willis, four years; Walter Griffin, four years; Andrew Willatzen, three years; Harry Robinson, two years; Charles E. White, Jr., one year; Erwin Barglebaugh and Robert Hardin, each one year; Albert McArthur, entering.

Others have been attracted by what seemed to them to be the novelty of the work, staying only long enough to acquire a smattering of form, then departing to sell a superficial proficiency elsewhere. Still others shortly develop a mastery of the subject, discovering that it is all just as they would have done it, anyway, and, chafing at the unkind fate that forestalled them in its practice, resolve to blaze a trail for themselves without further loss of time. It is urged against the more loyal that they are sacrificing their individuality to that which has dominated this work; but it is too soon to impeach a single understudy on this basis, for, although they will inevitably repeat for years the methods, forms and habit of thought, even the mannerisms of the present work, if there is virtue in the principles behind it that virtue will stay with them through the preliminary stages of their own practice until their own individualities truly develop independently. I have noticed that those who have made the most fuss about their "individuality" in early stages, those who took themselves most seriously in that regard, were inevitably those who had least.

Many elements of Mr. Sullivan's personality in his art—what might be called his mannerisms—naturally enough clung to my work in the early years, and may be readily traced by the casual observer; but for me one real proof of the virtue inherent in this work will lie in the fact that some of the young men and women who have given themselves up to me so faithfully these past years will some day contribute rounded individualities of their own, and forms of their own devising to the new school.

This year I assign to each a project that has been carefully conceived in my own mind, which he accepts as a specific work. He follows its subsequent development through all its phases in drawing room and field, meeting with the client himself on occasion, gaining an all-round development impossible otherwise, and insuring an enthusiasm and a grasp of detail decidedly to the best interest of the client. These privileges in the hands of selfishly ambitious or overconfident assistants would soon wreck such a system; but I can say that among my own boys it has already proved a moderate success, with every prospect of being continued as a settled policy in future.

Nevertheless, I believe that only when one individual forms the concept of the various projects and also determines the character of every detail in the sum total, even to the size and shape of the pieces of glass in the windows, the arrangement and profile of the most insignificant of the architectural members, will that unity be secured which is the soul of the individual work of art. This means that fewer buildings should be entrusted to one architect. His output will of necessity be relatively small— small, that is, as compared to the volume of work turned out in any one of fifty "successful offices" in America. I believe there is no middle course worth considering in the light of the best future of American architecture. With no more propriety can an architect leave the details touching the form of his concept to assistants, no matter how sympathetic and capable they may be, than can a painter entrust the painting in of the details of his picture to a pupil; for an architect who would do individual work must have a technique well developed and peculiar to himself, which, if he is fertile, is still growing with his growth. To keep everything "in place" requires constant care and study in matters that the old-school practitioner would scorn to touch. . . .

As for the future—the work shall grow more truly simple; more expressive with fewer lines, fewer forms; more articulate with less labor; more plastic; more fluent, although more coherent; more organic. It shall grow not only to fit more perfectly the methods and processes that are called upon to produce it, but shall further find whatever is lovely or of good repute in method or process, and idealize it with the cleanest, most virile stroke I can imagine. As understanding and appreciation of life matures and deepens, this work shall prophesy and idealize the character of the individual it is fashioned to serve more intimately, no matter how inexpensive the result must finally be. It shall become in its atmosphere as pure and elevating in its humble way as the trees and flowers are in their perfectly appointed way, for only so can architecture be worthy its high rank as a fine art, or the architect discharge the obligation he assumes to the public—imposed upon him by the nature of his own profession.

Frank Lloyd Wright.

EXHIBIT OF FRANK LLOYD WRIGHT AT THE CHICAGO ARCHITECTURAL CLUB, 1908.

Buffalo, N. Y.   THE LARKIN BUILDING.

The Larkin Building is one of a large group of factory buildings situated in the factory district of Buffalo. It was built to house the commercial engine of the Larkin Company in light, wholesome, well-ventilated quarters. The smoke, noise and dirt incident to the locality made it imperative that all exterior surfaces be self cleaning and the interior be created independently of this environment. The building is a simple working out of certain utilitarian conditions, its exterior a simple cliff of brick whose only "ornamental" feature is the exterior expression of the central aisle, fashioned by means of the sculptured piers at either end of the main block. The machinery of the various appurtenance systems, pipe shafts incidental thereto, the heating and ventilating air in-takes, and the stairways which serve also as fire escapes, are quartered in plan and placed outside the main building at the four outer corners, so that the entire area might be free for working purposes. These stair chambers are top-lighted. The interior of the main building thus forms a single large room in which the main floors are galleries open to a large central court, which is also lighted from above. All the windows of the various stories or "galleries" are seven feet above the floor, the space beneath being utilized for steel filing cabinets. The window sash are double, and the building practically sealed to dirt, odor and noise, fresh air being taken high above the ground in shafts extending above the roof surfaces. The interior is executed throughout in vitreous,

Buffalo, N. Y.   THE LARKIN BUILDING.

cream-colored brick, with floor and trimmings of "magnesite" of the same color. The various
features of this trim were all formed within the building itself by means of simple wooden
molds, in most cases being worked directly in place. So the decorative forms were necessarily
simple, particularly so as this material becomes very hot while setting and expands slightly
in the process. The furnishings and fittings are all of steel and were designed with the
structure. The entrance vestibules, from either street and the main lobby, together with the
toilet accommodations and rest rooms for employees, are all located in an annex which inter-
cepts the light from the main office as little as possible. The fifth floor is given to a
restaurant for employees, with conservatories in mezzanines over kitchen and bakery at either
end, opening in turn to the main roof, all of which together constitutes the only recreation
ground available for employees. The structure, which is completely fireproof, together with
its modern heating, ventilating and appurtenance system, but exclusive of metal fixtures and
furnishings, cost but little more than the average high class fireproof factory building—18 cts.
per cubic foot. Here again most of the critic's "architecture" has been left out. Therefore
the work may have the same claim to consideration as a "work of art" as an ocean liner, a
locomotive or a battleship.

LARKIN BUILDING—FOURTH STORY GALLERY.

LARKIN BUILDING—OFFICERS' DESKS—FLOOR OF MAIN COURT.
Buffalo, N. Y.

LARKIN BUILDING—METAL FURNITURE CLOSED TO ADMIT OF EASY CLEANING.

Buffalo, N. Y.   LARKIN BUILDING—METAL FURNITURE READY FOR USE.

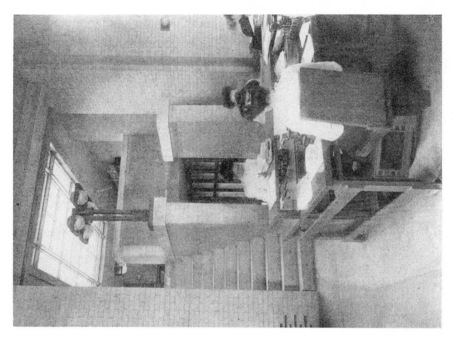

LARKIN BUILDING—TYPICAL GALLERY FLOOR.

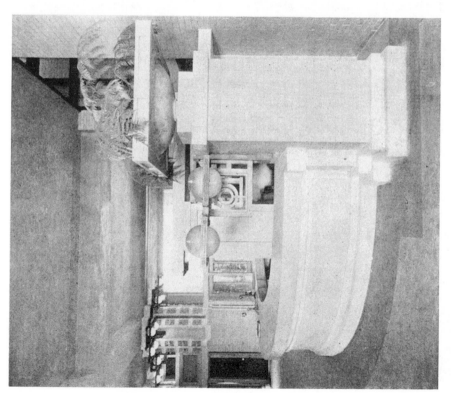

LARKIN BUILDING—INFORMATION BUREAU AND TELEPHONE CENTRAL.
Buffalo, N. Y.

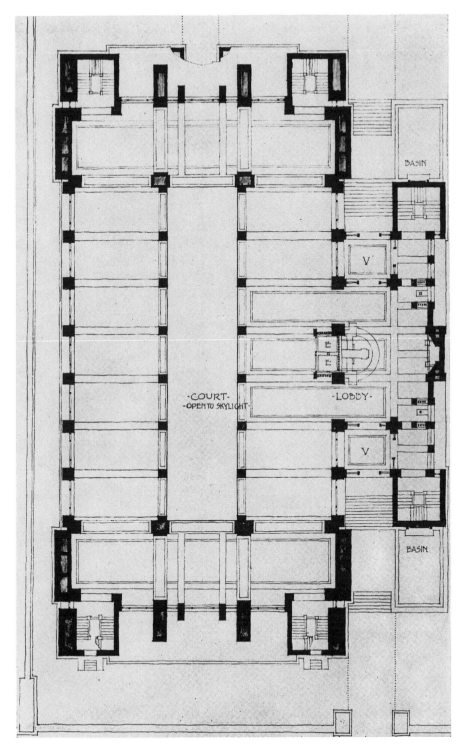

Buffalo, N. Y.   LARKIN BUILDING—MAIN FLOOR PLAN.

Buffalo, N. Y. THE LARKIN BUILDING—HOUSING AN INDUSTRY.

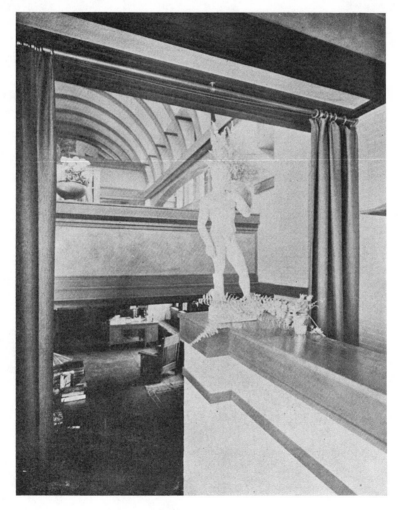

Springfield, Ill. HOUSE OF MRS. S. L. DANA.

General exterior view shown above. Interior of gallery, library beneath.

A house designed to accommodate the art collection of its owner and for entertaining exten-
sively, somewhat elaborately worked out in detail. Fixtures and furnishings designed
with the structure.

HOUSE OF MRS. S. L. DANA—VIEW FROM FOURTH STREET.

DANA HOUSE—DETAIL OF MAIN ENTRANCE, SHOWING VISTA INTO LIVING HALL.

DANA HOUSE—GENERAL VIEW FROM CORNER.

DANA HOUSE—FIREPLACE ALCOVE AT END OF GALLERY. BALCONY ABOVE.

DANA HOUSE—DINING ROOM.

DANA HOUSE—GALLERY AND LIBRARY.

BREAKFAST NOOK IN THE DANA HOUSE.

B. HARLEY BRADLEY HOUSE—LIVING ROOM.

Kankakee, Ill.   B. HARLEY BRADLEY HOUSE—PLASTERED EXTERIOR.

B. HARLEY BRADLEY HOUSE—LIVING ROOM FIREPLACE.

P. A. BEACHEY HOUSE, OAK PARK, ILL.—BRICK, PLASTER AND TIMBER EXTERIOR.

DINING ROOM OF BRADLEY HOUSE.

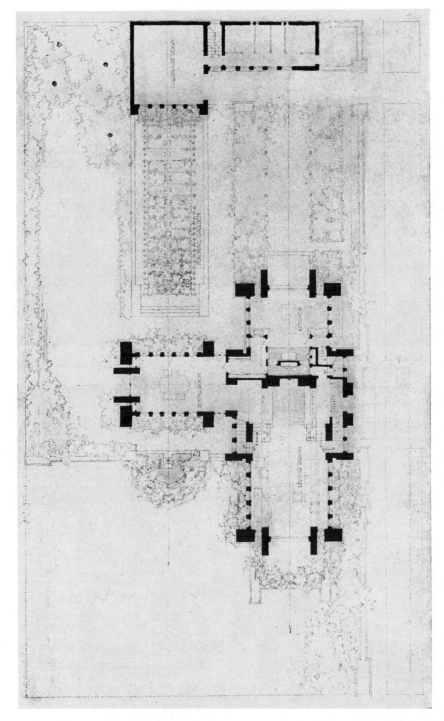

Oak Park, Ill.   H. J. ULLMAN HOUSE—GROUND PLAN OF PROPOSED RESIDENCE.

In this plan the dining room floor is at the garden level, with porch above the former; both dining room and porch being reached by steps from living room.

W. H. WINSLOW HOUSE—BRICK, STONE AND TILE EXTERIOR.

River Forest, Ill.

Oak Park, Ill.   THOMAS HOUSE.
   Basement entirely above ground. Ground floor entrance to living rooms on first floor,
                      bed rooms above.

ARTHUR HEURTLEY HOUSE.
Same type as Thomas House, with living rooms, kitchen and family bed rooms on main floor.
Two guest rooms and bath, children's playroom and servants' room on ground floor.

F. F. TOMEK HOUSE.

Plastered walls, tile roof. Basement entirely above ground. Ground floor entrance to living rooms on first floor. Designed for low, damp prairie. Bed rooms in upper story.

MRS. E. L. MARTIN'S HOUSE.

Oak Park, Ill.

A plastered house. The horizontal members utilized as protections for the plastered walls.
The eaves, plastic in form, suited to the method of construction.

F. F. TOMEK HOUSE—SHOWING CANTILEVER ROOF OVER TERRACES.

THE W. A. GLASNER HOUSE.
Glencoe, Ill.

A characteristic type of wooden dwelling, of which a number have been built to meet various simple requirements. In this case all the rooms and the porch are on one floor, with servants' room and laundry below. The side walls beneath the windows are covered with undressed boards jointed with inserted battens. The frieze and underside of eaves are plastered. Total cost about $5,500. The whole fits its site on the edge of a picturesque ravine.

MRS. E. L. MARTIN'S HOUSE.

Oak Park, Ill.

Showing porch managed as a semi-detached pavilion. A practical solution of the "porch problem."

MR. WARD W. WILLITS' HOUSE.

Highland Park, Ill.

ROBERT CLARK HOUSE—HOUSE, STABLE AND ENCLOSED GARDEN.

Peoria, Ill.

General View.

Detail of exterior of assembly room.

THE HILLSIDE HOME SCHOOL—SANDSTONE AND SOLID OAK TIMBER CONSTRUCTION.
Hillside, Wis.

MR. WALTER S. GERTS' SUMMER LODGE.

Birch Brook, Mich.

MR. CHARLES S. ROSS' SUMMER COTTAGE.

Lake Delavan, Wis.

HILLSIDE HOME SCHOOL—INTERIOR VIEW.

SUMMER COTTAGE—MRS. GEO. E. GERTS.

Birch Brook, Mich.

W. R. HEATH HOUSE.
Red brick with cement trimmings. Red tile roof.

Buffalo, N. Y.

MR. W. W. WILLITS' HOUSE—DETAIL.

Highland Park, Ill.   MR. W. W. WILLITS' HOUSE.
Living rooms within the terrace. View from south.

MRS. HELEN W. HUSSER, BUENA PARK, CHICAGO.

S. M. B. Hunt House, La Grange, Ill. Plan and two views of a typical, moderate cost house of the ordinary basement and two-story type with plastered exterior and undressed wood trim. The main floor is treated as a single room with separate working department, and has been reduced to the simplest terms consistent with reasonable comfort and privacy. The house has a trunk room opening from the stair landing—four bed rooms and bath on the second story, store room and laundry in basement. Total cost about $6,000.00 complete.

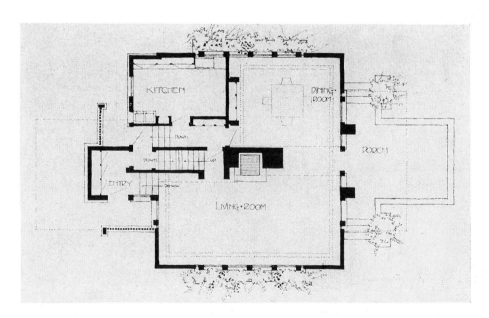

S. M. B. HUNT HOUSE—FIRST FLOOR PLAN.

La Grange, Ill.

LIVING ROOM SIDE.

S. M. B. HUNT HOUSE—PORCH SIDE.

La Grange, Ill.

D. D. MARTIN HOUSE—GENERAL VIEW.

Buffalo, N. Y.

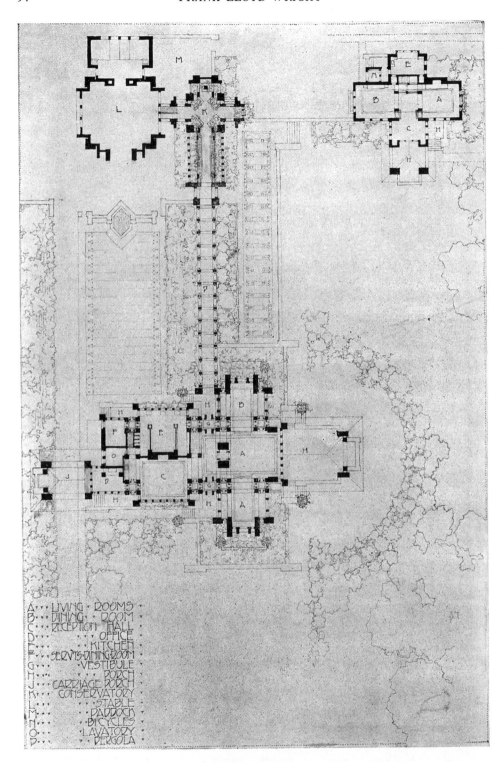

A···LIVING·ROOMS·
B···DINING·ROOM·
C···RECEPTION·HALL·
D···OFFICE·
E···KITCHEN·
F···SERV'TS·DINING·ROOM·
G···VESTIBULE·
H···PORCH·
J···CARRIAGE·PORCH·
K···CONSERVATORY·
L···STABLE·
M···PADDOCK·
N···BICYCLES·
O···LAVATORY·
P···PERGOLA·

D. D. MARTIN HOUSE—PLAN.

Buffalo, N. Y.

Details of conservatory.

D. D. MARTIN HOUSE.

Looking toward conservatory.

Buffalo, N. Y.

D. D. MARTIN HOUSE—HEAT AND LIGHT UNIT.

Reference to the general plan of the Martin house will show certain free standing groups of piers, of which the above is an illustration. In the central chamber formed by the piers the radiators are located, and the lighting fixtures are concentrated upon the piers themselves. Bookcases swinging outward are placed below between the piers; the open spaces above are utilized as cabinets, and from these the heat passes into the rooms. Fresh air is let into the central chamber through openings between the piers and the bookcases. The radiators and the appurtenance systems are thus made an artistic feature of the architecture.

(See page 45.) The Martin house is fireproof, the walls are of brick, floors of reinforced concrete overlaid with ceramic mosaic, roofs tiled. The vitreous brick used in the exterior walls is worked with bronzed joints into the walls and piers of the interior. The brick on these interior surfaces is used in a decorative sense as a mosaic. The woodwork throughout is of fumed white oak. A pergola connects the house with a conservatory, which in turn is connected by means of a covered way with the stable.

LIVING ROOM OF THE MARTIN HOUSE.

Fireplace opening with bronze doors to either hall or dining room or both. Facings of low toned gold mosaic; wistaria blossoms in bright gold.

D. D. MARTIN HOUSE—DINING ROOM.

D. D. MARTIN HOUSE—SOUTH ROOM.

Buffalo, N. Y.

D. D. MARTIN HOUSE.
Detail in conservatory.

D. D. MARTIN HOUSE.
Detail of library, bay and terrace.

Buffalo, N. Y.   THE BARTON HOUSE OF THE MARTIN GROUP.

This design is representative also of a type, total cost ranging from seven to ten thousand dollars. The main floor is treated as a single room, entered at the middle of the side. A central stair hall, with dining room and living room screened at either end, are formed within this room by architectural contrivances not extending to the ceiling. The kitchen and the porch balance each other as protruding wings on the minor axis. The second story contains four bed rooms, servants' room and bath. (See general plan, D. D. Martin House.)

Conservatory and stable.

D. D. MARTIN HOUSE.

Buffalo, N. Y.

Pergola and conservatory and entrance.   Stone bird houses.

BROWNE'S BOOK STORE—DETAIL OF INTERIOR.
Fine Arts Building, **Chicago.**

Entrance to office.

Oak Park, Ill.   OFFICE OF MR. FRANK LLOYD WRIGHT.
                            An alcove in the drafting room.

Oak Park, Ill.   RESIDENCE OF MR. H. H. CHENEY.
A one-story brick house set within terraces and small gardens, enclosed by brick walls.

LIBRARY OF MR. WRIGHT'S OAK PARK OFFICE.

STUDY FOR DINING ROOM OF THE DANA HOUSE.
Springfield, Ill.

To avoid distortion in rendering, the side wall has been shown cut away. The decorative
frieze around the room is treated with the Shumac, Golden Rod and Purple Aster that
characterize our roadsides in September.

PLASTER MODEL—HOUSE AND TEMPLE FOR UNITY CHURCH—VIEW OF END OF AUDITORIUM.
Oak Park, Ill.

A concrete monolith cast in wooden molds or "forms" and now in process of construction. A photograph on another page shows the work so far completed. After removing the forms the exterior surfaces are washed clean to expose the small gravel aggregate, the finished result in texture and effect being not unlike a coarse granite. The columns, with their decoration, were cast and treated in the same way. The entrance to either building is common to both, and connects them at the center. Both buildings are lighted from above. The roofs are simple reinforced concrete slabs waterproofed. The auditorium is a frank revival of the old temple form, as better suited to the requirements of a modern congregation than the nave and transept of the cathedral type. The speaker is placed well out into the auditorium, his audience gathered about him in the fashion of a friendly gathering, rather than as fixed in deep ranks when it was imperative that the priest make himself the cynosure of all eyes. The audience enters independently of, and at the rear of the auditorium, by means of depressed passages on either side. After services the audience moves directly toward the pulpit and out at either side of the auditorium itself. Unity House is designed for the various social activities of the church and for the Sunday school.

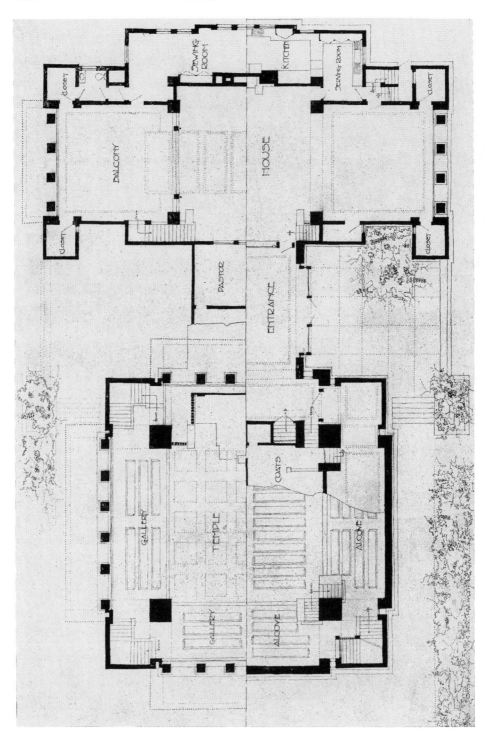

Oak Park, Ill.

BUILDING FOR UNITY CHURCH—MAIN FLOOR PLAN.

PERSPECTIVE STUDY—BUILDING FOR UNITY CHURCH.

Oak Park, Ill.

INEXPENSIVE CONCRETE HOUSE DESIGNED FOR THE LADIES' HOME JOURNAL—
PROCESS OF CONSTRUCTION SAME AS IN BUILDING FOR UNITY CHURCH.

BUILDING FOR UNITY CHURCH IN PROCESS OF CONSTRUCTION.
Oak Park, Ill.

MR. RICHARD W. BOCK'S ATELIER.

This structure is designed for concrete construction similar to building for Unity Church.

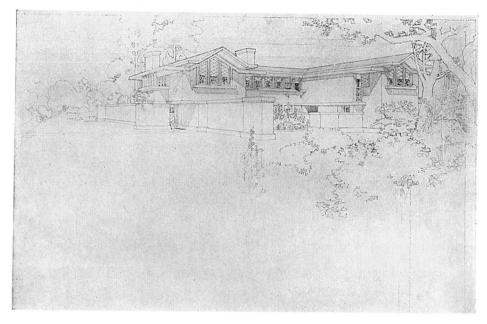

Glencoe, Ill.   MR. W. S. GERTS' HOUSE.

Racine, Wis.   THE THOMAS P. HARDY HOUSE.
Situated on the bank of Lake Michigan. The street front is opposite to the view here given.

THE ELIZABETH STONE HOUSE.

Glencoe, Ill.

HOUSE FOR MR. B. J. WESTCOTT.

Springfield, Ohio.

A simple treatment of the same problem as the Coonley house at Riverside, Ill. Living room
at center; dining room on one side and sleeping rooms on the other; service wing
extending from the rear of the living room.

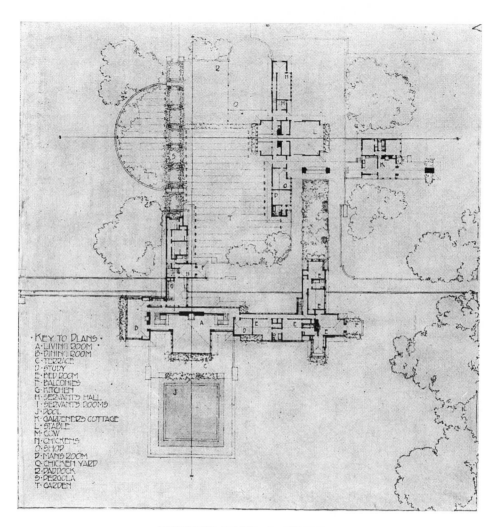

KEY TO PLANS
A·LIVING ROOM·
B·DINING ROOM
C·TERRACE
D·STUDY
E·BED ROOM
F·BALCONIES
G·KITCHEN
H·SERVANTS HALL
I·SERVANTS ROOMS
J·POOL
K·GARDENERS COTTAGE
L·STABLE
M·COW
N·CHICKENS
O·SHOP
P·MANS ROOM
Q·CHICKEN YARD
R·PADDOCK
S·PERGOLA
T·GARDEN

RESIDENCE OF MR. A. COONLEY.
Riverside, Ill.

A one-story house designed for the prairie, but with the basement entirely above ground, similar to Thomas, Heurtley and Tomek houses. All rooms, except entrance hall and play room, are on one floor. Each separate function in the house is treated for and by itself, with light and air on three sides, and grouped together as a harmonious whole. The living room is the pivot of the arrangement, with entrance, play room and terraces below, level with the ground, forming the main unit of the design. The dining room forms another unit. The kitchen and servants' quarters are in an independent wing. Family sleeping rooms form still another unit, and the guest rooms a pendant wing. Stable and gardener's cottage are grouped together and informally connected by a covered way which terminates in the gardener's verandah. An arbor crosses the garden to the rear, terminating in the service entrance. The stables, stable yards and gardens are enclosed by plastered walls.

RESIDENCE FOR MR. GEORGE M. MILLARD, HIGHLAND PARK, ILL.

Exterior of undressed wood throughout. The second story contains five bed rooms and two bath rooms. Man's room, laundry and store rooms in basement. This house is one of a type ranging in cost from seven to eight thousand dollars, complete.

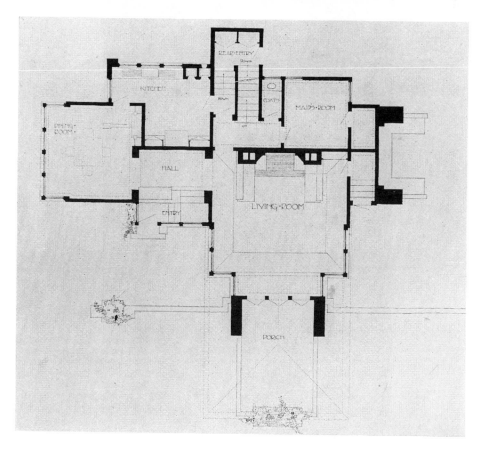

RESIDENCE OF MR. B. J. WESTCOTT.

Springfield, Ohio.

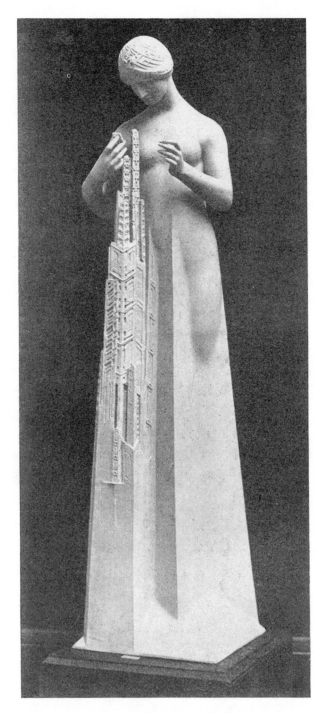

"FLOWER IN THE CRANNIED WALL."
A DECORATIVE FIGURE IN CREAM WHITE TERRA COTTA, DESIGNED FOR THE HALL-
WAY OF THE DANA HOUSE.

Richard W. Bock, Sculptor.

LOBE.—AMIENS CATHEDRAL.

SKELETON CONSTRUCTION.

THE NEW METHOD OF CONSTRUCTING HIGH BUILDINGS.

ITHIN the past three or four years a new method of constructing very high buildings in New York has come into vogue. It is known as the skeleton construction, and consists in the use of iron or steel columns, with thin curtain walls between, in place of solid thick brick walls. The curtain walls themselves are carried on wrought iron or rolled steel girders spanning the distance between the columns, which is usually about 15 feet. In addition, the weight of floors is also transmitted to the columns, so that the latter support the entire building and contents. The columns are encased with brick-work, and when the building is plastered and finished on the inside there is no visable evidence of novelty.

The advantage of using the composite construction is the room space gained in the difference between a thick wall and a thin one. In the ordinary method of building, the higher a brick wall the thicker it must be in its lower parts. The New York building law very properly requires a wall to be built on the principle of a mast of a ship, the off-sets at various stories in the thickness of a wall in heights securing what is in effect a taper from the bottom to the top. The lower story of a building is the most valuable for rental, yet it is in this story, of all the stories above the sidewalk, that the greatest area of a valuable lot must, under the old method, be wholly surrendered to enormously thick brick walls. Every inch gained in the width or length of the inside measurements of a costly building increases the availability of the structure, and therefore swells the income derived therefrom by the owner; but when this gain of space is feet instead of inches, in width and length as well, the reasons become obvious why the new method of construction, which takes up less than one-half of the area of plain brick walls, should immediately spring into public favor after an example or two had proved its strength, safety and probable durability. The great value of favorably located lots, fairly forces owners to build skywards in order to get an adequate return on their investment. The London and Lancashire Insurance Company not long ago erected an office building on a lot which the company purchased on Pine street, New York City, immediately adjoining the U. S. Sub-Treasury property. The lot measures 24.2 front by 74.4 deep, and the price paid for the same was $195,000. The lot is one foot

117

wider on the rear than it is on the front, and one side is one inch deeper than the other side, so that the actual area of the lot is about 1,834 feet, and makes the price figure about $106 per superficial foot. The old building was torn down, and a new building erected of the skeleton construction. The curtain walls between the vertical columns are 12 inches thick, the same thickness in the first story as in the tenth story. Lots on Wall street and lower Broadway are of greater proportionate value than that of the Lancashire Company, which has an area of only three-quarters of the unit of a city lot.

The era of high buildings began with the year 1870. Let any person who has long been a resident of New York draw on his memory and he will find that all high buildings which in the popular and received interpretation of that term are now so styled, are of a date subsequent to the erection of the Post Office building. Prior to that date there was a very limited number of fire-proof buildings within the limits of the United States. Those which did exist were chiefly Government buildings. Only ten years before that the first "I" beams were rolled in this country. Peter Cooper's Trenton, N. J. Mills, and the Phœnix Iron Co., of Pennsylvania, began to manufacture them about the same time. In the early fire-proof buildings—the Cooper Union, Harper's publishing building and the New York Historical Library building —the iron floor beams are of a shape very similar to what are commonly known as deck beams, with brick arches between. It was seen that if buildings were to be built higher than the conventional five or six story limit, to a height beyond the ability of firemen to successfully cope with a fire, such buildings must be constructed with something better for the floors, partitions, stairs and roofs than a mass of wooden beams, studs, plank, furring and lathing, and more scientifically arranged than a pile of kindling wood for burning, each piece being separated and exposed to the air. With the incoming of high build-

ings came a safer construction. Eight or ten stories in height—the height always being considered as above the sidewalk, and not including the stories below that level nor including towers nor stories above the level of the main roof—seemed to be the limit for a long time that owners could see their interest in going to. Suddenly a very much higher jump has been made, and it is a matter of general knowledge that Mr. Astor's new hotel, now erecting at 59th street and 5th avenue, will be seventeen stories in height. It is quite as generally known that the proprietors of the *Sun* are talking of putting up a new building, to be some twenty-eight stories in height, on their little corner which only measures 57 by 72 feet.

The accompanying plan shows the relative space occupied by the walls in

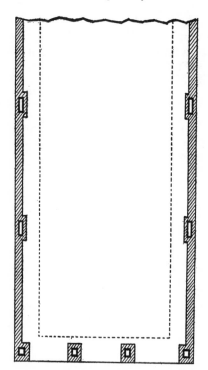

the new system and the old, the dotted lines representing the portion of the area of a lot that solid brick walls would occupy. High buildings are demanded, and to-day there is simply no limit to the height that a building can be safely erected. This result has been reached mainly through three inventions, all of which are distinctively American:

1. The modern passage elevator.
2. The flat-arch system for fire-proof floors; and
3. The skeleton construction.

The last enumerated one has only lately joined the combination in which the first two were so long inseperable, but it has come to stay, and the three work in unity for a common purpose. It is with the third invention that this article has to deal, but the other two form so important elements to a comprehensive understanding of the usefulness of the third, that a brief reference to them will be necessary.

Up to the year 1870 the elevator was not used to any great extent for passenger service. Many persons will recollect the old elevator in the Fifth Avenue Hotel, with its vertical iron screw extending the whole height of the elevator well, and passing through a sleeve in the centre of the car; very slow in movement, but safe, although frequently getting out of order. This was one of the first passenger elevators in this city. Improvements rapidly followed, until now great speed with absolute safety has been attained. It was the elevator that taught men to build higher and higher, for without the elevator a high building is impracticable. A story that long ago went the rounds emphasizes this fact. A gentleman had occasion to make a call upon an architect whose office was on the top story of a high building. The elevator service was temporarily stopped on account of repairs being made to the steam boiler, and the caller ascended by the stair-case, up flight after flight, towards the clouds until he finally reached his destination in an exhausted condition, when he feebly opened the door and inquired, Is Saint Peter in?

It was in the Post-office building in this city that for the first time in this or any other country was introduced hollow-tile flat arches between iron floor beams. This was the invention of Mr. Kreischer, a well-known manufacturer of fire-brick. His was not the invention of a flat arch in itself, but of a flat arch, whose end sections abut against rolled iron floor beams, and recess around the bottom flanges of the beams, having on top wooden sleepers and wooden flooring, thus forming a level ceiling underneath and a walking surface above. Previous to Mr. Kreischer's invention the method of filling in between iron beams was by means of common brick arches, leveled up on top with concrete, and floored over. On the underside the bottom surfaces of the beams were left exposed and painted. A ceiling of a room then consisted of a series of curved arches between iron beams, which were very unpleasant in their appearance and effect on the eye. If a level ceiling was determined upon, it had to be obtained by wooden or iron furrings and lathing, fastened up to the underside of the beams and then plastered. The flat-arch system provided a level ceiling at once, at a less cost and with much less weight of material than before. The iron beams were covered in and protected from fire, and the side walls had a lighter load to carry. A new impulse was given to fire-proof construction, and following the great fires in Chicago and Boston, the Kreischer system came into general use all over the country. In a legal contest that lasted for a number of years, it was finally decided in the U. S. Circuit Court that the Kreischer patent was void for want of originality under the crucial test of publications from all parts of the globe, that a patent must sustain when the law is invoked in its behalf. The decision of Judge Wallace prevented the inventor from realizing the profits of his invention. It did more, it deprived the inventor of the honor of having made the invention which abroad is recognized as an American system of fire-proof floorings.

At a meeting of the Royal Institute of British Architects, held in December, 1882, Mr. A. J. Gale described various things which he had seen during his tour in the United States. Among other things he stated that " In New York at the time of his visit there were many vast building schemes in hand. . . . The floors were mostly of fire-proof construction, consisting of iron beams filled in between with hollow tile flat arches, the iron being protected above and below, and joists being laid on the top surface." In connection with this statement, Mr. John Slater said : " It seemed to him that America was the country, par excellence, where suggestions were to be picked up by architects. To put the matter colloquially, it was the great place for ' tips,' and there could be no better place for an architect to visit than the States, after studying on the continent of Europe the artistic and archæological sides of his profession. The Americans were, in fact, so ingenious that their ingenuity was catching, and it appeared to be impossible for any one to visit the States without deriving much instruction. . . . They would be taught the wholesome lesson that everything English was not necessarily the best. It was only in regard to what might be called the constructional part of an architect's profession that he made these remarks." The Chairman, Mr. Ewan Christian, said that "having had the advantage of traveling in America, though only for a short time, he was very much impressed by the go-aheadedness of Americans. If a man in the States brought out a good invention connected with building or anything else, it was straightway adopted all over the country until something better was produced, when that, in its turn was taken up."

The skeleton construction will entitle Americans to as much future praise as have ever been so generously given them for past improvements made in the art of building.

The whole history of science is one continuous illustration of the slow progress by which the human mind makes its advance in discovery. It is hardly perceptible, so little has been made by any one step in advance of the former state of things, because generally it will be found that just before there was something very nearly the same thing discovered or invented. This is true of the modern Elevator in its steps forward from the hoisting apparatus of the ancients. It is true of the American flat-arch floor

system in the light of earlier publications made in France and other countries. It is true of the skeleton construction.

Without likening the skeleton to a cast iron front buried in a brick wall, its immediate predecessor can be seen in the devise frequently used to provide sufficient bearing strength in brick piers of too small an area to safely bear the load to be imposed without re-enforcement. A brick pier, of a size not larger than required for the safe support of the brick work above, is perhaps also required to carry the end of a line of girders supporting floor beams. An iron column is therefore placed im-

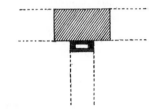

mediately adjoining the back of the pier.

If the projection of the column be undesirable, then the column is embedded within the back line of the pier.

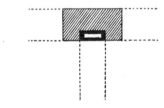

In the case of a flank wall on a street front, where the window openings are numerous and the brick piers too small to carry the weight of wall above and floor loads in addition, the piers have been

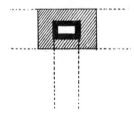

stiffened and strengthened or relieved of load by iron columns entirely con-

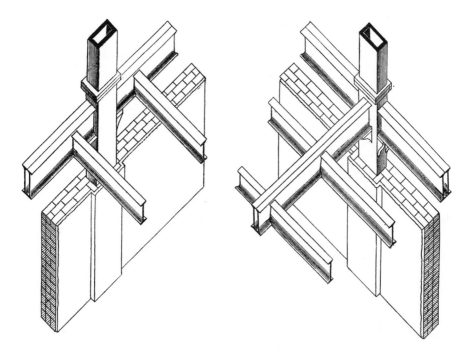

cealed within the piers, and iron lintels also concealed above the columns.

Such examples have been used repeatedly for many years, and contain all the essential features of the skeleton construction. The first complete cast-iron front ever erected in the world was put up in New York in 1848, yet that was but a repetition of iron columns and lintels long previously used as a substitute for stone and brick to the extent of a single story. So the skeleton is simply the evolution or expansion of the principal so long used in a smaller way. No patent stands in the way of the free use of the skeleton construction. A patent was issued in 1869 to a manufacturer of architectural iron work in New York, which covered the skeleton construction, but that patent expired by limitation five years ago, and the invention is now public property.

There are several variations in the use of iron skeletons. In some cases the frame is carried up to within three or four stories of the roof, and a solid brick wall used for the balance of the height, carried by the skeleton at the top line of the latter. In some cases the columns start from the base course of the foundations; in other cases from the top of the foundation wall, or the top of the basement story. There is still another method, such as was used in the *World* building, but which is not, strictly speaking, the skeleton construction, as the columns are not embedded in the walls but stand clear from the same; the walls are of solid brick and of great thickness, although supporting nothing but their own weight, which indeed is enormous on account of their great height. The floors are carried independently of the walls, and in this respect embodies the same principle as the skeleton construction.

One or the other of two methods is generally used in the skeleton construction. In one the girders are placed between the columns at each story and carry both the curtain walls and the ends of the floor beams. In the other the girders carry the curtain walls only, and are placed at every second or third story; the floor beams are supported by girders placed at right angles to the columns. In the foregoing cuts the two arrangements are so clearly shown that further description is unnecessary. The small details of bolting, etc., have been omitted, as these would add nothing to the information that the drawings are intended to convey.

The inside four inches of the curtain walls are usually built with hollow bricks, of the dimensions of common brick, so as to allow of the plastering being done directly on the wall, and thus obviates the necessity for the use of furring to prevent dampness from striking through.

At the foot of each of the vertical lines of columns it is the general practice to use a cast-iron flanged base to

distribute the imposed load over a greater area of bearing surface.

Crib footings of rolled steel or wrought iron beams are frequently used; and when placed below the water line they should be thoroughly coated with coal tar applied hot.

For the skeleton construction the existing building law makes no special provision. At the time when the law was enacted, in 1887, the use of composite structures was not foreseen. True, under that law, walls may be constructed of stone, brick, iron or other hard incombustible material, and by implication a combination of any of these materials, but the skeleton has been ruled to be one of the kind of cases to which the law does not directly apply, and is therefore subject to the decision of the Board of Examiners whose permission must be obtained before such a structure can be proceeded with. The Board regulates its action in skeleton cases in accordance with one of the amendments contained in the revision of the building law which failed to pass the last Legisture of this State. The columns are required to have a casing of brick work not less than four inches in thickness which must be bonded into the brick work of the curtain walls. The exposed side of the girders are required to be similarly covered in. The thickness of a wall is determined by its height, but where walls are carried upon girders, the heights are measured from the top of such girders, except that no curtain wall is permitted less than 12 inches in thickness. The metal work is required to be painted before being set up in position.

In the greater number of skeleton buildings erected in New York the columns are of cast iron; in the smaller number rolled steel or wrought iron of various forms of section. Some constructors advocate the use of cast iron only as the material for the columns which are used in the walls. High buildings are erected for permanency, to last for centuries. When columns are built around with brick work they are buried out of sight for all time, so to speak. The oxide of iron paint, so commonly used for coating iron and steel work is largely mixed with fish oil instead of linseed oil, and soon dries out leaving a coating of dry, broken scale or powder. Between the columns and the outer air is only a few inches of brick or stone work, through which dampness or rain finds its way. In wrought iron rust is insidious, and it honeycombs and eats entirely through the metal. Mild steel, such as beams are rolled of, rusts faster than wrought iron at first, then slower. Cast iron, on the contrary, slowly oxides in damp situations; rust does not scale from it, and the oxidation when formed is of a much less dangerous kind, extending only a little way into that metal, to about the thickness of a knife-blade, and then stops for good. There are other dangers to be apprehended, such as gases and creosote from flues, escaping steam from defective pipes, leaks or an overflow of water, all quite possible and probable to reach the columns. Wrought iron is seriously affected by such mishaps, cast iron practically not at all. Mild steel has come into use so recently that time has not yet enabled men to speak positively how short or how long it can retain its integrity in adverse situations. Damp plaster and cement corrode wrought iron and steel; lime is a preservative. If from any cause a column is affected in one place the entire structure above it is affected, but if a girder is affected the trouble is local for any one girder only carries a portion of the floor of one story and the bay or portion of the brick wall which reaches up to the next girder above. While failure in a girder would be far less disastrous than failure in a column, any trouble would be serious enough and fully warrants every precaution being taken in the first instance to avoid possible bad results. For wrought iron and steel columns a margin in material should be allowed to cover partial deterioration from rust. Instead of a low factor of safety, as 3 to 1, when weight is to be sustained by material that is to remain unimpaired, the factor should be as high as 5, to provide for the loss of a portion of the sectional area of such columns by rust, so that the remainder of the metal may be sufficient to safely carry the load calculated to be imposed. No part of the metal in a wrought iron or rolled steel column should be less than three-eighths of an inch in thickness, nor should such columns have an unsupported length of more than thirty times their least lateral dimension or diameter.

For beams and girders wrought iron has almost entirely superseded cast iron, and latterly rolled steel has crowded out wrought iron. The facility and promptness with which rolled beams can now be obtained; their admirable and scientific shape by which the greatest strength is obtained with the least weight of metal; the concise and simple tables of the bearing strength for the respective sizes and various lengths of beams freely circulated by the manufacturers; their reasonable prices; and the preference of architects and engineers to use wrought iron or steel when the load tends to separate or tear the metal asunder; all this has contributed to the extended use of wrought iron and steel for certain purposes. But for durability and lasting qualities under any and all circumstances of time and elements, particularly when buried out of sight in a casing not sufficiently thick to prevent dampness or wet or change of temperature from reaching the metal, as in the case of wall columns and beams for the support of the curtain walls, cast iron is the best material to use. For floor beams and for interior girders, wrought iron or rolled steel is matchless.

There was some fear expressed by members of the Board of Examiners when the first plans of the skeleton structures were presented for their approval, that the greater expansion of one material than of another, might work some trouble. The same bugbear had to be overcome when cast iron fronts were first introduced, when predictions of failure were based on the expansion and contraction of the metal. Events proved that the temperature of our climate, from the greatest cold to the greatest heat, exerts upon cast iron no appreciable effect, and for use in buildings is practically without expansibility. Cast iron, if of goodly thickness, offers a far better resistance to fire, or fire and water combined than wrought iron or steel. How well even thin plates of good cast iron will bear heat is shown in a familiar way by a common cook stove. Thin sheets of wrought iron will shrivel up almost like paper when brought in contact with flames. A comparatively moderate amount of heat will elongate and twist wrought iron and steel out of shape. When used for girders and floor beams they should be entirely encased in some non-conducting material. Whether columns of these materials should be encased is an open question. The advantage in one direction of a casing for wrought iron or rolled steel columns as a protection against fire, is a disadvantage in another direction, in that it may allow rusting to go on unseen to a dangerous extent. Covered or without covering, cast iron is the superior metal for columns. Cast iron is best for compression, rolled iron or steel for tension. The least thickness for a cast iron column should be three-quarters of an inch, and the greatest unsupported length for such column should not exceed twenty times its average diameter. Usually the box form of cast iron column is employed, but in many respects the **H**-shape is the best for use in skeleton construction. In order to make allowance for poor quality of cast iron, and for unseen defects in the castings, the factor of safety for cast iron columns should be 6 to 1, the same as the present building law provides for all posts, columns and other vertical supports of every kind of material.

When cast iron is used architects should insist on having the very best kind. Many columns are made in the Pennsylvania iron districts of iron run directly from the blast furnace, thus saving the expense of re-melting pig iron in a foundry cupola. Such columns are almost as brittle as glass, and when so made should be prohibited by law from being used in a building. Pig iron, when melted in a cupola, changes its nature and becomes a different grade of iron, getting rid of a certain amount of impurities, such as combined carbon, which makes iron hard, and phosphorous, which is one of the elements of weakness in iron. The re-melting is not only a purifying process, but it is an annealing process as well. By melting different brands of pig iron together the mixture is given desired qualities which they do not possess separately. This is the practice in all the architectural iron foundaries in New York.

The brick work which surrounds the skeleton cannot entirely be depended upon as a protection for the metal against the effects of fire. The covering is thin, and at best brick work is not fire-proof. That bricks resist far better than anything else is beyond question, but a brick wall is quite another thing. The mortar joints compose nearly one-fourth of the whole wall, and lime mortar is no more proof against severe heat than is limestone. Consequently the bond, by burning out, allows the wall to fall, making the damage as complete as though the bricks had been devoured by the flames. The manner in which bricks are hurriedly and carelessly laid up in a wall, not slushed in on all sides with mortar as they should be, but with one inner side of each brick having little or no mortar at all against it, leaves countless air spaces within the wall, and the air within these confined chambers is expanded during a fire. If heated air will run an engine, its expansive force can surely aid in the overthrow and destruction of a brick wall.

The skeleton construction imposes no new conditions on the architect. It calls for no skillful treatment to make it appear what it is. The metal frame, like the bones in a human body, is concealed from sight. Indeed, the architect is relieved from many troublesome conditions. He may design his structure without regard to width of piers, so that a front of brick or stone may be made nearly as light and airy in appearance as one of cast iron, and with as large window openings as desired. The building is so tied together laterally and vertically as to resist wind pressure or any other strain with impunity.

Already the architectural appearance of New York is being altered by the skeleton structures. New opportunities are opening up for architects to display their skill in treating problems of height, such as their professional brethren of a few decades ago never dreamed. It remains to be seen whether the æsthetic spirit will keep pace with the mechanical progress in the art of building, and bring forth designs of grace and beauty for the tower-like structures, notwithstanding any pre-conceived notions of disproportion between height and width.

William J. Fryer, Jr.

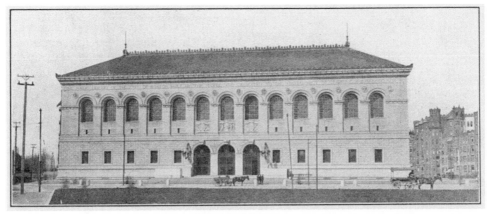

PUBLIC LIBRARY.

Boston.   McKim, Mead & White, Architects.

Architecture in the United States
I.
The Birth of Taste

Architecture, although the least plastic and animate of the arts, images at all times a nation's character, changing as that changes. It is the mirror of the national consciousness. It cannot lie. If it seems to do so it is only the more truly to betray the essential falsity of the social condition under which it had its origin. The parallel between our architecture and our national character holds good all along the line; it everywhere reflects the social tone that dictated it. The difference between Independence Hall, let us say, and a modern skyscraper, is the measure of the difference between the men and manners of Colonial days, and the men and manners of to-day. To trace, therefore, the development of architecture in the United States, from Colonial times until now, is to learn something of the ramifications of the public temper and the public taste during that period, while a knowledge of that taste and that temper, gleaned from other sources, will help to clear up many obscurities which such a survey presents.

Our architecture has not undergone that slow and orderly development which has usually characterized the progress of the art in other countries and in times past. Before our War for Independence, and for a considerable

time thereafter, the Georgian style, that is, the manner of building prevalent in England during the reign of the four Georges, modified into what we have come to call the Colonial style, was universally employed for buildings of every size and class. The architecture of the Georgian period represents the Renaissance of Jones and Wren in its last gasp; but with all its faults, something of the grand manner of an age of taste survives in it, and it is characterized by a quiet dignity arising from a certain simplicity of motive and a justness of proportion of which the builders of that day possessed the secret, or instinct, and which we appear to have lost. Certain it is that in the Colonial style we came as near as we have ever approached to achieving an American style of architecture, and its representative examples, for appropriateness and beauty have never been surpassed. I hasten to qualify this statement by reminding the reader that the problems which confront the modern architect are as difficult, compared with those presented to the Colonial builders, as the problem, let us say, of living the simple life at the Waldorf-Astoria, is difficult compared with living it on a New Hampshire farm.

Georgian architecture gave place to that of the so-called Classic Revival.

Fine Arts Museum.
Boston.

This curious phase of our development
has found but small place in our literature, but it has left many a souvenir
in the names of villages and cities.
(There are 27 Troys, 15 Romes and
12 Carthages), and in many old white
houses with tumble-down Greek porticoes, for this was the period of pseudo-
temples, their "orders" laboriously
worked out, by modules and minutes,
and translated literally, without the
change of a phrase, from stone into
wood and brick and plaster. It was
all false, affected, pretentious, yet oc-
casionally, in the right environment
was achieved an effect of sober dignity
—almost of grandeur—to which the
unmitigated and un-redeemed mid-Vic-
torian ugliness which succeeded it,

Independence Hall.
Philadelphia.

could never, under the most flattering
conditions, lay the smallest claim. The
late H. C. Bunner has happily suggested
the superiority of the elder vogue to
the later by this apostrophe of an old
white pillared house, addressed to a
new Queen Anne shingled cottage.

"I have had my day. I was built when
people thought this sort of thing was
the right thing; when we had our own
little pseudo-classic Renaissance in
America. I lie between the towns of
Aristotle and Sabine farms. I am a

Trinity Church.
New York City.
Richard Upjohn, Architect.

gentleman's residence, and my name
is Montevista. I was built by a prominent citizen. You need not laugh
through your lattices, you smug new
Queen Anne cottage, down there in
your valley! What will become of you
when the falsehood is found out of
your imitation bricks, and your tiled
roof of shingles, and your stained glass
that is only a sheet of transparent paper
pasted on a pane? You are a young
sham! I am an old sham! Have
some respect for age."

Even the Carpenter's classic period and the dim Victorian limbo were not without their glimmerings of light. These took the form of a few—a very few—really beautiful Gothic churches—of which Trinity in New York was among the finest—built by Upjohn, and his disciples; men inspired by the vital, but abortive Gothic revival in England. The influence they exercised upon our secular architecture was little enough, and rather pernicious than otherwise, since it produced the Gothic Farm House type, exploited in the pages of building manuals and agricultural papers—a thing of broken roofs, contorted chimneys, and long, narrow win-

Lenox Library.
New York City.

R. M. Hunt, Architect.

De Vinne Building.
New York City.
Babb, Cook & Willard, Architects.

dows. Of a different order, but scarcely more happy in results were the buildings inspired by the teachings of Ruskin, a man whom Mr. Cram characterizes as "of stupefying ability * * * quite the most unreliable critic and exponent of architecture that ever lived, but gifted with a facility in the use of perfectly convincing language, such as is granted to few men in any given thousand years." The existing Boston Art Museum is a typical example of the misdirected efforts of this particular group who "turned to detail and decoration the use of colored bricks and terra cotta, stone inlay, naturalistic carving, metal work, as the essentials

in constructive art, abandoning the quest for effective composition, thoughtful proportion and established precedent."

1880. I do not know why this apparently random combination of digits should mark an epoch in the history of manners and taste, both in England and America, but such is the case. Max Beerbohm wrote an essay on "1880", treating the period, in his elfishly humorous vein, as almost unimaginably remote—and remote indeed, it seems, so swiftly have the wheels of change revolved since then. Time, in the last analysis, is but succession, and

Marshall Field Warehouse.
Chicago.

H. H. Richardson, Architect.

Ponce de Leon Hotel.
St. Augustine, Fla.
Carrère & Hastings, Architects.

when changes succeed one another rapidly, time seems to extend; when slowly, to contract. The Italian Renaissance from its earliest dawn till twilight was scarcely two generations in length. But to return from this digression: It was in, or about 1880 that the aesthetic darkness of the "Scientific Century," by being made a subject for laughter became a subject for thought. The renascence of taste in England, inaugurated by William Morris, and the Pre-Raphaelites, and perpetuated by the "Aesthetes," was a fertile, and perhaps a fit subject for the satire of Mr. Gilbert and "Mr. Punch," since all movements at all revolution-

ary are apt to have their beginnings in exaggeration and excess; but the humors of "Patience" and of "Passionate Brompton," could not blind intelligent people to the enormous significance of the fact that men were again being born into the world with a craving for beauty—"mere" beauty, if you will. They found this beauty in Greek sculpture, in Gothic architecture, and in the paintings of the Italian Primitives; but in their own environments they

New York Life Insurance Company's Building.
Minneapolis, Minn.
Babb, Cook & Willard, Architects.

found it nowhere except in some scattered and random trifles brought in the holds of farfaring vessels from China and Japan. The storks, fans, and cat-tails, with which the Aesthetes adorned their dados, make us shudder now; but they testify to the sincerity of their admiration for the only vital art manifestation of any magnitude in the world at that time, and are eloquent witnesses of the fact that the appreciation of Oriental art was contemporaneous with the first concerted

Tiffany Residence.
New York City.
McKim, Mead & White, Architects.

Trinity Church.
Boston.   H. H. Richardson, Architect.

Saul is the finest statue he ever saw;" and Story says of one of Page's portraits, "No such work has been achieved in our time." In speaking of the aesthetic sensibility of the sixties, Henry James shrewdly observes, "The sense to which for the most part, the work of art or of imagination, the picture, the statue, the novel, the play, appealed, was not in any strictness the aesthetic sense in general or the plastic in particular, but the sense of the romantic, the

and serious attempt in modern Anglo-Saxon civilization towards the realization of beauty in the every-day life.

Even the most refined and sensitive spirits of the immediately preceding generation, though generally right on questions of morals, were generally wrong on questions of taste. The things with which the Hawthornes adorned their apartments and the presents given and received by Browning and his circle, there is no epithet fitly to describe. The letters written by New England's Brahmin caste abound in references to painters and sculptors of that day who are compared to the old masters to the latter's disadvantage. Charles Sumner writes to Story: "George Russell tells me that your

St. Nicholas Hotel.
St. Louis, Mo.
Louis H. Sullivan, Architect.

anecdotic, the supposedly historic—the explicitly pathetic."

In 1880 this point of view suffered a sea-change. Oscar Wilde, the particular prophet who carried the new gospel of aestheticism to our shores, wrong as he was in matters of morals, was right in matters of taste, and he found, here, a considerable number of men and women who were right, we are bound to believe, in both. Architecture, which is the mirror of man's mind in space, was not slow to reflect this new-born sensitiveness to beauty, but in localities and on a scale commensurate

The Villard Houses.
New York City.
McKim, Mead & White, Architects.

with the restricted character of the movement, which was limited to the towns and cities of the extreme east. Among the ugly and arid crags and crannies of the Boston, New York and Philadelphia streets, there began to appear some rare and delicate flowers of architectural art, the work for the most

The Condit Building.
New York City.
Louis H. Sullivan, Lyndon P. Smith, Architects.

part, of young Americans whose aesthetic sense had been nourished at the bountiful breast of Italy or France.

There is something touching in the refined and faded beauty of certain of these early essays in an American style, elbowed as they are on every hand by the big, florid, bedizened steel-frame skyscrapers of to-day. They seem to say to the passer-by "You'd love us if you'd only look at us," and so we would, New York can show nothing better of their several sorts, than Mr. Babb's De Vinne Press Building on Lafayette place, Mr. Ware's Manhattan Storehouse on Forty-second street, and Mr. White's pedestal and exedra for St. Gaudens' Farragut in Madison Square.

Not in these directions of restrained and cultivated originality, however, were we destined to develop just then, for Richardson, a flaming comet, was already blazing in the architectural firmament, attracting and scorching up all lesser luminaries, save three or four. Richardson compelled even the Philistines to sit up and take notice; to him belongs the credit of popularizing architecture in the United States. He was a great man, and the buildings he left are worthy of his genius; but his influence was as pernicious as it was pervasive and he delayed the normal evolution of architecture for many years. The style which he made his own, a modified and more massive Romanesque, neither lent itself readily to American needs and conditions, nor was it capable of expressing these with any degree of appropriateness and truth; it expressed only the powerful and romantic individuality of its creator, and in the hands of lesser men, fated, like all copyists, to seize on the idiosyncracy and miss the essential— it degenerated into a thing more crude, false, feeble, and pretentious than anything that had gone before. A short time after Richardson's death, when it was found that only Thor could wield Thor's hammer, most of the architects in the East, even Richardson's immediate pupils and disciples, turned elsewhere for their inspiration.

Messrs. McKim, Mead and White, who had never for one moment submitted to the Richardson obsession, continued to produce charming, scholarly, refined work, based, for the most part, on early Italian Renascence models. The Villard houses, in New York, reminiscent of certain places in

Farragut Monument.
New York City.   Stanford White, Architect.
Augustus Saint Gaudens, Sculptor.

beautiful, so rational, so suited in every way to its environment and purpose, that it may truly be called a masterpiece. In Chicago, Richardson had built, in his happiest vein, a great warehouse. Simple, severe, utilitarian, but most impressive, the work of a poet in stone, it seemed to symbolize the city's very soul, and it furnished the inspiration for many important buildings erected by Messrs. Burnham and Root, and Messrs. Adler and Sullivan. Of these the Auditorium Building is perhaps the best example.

After Richardson's death there was need of a new prophet in our architectural Israel, and to the eyes of a little circle of devotees in Chicago, he presently appeared in the person of Mr. Sullivan, who early developed a style of his own, which straightway became that of a number of others, (with a difference, of course)—young and eager spirits, not fettered by too much knowledge—not fettered, indeed, by enough! Outside this little circle Mr. Sullivan was either unknown, ignored or discredited by those persons on whose opinions reputations in matters of art are supposed to rest. Engaged for the most part upon intensely utilitarian problems in an intensely utilitarian city, he had no opportunity to captivate the popular imagination as

Florence, and the Boston Public Library, which, though composed of the same elements as the Library of St. Geneviève, in Paris, harks back to Alberti's Malatestian temple at Rimini, are two characteristic examples. The firm soon gained a substantial following, and the work produced was vastly better and more appropriate than the earlier excursions into Richardsonian Romanesque, though perhaps a little thin and anæmic to eyes grown accustomed to the bold and virile manner affected by the men educated in the methods of the Ecole des Beaux Arts. Of this manner Mr. Richard M. Hunt's old Lenox Library is perhaps the earliest example, and Mr. Whitney Warren's so different New York Yacht Club, is among the latest.

Meanwhile, other and different influences were at work elsewhere throughout the country. In Philadelphia and its environs the delicate and individual art of Wilson Eyre, and the more imitative, but admirable work of Frank Miles Day and Cope and Stewardson was mitigating, in spots, the ugliness of the earlier time. At St. Augustine, in Florida, Messrs. Carrère and Hastings inaugurated their brilliant career with the wonderful Ponce de Leon hotel, a building so original, so

New York Yacht Club.
New York City.
Whitney Warren, Architect.

Richardson captivated it in his Trinity Church, Boston. Yet by the power of his personality and the vitality of his genius, he has exercised as great an influence upon the national architecture as his illustrious predecessor—greater in fact, because more abiding, for Mr. Sullivan concerned himself with principles, not preferences.

Mr. Sullivan's theories and his accomplishments will be considered at greater length in a subsequent essay. It is sufficient to say, in this connection, that he has solved the aesthetic problem of the sky-scraper more successfully than any architect before or since. This problem had always been a thorn in the side of the academically trained designer, who usually endeavored to achieve diversity in the exterior where none existed on the plan by a series of superimposed motives, separated by cornices or string courses which had the effect of diminishing the apparent height. Mr. Sullivan was among the first to perceive the inherent irrationality of such a treatment. He saw, moreover, a great opportunity in the problem of the modern office building. Since loftiness was of necessity its chief characteristic, instead of suppressing he emphasized the vertical dimension.

The Guaranty (now the Prudential) Building in Buffalo, and the Condit Building in New York, are two embodiments of his idea. Although these have not been paid the sincere tribute of exact imitation, the force of Mr. Sullivan's example, more than that of any other man, put an end to the meaningless piling of feature upon feature. To emphasize, and not minimize the vertical dimension of a high building, has come to be the accepted practice.

The pre-occupation of the Chicago architects with the practical and economic aspects of the tall office building to the general exclusion of the aesthetic, had the odd effect of rendering their early essays in that field superior, as a general thing, to those of about the same period in New York. The latter show ornament for the most part misapplied, and an aesthetic pre-occupation misdirected. Mr. Root's old Monadnock building, for example,

is better architecture than Messrs. Carrère and Hastings' Mail and Express Building, though they stand at opposite extremes in the matter of cost and embellishment. The last-mentioned architects showed later, in their altogether admirable Blair Building, that they had learned from Mr. Sullivan or elsewhere their lesson.

Such architectural graces as other Western cities could lay claim to, up to the time that I have brought this chronicle, that is, just before the Columbian Fair, they owed, for the most part, to alien talent. San Francisco in particular, before the advent of men trained in the more scholarly methods of the East, was a veritable chamber of architectural horrors. It is said that in the early days it was the custom for the builder, at a certain stage in the construction of a house, to appear upon the scene with a wagon load of miscellaneous jig-saw ornaments, which he would then hold up, one by one, in the presence of its owner, until the latter had selected those that pleased him best. I have heard the theory advanced that the nickel and mahogany Pullman cars of the Southern Pacific first established the California criterion of taste, in the matter of house decoration— being the particular order of magnificence with which her sons were first and most familiar.

Mr. A. Page Brown's work in San Francisco, Messrs. McKim, Mead and White's New York Life building in Kansas City, Messrs. Babb, Cook and Willard's splendid office buildings for the same Company, in St. Paul and Minneapolis, and Mr. Sullivan's St. Nicholas hotel and Wainwright Building in St. Louis, to mention only a few typical examples, established a standard of excellence in these cities which had an effect upon the profession throughout the entire West, and when the time came for determining into what hands the exceptional architectural opportunities afforded by the World's Columbian Exposition should be entrusted, the most eminent Eastern architects were freely given the lion's share.

Claude Bragdon.

THE ARCHITECTURAL RECORD

VOL. XXVIII.   DECEMBER, 1910   No. 6.

THE NEW ARCHITECTURE

The First American Type of Real Value

A. C. DAVID

Photos by August Patzig

New York is a city in which many things happen, unprecedented in the history of urban humanity. No other city in the world has ever added 500,000 inhabitants to its population every three years. In no other city does such a high level of real estate values prevail over so long a strip of land as the level of prices which are being paid for lots on Fifth Avenue, from Thirtieth Street to Fiftieth Street. In no other city has anything like $200,000,000 been invested in new buildings in any one year. But unprecedented as are these and other evidences of the increases of population, wealth and business in New York, they are less remarkable to a discerning eye than a real estate and building movement which has recently been taking place on a small part of one avenue in the new mercantile district in that city. We refer to the transformation which has been made during the past two years on Fourth Avenue, between Union Square and Thirtieth Street.

The transformation which has been taking place on Fourth Avenue is not remarkable on account of the high level of real estate values which has been thereby established, because real estate on Fourth Avenue is still not worth more than a third of what it is on the best retail section of Fifth Avenue. The peculiarity of the movement on Fourth Avenue has consisted of the large number of new buildings of a single type erected in a comparatively short time. Within a distance of about a half of a mile, and during an interval of about two years, some fifteen mercantile buildings have been constructed. The largest of them covers a whole block front. The smallest of them a little less than half a block. The lowest of them is twelve stories high. The tallest of them is twenty stories high. The average for the whole group is sixteen stories. They have converted an avenue, which was formerly devoted to small retail stores and old furniture shops, into an avenue given over chiefly to mercantile business of the highest class. They will be used for the offices, the ware-rooms and the show-rooms of large manufacturing and importing firms and corporations, and they supply more floor space for such purposes than only a short time ago would have been needed during a period of ten years.

The interest of this quick transforma-

Photo by August Patzig.

THE MILLS & GIBB BUILDING.
4th Avenue and 22d Street, New York City.   Starrett & Van Vleck, Architects.

tion for the readers of the Architectural Record does not, however, consist in the evidence it affords of the business growth of New York. It consists, rather, in the opportunity presented on the new Fourth Avenue of appraising the value and effect of the forces which are molding modern American commercial architecture. For this particular purpose, it is much more useful than any other group of buildings which are concentrated within a similarly small space in any other American city or in any other part of New York. In the first place, they are thoroughly contemporary. In the second place, they are strictly commercial. They have not been erected by people who had any money to spend or any reason for spending money on architectural "effects." In the third place, with a few exceptions, they have not been designed by the architectural firms who have been most conspicuously successful in designing other types of buildings. They have usually been issued from the offices of architects who have specialized in commercial work, and who have made their reputation by their ability to plan such structures so that the smallest profitable expenditure of money will bring the largest return in available space, in economy of operation, and in adaptation to use. In certain cases they are owned and have been built by large wholesale firms, who will occupy them as their offices, and who have no reason to advertise their business by any architectural display. In other cases they have been erected by speculative builders, who have constructed them for the purpose of filling them with tenants and then selling them to an investor, and, of course, in all such cases the opportunities for unprofitable expenditure are cut down to an absolute minimum. These Fourth Avenue buildings have been planned and designed exclusively for the purpose of being made to pay; and on this fact one must insist to the limit, because it is the salient fact concerning them, and because they are distinguished thereby from many other commercial buildings which have been erected in other parts of New York.

Other than strictly commercial reasons have, for instance, dominated the appearance of the great majority of office buildings in the financial district and of many of the new edifices recently erected on Fifth Avenue. A bank, for instance, when it builds an office building, frequently sacrifices a good deal of space and money merely for the purpose of imposing on its customers an impression of its opulent stability; and this expenditure has its justification, because a big bank, like a big life insurance company, is a financial institution. Moreover, the fact that these financial "institutions" spend money on costly materials and details, and devote rentable space to the purpose of merely creating an "effect," has an influence upon the design and the appearance of competing buildings, the owners of which have no reason connected with their own business for any similar expenditure. A certain standard of ornate decoration is established, which tenants come to demand, and which the builder is obliged to supply at any cost to himself. Similar motives have operated on Fifth Avenue to take many, apparently, commercial buildings out of the exclusively commercial architectural class. The Gorham store has been described by a good judge as the best-looking store in the world, and this judgment may be true; but, obviously, it cannot be described as a strictly commercial building. Its customers are people of wealth and refinement; and the management of the Gorham company has, consequently, a good reason for entertaining their stylish customers in a really stylish habitation. So it is with the Tiffany store, and so it is to a smaller extent with many other Fifth Avenue commercial buildings. To be sure, certain other commercial buildings have been erected on Fifth Avenue which are veritably and vulgarly commercial; but they are vulgarly commercial not because they are frankly devoted to the transaction of business, but because they are business buildings, which are making an ugly and ostentatious attempt to advertise their importance instead of a comely and a discreet attempt.

This brings us to the gist of the matter. The better Fifth Avenue buildings are either modifications of European residential styles, as in the cases of the

Photo by August Patzig.

THE FOURTH AVENUE BUILDING.

4th Avenue and 27th Street, New York City.   Chas. A. Valentine, Architect.

Dodd, Mead & Co. Building.
4th Avenue and 30th Street, New York City.
Babb, Cook & Welch, Architects.

bility it never will have. A specifically commercial architecture has no reason for existing unless specifically commercial requirements in a building are allowed full expression. Such can never be the case in cities, which restrict the height of buildings either by ordinance or by any interpretation of rights under the common law, such as the English custom of "ancient lights." If American cities had begun by restricting the height of buildings we should never have had any specifically commercial architecture in this country. The tall building is the economical building. It renders meaningless all the architectural values upon which the traditional European street architecture has been based. Precisely and exclusively because it was allowed to shoot upwards, American commercial architecture was emancipated from paralyzing restrictions and has become a specific and original type,

103 Park Avenue.
Park Avenue and 41st Street.

Tiffany and Gorham buildings, or they are modifications of European (French) apartment house architecture, as in the case of the Altman's store. They are buildings which are commercial in function, without any pretense of being business-like in appearance; and in this respect they are following in the footsteps of the traditional European methods. Substantially all European buildings which have been used for business purposes have been designed as modifications of urban residential styles. Europe has never had any specifically commercial architecture, and in all proba-

dominated by novel formative and essentially real, practical requirements.

It was, of course, evident from the very beginning of the American skyscraper that some such development was taking place, although the first indications of it appeared in Chicago, rather than in New York. The earliest tall buildings erected in Chicago were dominated by practical requirements, but they were far from being complete expressions of the new American commercial architecture. In the first place, the requirements for such buildings had not at that time been fully defined and standardized, and, in the second place, the buildings were in appearance, unnecessarily uncouth and ugly. The early New York skyscrapers, on the other hand, were designed to a considerable extent independently of practical considerations. From the start the New York architects, supported by their clients, were seeking in their skyscrapers to make some kind of an irrelevant and costly architectural display; and they frequently sacrificed practical advantages and spent an unconscionable amount of money in a kind of architecture that diminished rather than increased the commercial value of the building. It was not until almost ten years later that New Yorkers began to realize that commercial buildings of a certain kind could be made more, rather than less, attractive by a loyal and intelligent attempt to make them serve an exclusively commercial purpose.

It is not our purpose to write a history of the architectural development of the American skyscraper. Many architects have contributed to the process, and it has been helped by many improvements in technical methods. If it had not been for the enterprise and adaptability of manufacturers of front brick, terra cotta, steam-heating plants, elevators and the like, the new commercial architecture would not have been possible; and the earlier architects were hampered by the lack of many materials and devices upon which both the utility and the good looks of the new commercial architecture depends. But a certain result has been reached; and what we wish to call attention to is the fact that this result is summed up better on this half a mile of

Three of the Most Recent in the 4th Avenue Development.

teresting group of commercial buildings concentrated in one spot, either in this or any other country, we do not mean that they constitute a satisfactory solution of the problem of the design of skyscrapers, or that any one of them is a beautiful and exhilarating piece of architecture. But certain qualities can be claimed for them as a group, which justify the description. They are really commercial buildings, because they have been built to pay, while, at the same time, they have by the use (for the most part) of entirely appropriate means been made measurably attractive. In the course of time the problem of meeting in the most economical manner the complex group of practical requirements, upon which the earning power of such build-

The Parker Building.
4th Avenue and 19th Street, New York City.
R. H. Robertson, Architect.

Fourth Avenue than in any other similarly small neighborhood elsewhere in New York or in the United States. New Yorkers are fully justified in talking very big about these buildings. There is no group of purely commercial structures in the world which do more to earn their living, both in use and in appearance, than does this group on Fourth Avenue. It is American commercial architecture at its best, and American commercial architecture is not only the best, but the only genuine commercial architecture in the world.

By insisting that these Fourth Avenue buildings are, on the whole, the most in-

The Everett Building.
4th Avenue and 17th Street, New York City.
Starrett & Van Vleck, Architects.

ing are based, will be still more completely solved, and architects will be able to make the resulting design still more appropriate; but even if these Fourth Avenue buildings are still far

The mercantile buildings erected on Fourth Avenue differ from the great majority of office buildings, in that the rents which can be charged for space therein are smaller than the rents which

Photo by August Patzig.

THE COOPER HEWITT BUILDING.

4th Avenue and 28th Street, New York City.   Clinton & Russell, Architects.

from completely representing the full development of their type, they assuredly point in the direction which will lead to the ultimate attainment of the goal.

can be charged in structures used exclusively for office purposes. In the latter several dollars a square foot can frequently be obtained. In the former, sixty or seventy cents a square foot is usually the limit. Of course, the difference in the value of the land on which the two types of buildings are erected will account for a large part of the difference in rent. Nevertheless, the architect of a loft building is forced into rigorous economies which the architect of an office building can sometimes escape. An additional expenditure of $50,000, which would constitute a small portion of the cost of the office building, would constitute a much larger proportion of the cost of a mercantile building. The expense of the latter must be kept down to somewhere between twenty and twenty-three cents a cubic foot, while, at the same time, the standard of construction, at least in the case of buildings seeking the better class of mercantile tenants, must be very high.

The practical conditions which these buildings are required to meet may be grouped under five heads: (1) those following from the necessity of obtaining a maximum amount of clear and available floor space, (2) those resulting from the exactions of the insurance companies, (3) those resulting from the building laws, and (4) those resulting from the necessity of economical operation. Finally, speculative builders have discovered it advisable to pay some attention to design, because, other things being equal, a structure which presents a good appearance sells better than one which does not.

Of course, the prime object is to secure the maximum floor space, made properly available by accessibility, the absence of impediments, abundant light and proper distribution. In large lofts, containing 10,000 or more square feet there may be large numbers of employees, engaged in various kinds of work, all of whom have to be overlooked by a floor manager. The ideal loft, consequently, is square in outline; and anything like an L-shaped plot is usually avoided. Among the new Fourth Avenue buildings all except one are built on square or rectangular lots. Starting with a square lot, the great effort of the architect must be to secure the largest possible amount of light for the different floors, because on such a supply of light

the maximum availability of the floor space will depend. The amount of light which he can get will, of course, depend upon the number of directions from which good light can be secured; and the consequence is that the control of a corner is of the greatest practical importance in designing an ideal loft. With that advantage more or less light can be secured for three sides of a floor; and the amount will be more, rather than less, when one side fronts on an exceptionally wide thoroughfare, like Fourth Avenue. As a matter of fact, all but two of the important buildings recently erected on this avenue are built upon one or more corners. Usually the space obtained on any single floor is thrown into one large loft; but sometimes such is not the case. In planning the use of his floor space, the architect is obliged to consider the possibility of subsequent subdivision.

The height, no matter how many directions from which it is obtained, is, of course, made available by windows. The great object of the plan is to obtain the maximum area of exterior openings; and these windows must be arranged, if possible, so as to make every square foot of floor space available without the use of artificial illumination. The consequence is that large mullioned windows are used, so as to fill the entire space between the piers with glass. Until recently the height of the windows was determined by the height of the steam radiators from the floor; but more recently the architect has been able to lower his window sills by using a system of indirect steam radiators, which flattened out the space needed for the heating arrangement. The net result has been to leave practically only the pier and the floor lines solid on the exterior, all the rest of the façades being thrown into window space. The dominant consideration of a maximum amount of light has also tended to increase the height of the ceilings to the very limit of economy, because of the aid rendered thereby not only to the lighting, but to the ventilating system. The arrangements for ventilation are very carefully planned and insure good air in all kinds of weather.

Photo by August Patzig.

THE MILLS & GIBB BUILDING.

4th Avenue and 22d Street, New York City.   Starrett & Van Vleck, Architects.

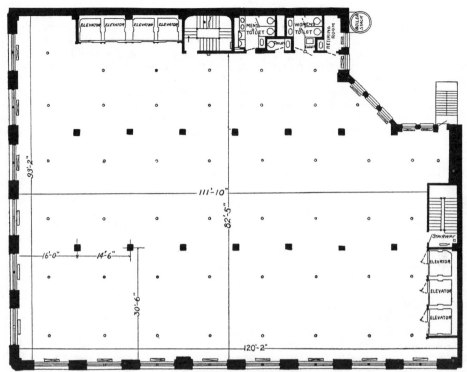

TYPICAL UPPER FLOOR PLAN.

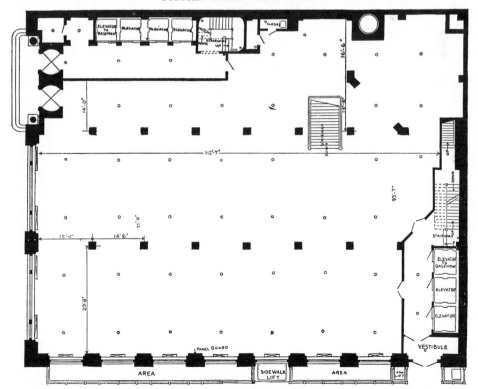

TYPICAL GROUND FLOOR PLAN.

Of course, the amount of clear and available floor space is affected by many factors besides the amount of light. The interior columns must be arranged along the fewest possible number of lines, and the various conveniences and services connected with the building must be planned so as to supply an adequate service, without diminishing any more than necessary the rentable floor space. The planning of these services is, perhaps, the most difficult part of the architect's job, because the chance of economy varies with the class of tenants for which the building is prepared, the size of the lot and its shape. The number of elevators needed, for instance, will vary according to the use to which the lofts are put. Two elevators have been considered enough for a building 100x100, but of late years such a limitation of the elevator service has been found dangerous. If the floors are used for manufacturing purposes or are subdivided into offices, the number of employees increases; and as they usually arrive and are dismissed at about the same hour, the elevator service has to be proportioned to the exigencies of emptying the building, if necessary, within a few minutes. A large area has to be devoted, also, to the freight elevators. They have to be provided with a separate entrance, which is situated, if possible, on the side street, where trucks may have less difficulty in unloading and loading. Another difficult matter to arrange economically is the toilet accommodations. Two toilest have to be provided on every floor, one for each sex; and in case the building is used for manufacturing purposes, the factory law requires the furnishing of additional toilets elsewhere in the building.

Second only in importance to the planning of a maximum amount of clear and available floor space is the satisfaction of the exactions of the Board of Fire Underwriters, so that the tenants may obtain the lowest possible rate of insurance. The standard of fireproof construction is thus pretty well fixed, but it tends constantly to become higher on grounds, not only of fire protection, but because of the resulting economies of maintenance. The tenants in such buildings carry large amounts of stock, much larger than the tenants of an office building, and the saving for them is very considerable, in case the building measures up to the highest standard of fire-proofing. Some of the best of Fourth Avenue buildings are models of substantial, safe, economical and at the same time quick construction. In a number of them granolithic or concrete floors have been used. Metal trim of a very simple stock design and painted to represent wood has become almost universal. Ornamental designs are avoided in the plastering, and the plaster corners are protected by metal beading. Speed of construction and necessary quickness of occupancy makes it necessary to standardize all details, and to omit as much paint as possible. Of course, an automatic sprinkler system and full local fire protection have to be provided for every floor.

Floor loads, stairways, fire-escapes and the like are all designed so as to conform to the requirements of the local building law. The steel frame has to be of sufficient strength to carry a live load of one hundred and twenty-five pounds to the square foot. A substantial saving can sometimes be brought about by full co-operation between architect and engineer in the design of the frame-work. An economy usually results from combining the stairway and fire-escape provisions of the law. Two stairs are demanded for each 5,000 square feet of space; and in buildings of larger area, the exterior fire-escape, which is also demanded is converted into an outside stairway.

Changes of considerable importance have recently been made in the equipment of these loft buildings. Until recently it was almost the universal custom to install a heating, lighting and power plant in buildings of this character, because the policy of the public utility companies made such private installations profitable. Now, however, contracts can be made to obtain the power from the street, which makes it more economical to buy it; and the consequence is that such plants are now generally omitted. Space is still left for them so that they can be installed at some future time, in case the economical operation of the building should demand it; but the day will probably come when a cheap supply of power from a central plant will be so well assured that such a

The Brogan Building.
4th Avenue and 20th Street, New York City.
Neville & Bagge, Architects.

space will no longer have to be reserved. When this time does come, it will be possible to effect additional economies in interior arrangement.

The foregoing are some of the essential practical requirements, which have

to be met by the architects in the design of these buildings, and when they are all met he is not left very much discretion in adapting his interior arrangements to a pleasant exterior effect. The exterior consists of a frame work, usually about sixteen stories high of piers and floors, the lines of both of which are separated by fixed distances, and both of which cannot be disguised by much ornamentation. The use of large detail is forbidden both by the expense and by the knowledge that no detail can be scaled large enough to count effectively at such a great height from the street. There is only one architectural device of importance which they are permitted to use at the expense of practical availability of the building. They have been permitted to place cornices on some of the buildings whose projection is sufficient to hurt the light on the top floor. The consequence has been that the top floor is often used in part for the janitor's quarters, for store-rooms, or for extra toilets, whenever they are needed.

At the same time it must not be inferred that the architect, even if he would, could ignore aesthetic considerations. A certain standard of architectural decency tends to be imposed even on speculative builders. They find that a building which has been made measurably attractive in appearance at some moderate cost will sell better than a building in which such considerations have either been ignored or have been met by clumsy and vulgar methods; and the means whereby some measure of architectural attractiveness can be obtained within the necessary limits of expenditure are now pretty well settled by common consent. Thus the appearance of these buildings, like every other aspect of them, tends to become standardized.

In the effort to render a sixteen-story building attractive at a minimum of expense, the architect has to depend upon a few simple and obvious devices. He can in the first place group his window openings to some slight extent and by these means he can emphasize the corners of the building and give them a certain solidity. In many cases this device has not been used, but in those

Photo by August Patzig.

THE THREE THIRTY-FOUR FOURTH AVENUE BUILDING.

4th Avenue and 25th Street, New York City.   Geo. B. Post & Sons, Architects.

buildings, such, for instance, as the Braender Building on the southeast corner of 24th St., whose architects have used it, the effect is excellent. In no other way can a structure of this kind be made to look like a tower rather than a cage, and the cost of the arrangement is practically negligible. It gives the

The Ashland Building.
4th Avenue and 24th Street, New York City.
Wm. C. Frohne, Architect.

building a salient line and direction, from which it can derive some propriety and dignity of appearance.

A tall loft building can do without emphatic lines, but it cannot do without some attractiveness of coloring. The great effort of the architects has been to obtain a good-looking material for the main shaft of the edifice, and in this effort they have been enormously helped by the advances recently made in the manufacture of front brick and glazed terra cotta. In one or two cases stone has been used, and with admirable results, but the cost of stone is usually prohibitive. An architect can now choose between many varieties of brick and terra cotta, all of which give the building a pleasant color and surface, and all of which are susceptible within limits of decorative treatment. It is particularly in this respect that the Fourth Avenue buildings exhibit a considerable average advance over any similar group of their predecessors. A better colored brick or terra cotta has usually been specified; and the material has been treated with discretion and good taste. In some cases decorated patterns have been obtained in the laying up of the brick itself. In other cases white glazed terra cotta decorated with superficial ornamental patterns has been effectively employed. In still other cases a brick building has been trimmed with colored and glazed terra cotta. The variations on the central idea are numerous and ingenious and permit the display of a high degree of aptitude for purely decorative design. What is needed and sought is essentially an attractive and effective arrangement of color and pattern. And in seeking these appropriate and economical means of ornamentation, the architects have abandoned an error, which was very prevalent until recently even among the designers of strictly commercial buildings —the error of overloading the top stories of a sixteen-story edifice with masses of ugly and bloated terra cotta detail in high relief. Ornamentation of this kind was ineffective from the street, and from the upper windows of an adjacent building it was frankly hideous.

We trust that readers unfamiliar with conditions in New York will now be able to appreciate the importance of this group of mercantile buildings as representing a significant and prominent architectural type. The dominant idea to keep in mind in respect to them is that they are from every point of view essentially a normal and natural growth. In almost all other departments of American architectural design the process of improvement has depended on the somewhat forcible imposition on the American public of European technical standards and traditional forms. But in respect to these commercial buildings this usual source of architectural amelioration has availed nothing. Indeed whenever the attempt has been made to impose these standards and forms on commercial buildings the result has been perverting and in some instances corrupting. Neither has very much progress been made by means of a rigorous application of merely logical ideas. The advance has come about by way of a candid and unpretentious attempt to design buildings, which satisfied every real practical need at the lowest possible cost. The result of this attempt up to date is a group of buildings which really earn their living, and they do so without either any subservience to tradition or any revolutionary departure from it. They are absolutely a case of the survival of the fittest—the fittest, that is, under existing conditions. The conditions will change both aesthetically and practically, but any future advance of American commercial architecture will depend upon a further development of the ideas and the methods which have made these Fourth Avenue buildings what they are.

Photo by August Patzig.

4TH AVENUE, LOOKING NORTH, BEFORE THE RECENT DEVELOPMENT.

FIG. 4.   ACOMA PUEBLO, NEW MEXICO.

A Type of Original American Architecture

The architecture of a people is as much a part of themselves as their habits of living; in fact, being free from alien or abnormal influence, the architecture of a people is one of their habits of living. It develops with the necessities born of the conditions under which it exists, and given this opportunity assumes the dignity of a type.

Doubtless the first thought raised by the words, "American Architecture," will be something ranging from the rude log hut of Lincoln's infancy, or the stately Mount Vernon home of Washington, to the modern steel-skeleton sky-scraper, all of which are types created by American ingenuity to overcome American necessities.

The particular type of which it is here proposed to speak is one very remote from these things, however, one more truly American, indigenous to the soil, and influenced by no borrowed motif, but the rather furnishing its own.

This briefly concerns the domestic architecture of the Pueblo Indians of the Southwest; a race probably older, certainly distinct from any other of the aborigines of the United States. These people are being civilized, Christianized, or subjected to some other process of elimination, so that they will soon become extinct, and with them their architecture will become a memory.

While many interesting examples of the original type are still to be found, the newer work shows the alien influence; and as the older buildings decay they will be replaced by work of another class.

The authorities of the University of New Mexico, contemplating a scheme for the future needs of that institution, have considered the adaptation of this style of architecture to institutional needs, and in this have the approval of some archaeological authorities.

The type is developed from the material most readily obtainable; and it most perfectly satisfies the conditions it

Fig. 1. Acoma Pueblo, New Mexico, Showing the Primitive Stairs of the Houses.

Fig. 5. Laguna Pueblo Houses Built of Stone, from which the Plaster has Fallen.

has to meet. The walls are built of stone or sun-dried adobe brick, laid in stiff adobe mud, built very thick, and plastered smoothly inside and out with the same adobe mud. Often the walls are then whitewashed with lime, and sometimes decorated with paintings. The adobe plaster when dry forms a very hard surface, reasonably waterproof, and perfectly airtight.

The floors for upper stories and roofs are formed by building in large timbers at the desired height; these support smaller timbers and the whole is covered with adobe and packed tightly. Arranged to drain toward the walls with scuppers to discharge the rainwater, these roofs do very well in a country of little rainfall.

Two or three-story buildings are the rule, passage from one story to another being obtained by pole ladders and by steps up the walls. The older Pueblo houses were often built about and facing a central plaza, thus giving a barren outside wall to strangers and neighborly comfort to those inside. Good examples of this are shown in the illustrations of

Acoma Pueblo (Figs. 1-4). In this type the lower stories were originally built entirely without door and window openings in the walls, access being from scuttle holes in the roof.

The householder being on his roof, defense of this type of building was a simple matter of keeping the enemy from scaling the walls.

The successive stories retreat from the front, leaving open porches before each apartment. This is well illustrated in Fig. 2.

Some villages built in less strenuous times, perhaps, as Laguna and Zuni (Figs. 5-7), depart from the fortress type, enclosing the plaza, and follow more or less regular streets.

The photographs from Zuni Pueblo (Figs. 6 and 7) show an adobe built village; and that from Laguna (Fig. 5) shows some old stone walls, from which the plastering has fallen, as well as some newer work.

A very pictureque example of an isolated group is shown in the photograph

Fig. 2. Showing How the Successive Stories of the Houses Retreat, Acoma Pueblo, New Mexico.

Fig. 3. An Acoma Pueblo Village.

Fig. 6. Zuni Pueblo, New Mexico—An Adobe Village.

Fig. 7. Zuni Pueblo, New Mexico—Another Adobe Village.

of Taos (Fig. 8) in the northern part of New Mexico.

The illustrations given here are intended as examples of a type only, and are in no sense considered exclusive specimens.

Some excellent reproductions of the Pueblo style have been made by the Santa Fé Railway Company at the Grand Canyon of Arizona. The effects are obtained in cement and stucco on metal lath.

If it be true, as we have read, that the characteristics of good architecture are that a building shall be in harmony with its surroundings; that the exterior shall be in right relation to the interior, the elevation being a natural development of the plan; and that it shall be free from meaningless and meretricious ornament, then Pueblo American architecture is good architecture, and deserves a moment of consideration; and it further possesses the merit of being a frank and logical expression of its purpose, and of the materials used.

Vere O. Wallingford.

Fig. 8. Taos, New Mexico.

The Value of the Curve in Street Architecture

A geometrical definition says that a straight line is the shortest distance between two points. So that any one who makes a road or other surface for traffic between two points usually lays it out between straight lines, or as near an approximation to them as he can get. Where there are many surfaces for traffic within a limited area, as in a town, the advantages of a straight line are increased; saving of time in travel becomes multiplied by the number of those who travel, whether pedestrians, horses, or street cars; the system of interwoven

generally revel in every kind of curvature, and, in the old world, streets follow their example. In every one of these we can trace to a greater or less degree artistic possibilities of a kind not to be found in the straight line. Lines of beauty do, or ought to, move in every park road or garden path that is not straight. A mere street curb is able to express a sweep of line that is living and dignified and a real pleasure to every one who can see it as it is. The really superb effect that can be produced by the foreshortened lines of common mac-

Embankment of the Arno at Pisa.

A Superb Sweep of Masonry Lining the Reaches of a River.

lines becomes simpler, and the spaces between them more useful and tractable; dimensions, angles and areas are easier to calculate and record; and drainage, sewage, and other practical problems are simpler to solve. As an artistic motive in surfaces for traffic when properly treated, the value of the straight line has been understood since the beginning of architecture; and it is as plainly seen in the Hypostyle Hall at Karnak or the Mall in Central Park as in the streets of Paris or the avenues of Schönbrunn.

For all that, as a motive for surfaces of traffic, the straight line is very much in the minority; cow tracks, country roads and paths in suburban gardens

adam is to be seen in any well-laid-out park here at home or in Europe, but particularly in France. The lines on the driveways in the Bois de Boulogne, for instance, have a grace and vigor and motion that will be a novel delight to any one who will go and discover them, and the simple borders of box or ivy along the entrance drive or path of a Parisian suburban lot have a grace that would be striking in itself without the laurels and aucubas they enclose. When a river winding through a town has its reaches fortified and accented by stone embankments, the sweep of line and surface of massive masonry is often a thing no less than magnificent, as most of those will agree who have seen the Arno

Franz Joseph's Quay, Vienna.   The ugliness of
angles that should have been united in one large
curve.

Genoa.

at Pisa, the Tiber at Rome, or the Thames at London. The gentle reader is advised when next he takes a train to mark the superb sweep of the parallel tracks round a curve, and though they are nothing but segments of circles, he will see them foreshortened into ellipses, and acquire what Nero offered riches for —a new source of pleasure. Unfortunately, he will acquire also a new source of pain, for he will learn to feel discomfort when he sees lines on the ground, that should be curves, wrenched into kinks, or badly drawn, or in any way spoiled or lost altogether.

So the straight line is not by any means the only source of beauty in country roads or city boulevards. It has its practical disadvantages besides, for it is often not for purposes of actual utility, by any means the shortest distance between two points. This has been known from time

immemorial by all sorts of practical people, from the cow who prefers a spiral track up a hill to a direct track that is not half the length, to the railroad engineer who builds a horse-shoe curve in the hollow of a mountain. In fact, when it comes to laying down lines of traffic, the straight line is only the shortest when it does not entail a losing struggle with the laws of gravity. What this means, needs but a little figuring to show. If it takes a certain force to overcome a certain grade, it would, if other things were equal, take twice as much to overcome a grade of twice the steepness, because the weight has to be raised through twice the height. It is found that if a horse can draw 1,000 lbs. on a level, he can only draw 910 lbs. on a grade of 1 per cent., 550 lbs. on a grade of 5 per cent., and only 100 lbs. on a grade of 10 per cent. The resistance to the tractive power of a locomo-

Regent Circus, London.

Regent Circus, London.

tive due to gravity alone is 2 lbs. for every ton of the train on a grade of 1-10th per cent., and 32 lbs. per ton on a grade of 1.6 per cent. Such figures as these will give an idea of the power expended in every street of the town merely to overcome the unceasing resistance of gravity by pedestrians, horses and street cars, all of which can be expressed in foot-pounds of the strength of men and animals and coal. If the power thus used up on streets like Amsterdam Avenue, New York City, could be saved it would be worth millions of dollars annually, and add so much in wealth and en-

Thus for practical purposes, for economy of strength of men and animals or power of machinery, and even of time, for convenience and economy of planning of buildings and utilization of space the straight line is often anything but the shortest distance between two points.

Somewhere in the earth, ever since men have made structures to house themselves or their dead, or their ideas of a deity, the curved mass of masonry —usually taking the simplest form of a circle or part of one—has found expression, either growing out of practical

Via Serbelloni, Bellagio. The picturesque effect of houses built along an ancient cow-track.

Amsterdam Ave., from 116th Street, N. Y. C. Showing cars climbing painfully in and out of the valley of 125th Street—the gridiron unmitigated.

ergy and comfort to the community to be expended in profitable directions. Apart from the saving of energy, it will often take actually less time to trot or steam at full speed along a roundabout but easy course than to climb on foot or wheels slowly and laboriously up a short but steep one. Besides, buildings along a steep street are more difficult to plan and expensive to build, and the back yards must either remain sloping and lose part of their usefulness, or be raised into levelness and practicability by terrace banks or retaining walls; all which means further expense and loss of space.

needs of material or uses, like the piles of the mound-builders, the Indian topes, the amphitheatres, the Colosseums or the Albert Halls, or the circular meeting places of radiating streets like those in Washington or the Place de l'Etoile in Paris, or made wholly or in part for their own sake, like the Temple of Vesta, the colonnade of St. Peter's, or the apse of a Gothic cathedral. Never a building age but has, in one way or another, felt and submitted to the fascination of the line that always changes, that presents successions of innumerable columns or windows or even mere unbroken surfaces at different angles, each with its own variety of light and shade, yet all in graded order, and gaining from the foreshortening of a number of equal things the variety of a series of unequal ones, changing successively in exact proportion. Every pillar in Bernini's colonnade, and every exterior stone in the Castle of St. Angelo has a presentation, an individuality and a distinction that it could not acquire in a structure of rectilinear plan. Never a Mr. Howson Lott who devises a path of superfluous wriggles up to his front door, and aggravates his indirectness by the latest and rigidest kind of cement pavement,

The straightest-looking lines are those which are really curved. A column must have an entasis or it appears concave, and a long wall or step must rise in the middle lest it seem to sag, and the Parthenon, exemplar of severe verticalness and horizontality, had not a straight line in it. The parallel beams of the sun at sunset appear to spread towards the zenith, and converge to the opposite horizon; the lines of a street, eaves, windows and curbstones rise and fall to their vanishing points whichever way one turns. The plane-appearing superficies of the sea is round, and so is the right line of the horizon. The fact is,

Kingsbridge Road, N. Y. C., Looking South. The ugliness of successive angles in a road that should have been made in natural curves.

From the Doge's Palace, Venice.

but feels strongly, if illogically, the charm of the foreshortened curve, so pleasing to the eye and so exhilarating to travel along. No one of artistic feeling or performance who does not delight in the eternal and indispensable curve of the sky or the cathedral dome, of household utensils or decorative detail, whether of the surface of a vase or the stupendous ellipse of a planet's course. People go out of their way to make curves in anything, from an argument to a garden walk, from the plan of a church to some new distortion of the feminine form divine. And perhaps all this groping after the curve is less mad than methodical, a yearning for something eternal and essential. Is there such a thing as a straight line, after all?

there is no such thing as a straight line. They are all merely phenomena, apparitions, not realities, tiny segments of vast circumferences serving for our small and temporary uses. The more sides a regular polygon has, the nearer it approaches a circle; and when the number of sides becomes infinitely great and their dimensions infinitely small our polygon becomes a circle. Thus every straight line on the earth, every tangent at the end of one of its radii, is but another contribution to its general roundness, and the gigantic path of the sun's light to one of its planets is but an infinitesimal part of an infinite circle of the universe.

Yet with all this instinctive search for the bending line, its use in and out of season, building designers seem often loth to use it, particularly on a large scale; or perhaps it does not occur to them. There was, for instance, a noble opportunity for a sweep of columns or arches or other architectural motive lost at St. Louis, where the transverse avenue between the principal groups of buildings would naturally be a circle struck from the centre of the great fountain; but the obvious and opportune curve is broken into six straight lines and four angles, two of them re-entering and all more or less difficult and thankless to treat. The bridges of Paris and Rome rise to an angle in the middle instead of the more graceful and convenient curve of those in London. Compare the splendid sweep of the Arno embankment at Pisa with the ugly angles on Franz Josef's Quai at Vienna. How much more restful and pleasing would have been these lines of buildings, curb and car-track, had they been reduced to one great segment of a circle. A railroad engineer is compelled to make a curve at every change of direction, as a train will not travel along a kink, but the city engineer, or whoever plans new roads or streets, never uses a curve that can be avoided; it is troublesome to lay out on the ground and record in the office. So our towns are disfigured by endless successions of streets meeting at awkward angles in road surface and building line. If we wish to see a street of graceful line that is not straight, we must usually go to the old world where they have grown up everywhere along ancient farm roads or sheep paths. The character of such a street is entirely different from that of a straight one. The sides bend round a corner and disappear from view, provoking the never-fading curiosity to discover what is beyond. The façades of the buildings are presented at different angles, and, on one side, to greater advantage than where they are all in the same plane. How much of its charm does the Grand Canal at Venice owe to its windings, and how much would some of the palaces lose were they to be marshalled along their watery highway straightened out, until one could see from the railway station to the ducal palace? How much of their

fascination do so many country towns of Italy or England owe to the curvature of their streets? Look, for instance, at the picture of the Via Serbelloni at Bellagio, where the houses have obviously strung themselves along the track of farm wagons rotted away, maybe, these thousands of years, but which took the easiest route uphill. What a charm did those long-forgotten feet or wheels lend to the irregular course they unthinkingly marked out! Look at the picture of the street seen through the ancient gateway of Bologna! This long-buried Strada dell' Abbondanza at Pompeii so nearly approaches the superb in the sweep of its lines and the regularity of its massive piers that it is hard to believe that it was not designed and constructed for the effect such a highway ought to have. They seem to have understood the value of equal spacing and continuous cornices on a curve in England better than on the Continent; they have found the conditions there, and gladly accepted them for a motive. There is the famous example of Regent's Circus in London, or the Crescent at Bath, where the resulting effect is very striking in its logic and order. In the West End of London are many curved streets of houses of similar and commonplace design, yet looking very handsome and dignified with their unbroken horizontal lines and repetition of vertical ones. In the same way, and on a very large and complete scale, the circle is used in the Piazza Castello at Milan. These curved streets separate themselves into two classes, the monumental or conscious and deliberate (which is comparatively uncommon), and the accidental or picturesque, which is found in almost every town in Europe, and many at home. All travelers see, and most travelers admire them, more or less, consciously or unconsciously, for they are full of charm and artistic suggestion. Yet, though every traveler with half an eye for the picturesque has felt their fascination, though they have been sketched and painted and engraved and oleographed, though irresponsible Cook's tourists have snapped them with portable kodaks, and serious professionals have photographed them with clumsy box cameras, it does not seem to have occurred to any one, in this country at least, to take them for a motive of design, to deliberately and aforethought make something of the same kind where circumstances permit and encourage. Yet we have within our borders places and conditions that invite such experiments. Amsterdam Avenue runs resolutely north and south, but achieves a straight course only by dipping into many valleys and scaling steep ascents, and numerous cross streets are so set in their determination to run east and west

of beauty, very often little thought of convenience or cost of construction, and no real designing except for such practical needs as those of sewage and surface drainage. The idea of seriously attempting to adapt the city plan to its site seems to have cost no one a moment's sleep, but the resolve to adapt the site to a plan—that of the gridiron—appears to have guided every ruling pen and every T-square that has had a share in placing the streets of Greater New York. Yet the undeveloped part of our city offers opportunities for urban scenery and the practical uses of a city,

The Parade, Dover. Strong cornice lines on a curve.

The Strada dell' Abbondanza, Pompeii.

that traffic is inconvenient on them at all times and really perilous in winter.

Thus the curve in street planning is a thing not to be avoided, but gladly accepted, when conditions suggest it, when a change in direction becomes imperative or a steep slope is to be surmounted. Here in Greater New York north of 155th Street, and in some places south of it, are great areas of rough land through which streets have been cut or planned, or will be planned and cut, with ruthless and blind angularity and regularity, with no thought

for uniting the glories of architecture and the greenery of parks with convenience of traffic and places to travel to that no modern city can equal. But if this splendid inheritance is to be used and developed, and not squandered by mishandling, the problem of investing it must be studied by minds untrammeled by tradition; that know and can employ the lessons of previous ages and works with zeal and judgment, but will not be bound by them in conditions that they do not fit, that are local and unique and our own.   *H. A. Caparn.*

THE 1870 CULMINATION IN FRANCE.

A COMPARISON OF MODERN AMERICAN ARCHITECTURE WITH THAT OF EUROPEAN CITIES

By PROF. STANLEY D. ADSHEAD
of
(The Liverpool University.)

BEFORE COMPARING the architecture of America with that of the modern European city, it will be well to review the historical sequence of architectural thought since the Renaissance, and so endeavor to discover the underlying causes which have conduced to bring about the finest results.

A retrospective glance at the growth of architecture in Italy, France and England from the dawn of the Renaissance, shows us that in Italy architecture arrived at its highest state of perfection in the hands of San Gallo, Sansavino, Sanmichele, and Peruzzi, all students of the remains of ancient Rome. Later we get Palladio after whom there set in a decline. In France there was attained a culmination when Perrault completed his wing at the Louvre. The subsequent decline which followed however, during the reign of Louis XV. was rapidly stayed by Gabriel, who, renewing the study of Italian art and assisted by artists from that land, brought architecture to a second culmination in the Petit Trianon at Versailles.

A still higher pinnacle was reached when Percier and Fontaine influenced by the grandiose imperial ideas of Napoleon used the imperial work of ancient Rome for their inspiration and so fostered the Empire style. This was perfected in the Louvre in Madame Beauhamis palace and in the work of the period at Fontainebleau. There then came a reversion, over much archaeology tended to pedantry and ultimately there again followed a decline.

Attention must now be directed to the Ecole des Beaux Arts, under its influence were produced men like Labruste, Leon Ginain, Duc and Charles Garnier, whose several most important works were the Library of St. Genevieve, the Ecole de Medican, the Law Courts and the Opera House. Their work was characteristic in that it assimilated the Greek revival with the modern conditions that prevailed. This was the third epoch-making period in France, the style was called Neo-Greek, it reached its culmination in 1870, and here for the present we leave French art.

In England the first culmination was attained with the later works of Indigo Jones. With Wren we get the commencement of a decline hurried to its completion by Gibbs and minor men, ultimately to result in the exhuberant but somewhat vulgar splendour of the Queen Anne style. Dance, Adams and Chambers were the prime movers in a national revolt, and their work which was a reflex of contemporary French art was in reality a revival of work in Italy and Rome. It resulted in a style of English architecture much purer in form. These men were followed by Soane, Cockerell and Elmes, and later by Pennethorne and Smirke. About this time were published the researches of Stewart and Revett, a work which finally resulted in the eclectic pedantry of 1850 and thereabouts.

With Cuthbert Brodrick of Leeds and perhaps Sir Charles Bary the continuation of pure classic architecture in England practically expired. The Gothic revival had set in, its accentuation of construction, following as it did a phase of art entirely aesthetic was the keynote to its success, and by 1870 all other schools had practically disappeared.

In countries like Holland, Germany and Austria a similar sequence had ensued, but these countries lying outside the direct Renaissance track merely repeated the rotary process of countries like France and England in a less conspicuous and more local and unsophisticated way.

Thus is will be seen that in the sequence of architectural thought, purity in style arrived at by reference to the achievements of the past may culminate in pedantry; but it does not follow that it will always arrive at so advanced a stage. It is certain, however, that sooner or later there will set in a decline. This may be brought about by a gradual tendency to provincialism as in the case of the Georgian style in England which was after all but an exaggeration of the work of Jones and of Wren; or as when the style of Louis Quinze in France following that of Louis Seize resulted merely in a confused accentuation of the points of interest in the latter. Or again

the collapse may be sudden, and may mean utter disruption, as when the pedantry of Wilkins was swept away by the Gothic revival, or as when the Neo-Greek was annihilated by L'Art Nouveau and the secessionist movement which has seized hold of the French.

It has been necessary thus to review the historical sequence of architectural thought in Europe during the Renaissance in order to discern the conditions most favorable to an epoch making period. We are now in a position to proceed with our investigation as to the comparative merits of the architecture of the different nationalities in modern times.

Germany and Austria during the 17th and 18th centuries lay outside the geographical line of Renaissance progress, and Germany's war with France rendered this isolation the more complete. Little wonder then that Germany and Austria since 1870 should have been obliged to sacrifice all traditional association in architecture to meet the demands of an extraordinary organic activity which had internally arisen, and little wonder that these countries should have laid aside those "motifs" and ornaments which have permeated architecture since the Periclean Age, and in lieu thereof have turned about to find others more expressive of the rejuvenation which the countries east of the Rhine and north of the Danube were undergoing. At first Holland, Belgium and Germany were ransacked and their most blatant extravagances produced during the early periods of the Renaissance were re-erected in exaggerated form. Frankfort station, the Town Hall of Wiesbaden and the Ringstrasse at Cologne were the result. About the year 1890 German and Austrian architects, wearied with the resuscitation of Renaissance forms derived even from the most exotic and quaintest of styles, and feeling that every possibility for the display of striking individuality had been extracted from these sources, had their attention suddenly directed to the fascinating attractions of that style of architecture which had come to be known as L'Art Nouveau. The possibilities it afforded for the expression

TYPICAL MODERN FRENCH.
THE SCHOOL OF PASCAL.

of their many original and scientifically developed conceptions could not be gainsaid, and L'Art Nouveau as originated in Glasgow, as advanced by the Arts and Crafts movement in London, as illustrated in the pages of the Studio, and as first exemplified in Vienna by Wagner and in Berlin by Otto Reitz, was seized hold of and travestied by the architects of Dusseldorf, Cologne, etc., with an enthusiasm almost childlike in its ingenuousness. One can only regard it as the outcome of an honest yearning after instinctive expression but which in an intellectual age must necessarily be an affectation.

von Thiersch. This is the latest of some half dozen works by this architect, amongst which may be mentioned the Law Courts of Munich, perhaps less successful, and the Festhalle at Frankfurt. Frederick von Thiersch stands practically alone in Germany as an architect who has confined his studies to the epoch-making periods in the architecture of Europe which we have reviewed; he has met the new conditions of his time, concrete construction and the like, and has succeeded in combining with them a scholarly tradition and considerable imagination.

THE 1870 CULMINATION IN FRANCE—LE PALAIS DE JUSTICE.

fectation. But quite recently there has been a return to the study of a later type of Parisian "Hotel," in reality a revival of the Louis Seize; in some cases it has been assimilated with L'Art Nouveau. This return to a more reasonable style augurs well for Germany and Austria, as an instance we would refer to the Hotel Adlon in Berlin, to premises such as the show rooms of Schneider and Hanan at Frankfurt, and others there in close proximity to the Kaiser Platz. But later and still fresh from the chisel of the mason and the brush of the artist we get the Kursaal at Wiesbaden, by Frederick

He was educated at Rome and there is no doubt that he is a scholar well acquainted with the best periods of the architecture of France. Were all the modern buildings in Germany equal to or based upon similar principles to those which have inspired the work of this one man, the architecture of Germany would in the modern world be unsurpassed; but as yet his works are but few, they have been but recently erected, and Frederick von Thiersch stands alone. From Germany and Austria we pass on to England.

Since about 1860 no country in

Europe, perhaps with the exception of Germany, has undergone such internal disruption in the matter of her architecture as has England. The Gothic revival which followed the pedantry of Pennethorne and Smirke utterly dislocated the sequence of events which had risen and fallen since the time of Jones. About 1890 there was a general concensus of opinion that Gothic architecture was doomed, that it must be superceded by work based on classic thought, and that to be truly national it must be drawn from an English source. About the same time a phase of L'Art Nouveau originated in Glasgow and associated with the names of Macintosh, Walton and others, passed on to London and was there taken up in its German aspect by men like Percy Adams, in its more English aspect by men like Harrison Townsend and in a more restricted way by John Belcher, R. A. Offshoots, are to be seen in the domestic work of architects like Letherby, Voysey and Schultz; but in England L'Art Nouveau had never seriously captivated the attention of the architects at large; it was always with some interesting development of classic architecture that they were concerned. We say interesting, and in doing so desire to lay stress upon this word. The desire for interest rather than for refinement, the lack of appreciation of scale and the disregard of the importance which attaches to the expression of pure style are factors which have retarded the progress of English architecture above all others. Unlike Germany, England has never given way to a desire for childish display, her mistakes have been due almost entirely to her excessive desire for interest, to her love of self-assertion, and to her naive ignorance brought about largely by the system of education provided by the state.

Between 1880 and 1890 the English classic "motifs" were drawn from the early Renaissance of Jones, and from the picturesque architecture of the same period in Holland and Belgium. The leading spirits at the time were Norman Shaw Nesfield and Ernest George; certainly they are able men, and have had a well deserved and distinguished career,

but one feels that artists as they are it were a pity that they had not lived during more favorable times.

Following the period 1890, England has certainly produced a few good architects. We describe them as good architects because they were artists in the sense that they have shown great ability to express themselves, but their education has been an undisciplined one, and they have had to serve a public whose environment amidst the confused architectural effort of their immediate past, has rendered them quite incapable of appreciating anything more than an ostentatious display. Little is it to be wondered at then, that architects like William Flockhart, Beresford Pite, Lanchester and Rickards, and Bentley, who, whilst producing work, which judged from a narrow standpoint is at times astounding in its originality and in its sense of appreciation for abstract form, yet, when placed alongside the great works produced during the epoch-making periods to which I have referred, is found to be lacking in breadth, scale, and in the kind of interest which is associated with a wide acquaintance of the meaning and import of traditional style.

Passing to France and reviewing her architecture since 1870 we see that what is called the secession has set in. At first there was a return to the architecture of the "hotel" as erected in the time of Louis XVI. Architecture in France was still as it had been since the degeneracy in Italy, the finest. the purest, and the most distinctly traditional of any architecture in the world; but at this stage France was called upon to produce the exhibition architecture of 1889 and 1900. All this has tended to that phase of expression known as the "Tour de force." At first it was applied to the Louis Seize details which were the stock in trade material of the designers of the day, and as outstanding results we get the Grand and Petit Palais.

The new style appeared contemporaneously with L'Art Nouveau which sweeping through Germany and Austria had invaded France, France being the last country to accept the new phase. To the credit of France it must be stated that alongside this secession movement older and more philosophic men were still adhering to the traditions of the epoch of 1870 and thereabouts. The works of M. Pascal in the Libraire Nationale and of Wewes in the Ritz Hotel, of Nenot and of other men are examples of the work of this school which is still being done. At the present day a phase of art which is an amalgamation of

done, that appreciation for scale which is so obviously lacking in the architecture of Germany, England and other European countries of first importance.

Lastly we turn to America. There is no need to dwell upon the growth of American architecture during the Colonial period, nor, indeed, during the early life of the republic. The real interest of American architecture in its modern

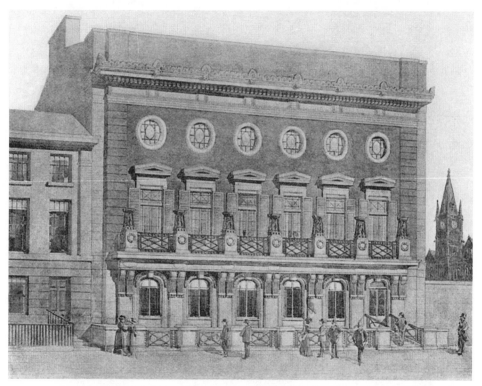

A NEW DEVELOPMENT IN ENGLISH ARCHITECTURE.

Louis XVI detail, L'Art Nouveau inspiration and other influences emanating from an ingenuous desire to express structural form has seized upon the architecture of France, has obsessed the Ecole des Beaux Arts, and threatens to bring the national architecture into realms where the highest aspects of the art are unappreciated and unknown. Yet with all this tendency to realism, as opposed to aestheticism, the modern architecture of France still preserves, as it always has

phase commences with the work of Richardson, Hunt and McKim.

Until about 1870, America followed closely in the steps of England. It was at about this time that Bowling Green Buildings and other works in a similar style were erected; they were based on "motifs" derived from contemporary work in Europe. At the time, in England, classic architecture was still hankering after the work of Cockerell, in France the Neo-Greek was in full swing,

A NEW DEVELOPMENT IN ENGLISH ARCHITECTURE.
William and Edward Hunt, Architects, 1910.

A New Development in English Architecture.

dered a service to America which she could never requite. The works of the firm of McKim, Mead and White, of which he was the head, are well known and have been fully reviewed. It is not on the merits of each of these works that we wish to dilate, this has already been done, but to direct particular attention to the source of inspiration from which they were drawn. McKim was in the first place a philosopher and in whatever phase of art he happened to be at work, it was always a derivation from the finest source. In the second place he was a student, and to no one were the resources of the past better known, added to this he was a refined and sensitive artist. However closely he based his work on the masterpieces of the past, he was always original; even such buildings as the Tiffany building, the Pulitzer residence and the general waiting room of

A New Development in English Architecture.
Wm. and Ed. Hunt, Architects.

and in Brussels the "Palais de Justice" was being commenced.

The Gothic revival followed and culminated in the works of a genius, Richardson, who produced Trinity Church, Boston, a modern Gothic building unsurpassed by contemporary work of the kind on either side of the Globe. It was from this period, about 1870, that the modern movement in America dates. Our attention is here for the first time directed to the work of Charles Follen McKim, and the wonderful progress of architecture in America since then is entirely due to this man. In McKim we have a genius who is at once philosopher, artist and scholar of the highest rank, and it would not be paying too high a compliment to his name, now that he is gone, to say that he should be numbered with the few greatest architects that the world has yet seen. Had he merely directed attention to the importance of renewing the study of classic art, he would have renthe Pennsylvania railway station, New York, based with almost pedantic correctness on the Grimani Palace, the Cornaro Palace and the Baths of Caracalla respectively, were in his hands made original and modern, in a sense that tradition was woven around a new idea.

His scholarly use of traditional "motifs," his keen sense of proportion, his correct use of detail and his appreciation

that evolution in thought is not synonymous with change in local condition and the trivialities of a chance intrusion.

To express character in his building, and that in its finest and deepest sense was with McKim the first requirement in design. If it should so suit him, the expression of the stanchicon, the rainwater pipe, the chimney, and even the roof is calmly set to one side.

MODERN GERMAN.

for color enabled him to stamp an unmistakable personality on everything he touched. It follows therefore that his work was intellectual and academic rather than instinctive and provincial; and if it does not reflect all the accidental issues, so important to the realist, it was because as a philosopher he recognized that the finest things in architecture are like the facets of human nature, permanent, and

But the honor of infusing into American architecture fresh "motifs" extracted from a European source must also be shared by other men. To Carrère and Hastings a great debt is due. Unlike the firm of McKim, Mead and White who showed a leniency towards the Italian and Venetian Schools, and later the works of Greece and Rome, Carrère and Hastings confined their attention to the epoch-making periods in France. To them is almost entirely due the credit of having persuaded the younger architects of America to study at the Beaux Arts. Whilst the work of this firm does not always carry with it that conviction which is inseparable from the work of McKim, it is not our place here to make distinctions. Carrère and Hastings may not always have arrived at that perfection in proportion which when endeavoring to captivate the beauty of an original example, and at the same time assimilate the conditions of a new problem, needs such a strain upon their imagination to attain. That such works, as the En-

Modern German—A Typical Bank.

trance Hall of the New York Library, the Traders' Bank at Toronto, the Blair Building, the House of Representatives at Washington and the houses for Root, Wm. K. Vanderbilt and Murray Guggenheim, show them to be architects of the very highest rank. Not only have they solved the modern problems, but they have shown a fine discrimination in that they have chosen for their inspiration the culminating periods in architectural progress, and in particular that period which commenced with the work of Perault, and terminated with work of Gabriel in the Petit Trianon at Versailles.

Contemporaries of McKim, Mead and White, and of Carrère and Hastings

are Post, Cass Gilbert and Burnham, such men we must recognize as the pioneers of the modern American school. It becomes difficult to discriminate between the pioneer and the disciple, but the following names chosen at random are doing work which is representative of its best traditions—Howells and Stokes, Rankin and Kellogg, J. G. Howard, Guy Lowell, Kilham and Hopkins, and Parker, Thomas and Rice. This is an incomplete list, but these are the names of some of the architects whose work the schools of America should follow if the great tradition founded by McKim is to be handed on.

So rapid has been the progress of American architecture, and so sudden are the changes that have come about, that it is difficult to forecast even the possibilities of to-morrow. The immediate influence of McKim and of Carrère and Hastings, which up to the present has practically been responsible for all that America has done, is to-day on the decline; indeed, judging from the most recent architectural erections in New York, it would appear that the later American students from the Ecole des Beaux Arts, whose influence is just commencing to be felt are obsessed with the latest secessionist ideals which are at present bringing into a state of confusion the architecture of France. This is undoubtedly an unfortunate circumstance for the future of America.

In reviewing the architecture of America attention has been confined to the individual works of a few men, nothing has been said of it as a whole. American architecture sadly lacks composition, but this can only be attained by ownership control in one of its many forms, its absence is no fault of the art. The American city is mediaeval in its composition, classic in detail, and is built on a classic plan.

Space will not permit of our investigation into the condition of modern architecture being carried further, but to sum up, our verdict is as follows: in Germany and Austria it is archaic in its technique, ingenuous in its method of expression, and its aim is realism as opposed to aestheticism. At its best it is a simple phase of art, and like the impressionist school of painting is narrow in its intention, and therefore incomparable in result with the more academic works that have been produced by less provincial schools.

The modern architecture of England in confused in its intention; it does not, like that of Germany and Austria depend entirely upon innate and subjective inspiration; but at the same time its source which have inspired all the greatest architectural works of the past. With the modern French student the expression of construction and physical intention counts first, whilst those more abstract but no less important qualities which count so high in the valuation of the greatest works take but a second place.

Modern American architecture is in the first place an intellectural art. As seen to-day, it is the outcome of a selected

TRADITIONAL CLASSIC IN GERMANY.
Weisbaden.

The New Kursaal.
Frederick Von Thiersch, Architect.

is digressive; this no doubt is due to the effect of the Gothic revival from which it has but recently recovered.

The modern architecture of France still preserves its national appreciation for scale, its most striking tendency is to evince a too evident desire for effect and it is inclined to be theatrical. In its method of expression it affects a realistic type of art, and there is no doubt that in its strenuous efforts to succeed in this direction, it sacrifices those principles appropriation of European masterpieces of the past. Having no tradition of its own on which to base a style of monumental art, it has been faced with two alternatives. It might, like Germany after the war of 1870, have depended upon itself and refused the open door, or relying entirely upon a process of adaptation have decided to look abroad and choose from a well selected source. Needless to say the national intellect inclined it towards the latter course, and as a result,

American architecture as we see it to-day will ever be regarded as an epoch-making period in the progressive stages of the architecture of the world. In making a statement like this we must needs assume that the epoch-making periods in the history of architecture have arrived at such times as has been pointed out, and if we assume that the sequence of thought will repeat itself in the future as history shows it to have done in the

hence any reversion to pure styles is not likely to be acceptable to more than a small section of her architects for very many years to come. The future of American architecture depends upon the energy and intelligence of the followers of the movement started by McKim. The secessionists are no doubt causing some confusion, but the common sense and natural intelligence possesssed by this nation will prevent excesses such as

TRADITIONAL CLASSIC IN GERMANY.
Weisbaden.

The New Kursaal.
Frederick Von Thiersch, Architect.

past, then the high place given to American architecture of to-day is well sustained. In conclusion let us glance ahead, the architecture of France is threatened with dissemination the secession movement which is absorbing the attention of the Ecole des Beaux Arts will no doubt keep French architecture clear of effete aestheticism, but at the same time, if carried to extremes, it will bring about ultimate disintegration. Germany is heart and soul in the throes of L'Art Nouveau,

have been witnessed elsewhere. In looking to the future of the architecture of England, we recognize that there exists at the present moment a well established school whose efforts, however, are confined to domestic work alone. Lutyens and Baillie Scott may be regarded as the most prominent leaders of this school. Their work is based on the cottage to be found anywhere in England up to a hundred years ago. Judging from Lutyens latest designs the residence of the future will be more refined and based on a later style. Monumental architecture in England has perhaps a brighter future than in any other country of first importance. There the secessionist movement so pronounced in France, and L'art Nouveau so strong in Austria and Germany are receiving but scant attention. In looking at the future of English architecture it is to the younger schools and to the vigor which they display that our

a revolt against the picturesque classic, of Norman Shaw, the coarseness of the Queen Anne and the naive simplicity of L'Art Nouveau. Originally eminating as it may be said to have done, from the offices of such men as Verity, Burnet and Pite, it now has a definite programme of its own. Its aim is to recapture some of the refinements of Saone, Cockrell and Elmes, it is inspired by the American schools, by the hard beauty of the Neo-

TRADITIONAL CLASSIC IN GERMANY.   The New Kursaal.
Weisbaden.   Frederick Von Thiersch, Architect.

attention must be directed. Prominent amongst these is rapidly arising a school of academic thought, whose aim is to produce architecture academic and monumental as opposed to that which is provincial and picturesque. It is on the growth of this school that a brilliant future for English architecture depends. The executed works of its pioneers are as yet but few, but their energy is the energy of renewed youth. The movement has arisen out of

Greek and by the work of such modern French architects as Pascol, Nenot, Mewes and Breasson. It is early to mention names but it would be an omission not to mention the Liverpool School of Architecture in connection with this new movement. Of executed works the office building at the corner of Wigmore Street and Portland Street by Mr. Hunt and the Berkeley Hotel by Messrs. Richardson and Gill are excellent examples of what is being done.

MODERN ARCHITECTURE.—A CONVERSATION.

RCHITECT (*perturbed, entering School of Modern Architecture*).—The present condition of our art is most perplexing and unsatisfactory. What comfort, I wonder, is there here?

CLASSICIST, GOTH, ROMANESQUER *look up from their drawing boards and smile pityingly.*

ARCHÆOLOGIST (*greeting him*).—Unsatisfactory? Perplexing? We don't find it so here. My dear sir, possibly (*smiling with air of superiority*) you are not acquainted with the great work we have accomplished by strict attention to archæology. The imitative....

ARCHITECT.—But the creative....

ARCHÆOLOGIST.—The creative in archæology! My good sir, what place is there....

ARCHITECT.—Pardon me, but I speak of architecture....

ARCHÆOLOGIST.—And, pray, what is architecture but the strict application of archæology to modern requirements? If architecture is not applied archæology, what is....

ECLECTIC (*entering*).—Wouldn't a judicious blending of styles meet the case?

Chorus of dissent from CLASSICIST, GOTH *and* ROMANESQUER.

ECLECTIC.—That's the trouble with you dry-as-dusts. You have only one idea. You have no conception of how freedom invigorates a design. The Gothic, for instance, is all very well, but it needs broadening and stiffening in the joints, if I may say so. Now, I've used it with great success in an exquisite cast-iron front tenement I turned out the other day for a wealthy New Yorker, but I Romanesqued the entrance somewhat, and with the aid of a heavy modillioned cornice....

GOTH.
CLASSICIST. } Vandal!
ROMANESQUER.

ECLECTIC.—Gave quite a modern air to the thing. But in Philadelphia....

ARCHÆOLOGIST (*severely*).—Stop, sir. The name of that piebald city may not be mentioned within these precincts.

ECLECTIC.—Oh, very well, then. Out West....

WESTERN ARCHITECT (*rising from group of listeners*).—Permit me, sir. In the West, you will be interested to know, several of our brainiest architects are now engaged in the creation of an original "American Style," and what with the Chicago system of construction on one hand, and the inventive genius of our people on the other, this copying of effete forms is about ended.

171

Chicago, Ills.   NEW GERMAN OPERA HOUSE,   Adler & Sullivan, Architects.

CLASSICIST.—Effete forms, sir! Ah, how faint is your appreciation of perfection!

GOTH } (*in rapture, each look-*
ROMANESQUER } *ing in a different*
direction).—Perfection!

CLASSICIST.—I maintain that hope for architecture to-day lies in the use of certain forms perfected by the Greeks. The tendency of the time to proceed without precedent is subversive of true art. If we are not grammatical....

ARCHÆOLOGIST.—I beg you, archæological.

CLASSICIST.—Have it so if you will —we are barbarous.

GOTH (*to Classicist*).—But you will admit that Greek architecture is quite undeveloped, one may say is really primitive on the constructive side.

ARCHITECT (*eagerly*). — That's it. How am I to harmonize Grecian precedent and modern requirements, which my clients insist shall be satisfied?

CLASSICIST. — Unreasonable beings; art is not for them.

ECLECTIC.—Nonsense! Harmonize! There is no need to harmonize. Our duty is to select. What do the styles exist for if not for that? I am making a design now for an eleven-story office building for a religious "daily" in what I call the "classic spirit." That's as near as you can get to antiquity. Doric on the ground floor, you know, with a broken pediment and a bull's-eye to get light; Ionic columns above in brick; then Corinthian, with a mansard roof supporting a spire-like tower surmounted by a forty-foot statue of the Freedom of the Press. Greek elegance with Gothic aspiration. I say, you *must* break away from precedent a little in these matters. Our effort should be confined to retaining the spirit.

CLASSICIST (*in horror*). — Shade of Ictinus!

ICTINUS (*appearing*).—Who called me!

CLASSICIST.—Oh, my master!

ICTINUS (*sorrowfully*). — Slave, I dreamed that I bequeathed to you a lordly kingdom; but it was only a bondage.

CLASSICIST.—But, master, I have followed in thy footsteps. Thy diameters....

ICTINUS.—Diameters! Poor fool! Think you that we live by a formula?

CLASSICIST.—Master, I have measured every column in thy masterpiece and found....

ICTINUS.—Yes, feet and inches; not our spirit.

CLASSICIST.—But how are we to work?

ICTINUS.—In thy own delight, and with reason, as we did, and as the great ones that followed us did.

CLASSICIST.—But to-day our architecture . . . .

ICTINUS.—Your architecture! where is it? Show me some work that is really yours—that your soul delights in. Therein will be the hope for your art.

ARCHÆOLOGIST.—But are we to ignore the Past?

ICTINUS (*smiling*).—No, indeed. You cannot. Useless to try, even. But you question the Past only for its What, not for its How. You seek for the dead matter of Art, not for the living spirit, which is the same yesterday, to-day and forever.

ECLECTIC.—Permit me to suggest. You leave out of view, perhaps, our tenements and office buildings.

ICTINUS (*shuddering*).—No, great Apollo; no. Believe me I don't. They darken our life yonder. O! Ilissus, and thy quiet places still haunted by our dreams of beauty, hast thou no message for these barbarians. Ah, friend, I see you are the rash one here. You voyage restlessly among old lands; these your companions abide some·here some there. Those tenements and office buildings of which you speak can—be—made—artistic—I—suppose; but they cannot inspire great art. You cannot clothe the petty things of life with majesty. The hands build greatly only where the feet tread reverently. And, really, it seems to me you modern barbarians have no great architecture because there is so little in your lives that demands—and the demand must be imperious—grand expression. Your office buildings and factories and stores are matters of percentage. Art is not. Your theatres—O shade of Æschylus! —are also per cent affairs, where the

·The "Banks" Building ·Front St New York·   ·R·W·Gibson Architect· 18 Wall St·N·Y·

curious and idle make exchanges with . . . .

MODERN ARCHITECT.—The theatrical manager.

ICTINUS (*warmly*).—Friends, why look for a source of great art there? Your day is not favorable. Perceive that. By and by some vision may come to you as the Vision of Beauty came to us and you may follow it as we did.

GOTH.—And as my masters did that which came to them.

ICTINUS (*pointing before him*).—Look! Look! O! city of the Purple Crown, again I behold thee, and thy temples and sanctified places. Thy olive groves adorn thee, and the wide blue sea worships at thy feet. And the air is filled with the voices of thy heroes, my city, and of thy poets. The eternal gods are there, and their gift is beauty. Oh, this is life again! Feel it!

CLASSICIST.—What is he talking about?

ARCHÆOLOGIST.—Why, where is he gone to? I wanted to question him about the length of the stadium.

Harry W. Desmond.

Baron Haussmann and the Topographical Transformation of Paris Under Napoleon III.

III.

The Premier Réseau and the Rectification of the Grande Croissée

It has been necessary to discuss at length the development of the plan of Paris before the advent of Haussmann. The dominant characteristic of his administration was its broad appreciation of the work which had preceded. He realized perfectly that he was only one of the many masters who had assisted in the solution of this vast problem, and taking up the task where the older men left it, he finished it in a manner which would have given them supreme satisfaction.

When Haussmann came up from Bordeaux, in June, 1853, leaving his brilliant administration of the Gironde, he found the situation well understood. The Emperor had taken up the Napoleonic traditions. Like the great Bonaparte he was filled with a desire that the capital of his Empire should be "quelque chose de fabuleux, de colossal, d'inconnu jusqu' a nos jours." A crude sort of magnificence would doubtless have satisfied him; but his sense of proportion was correct. He knew that he had a great, growing and proud city under his hands, and that its map must be drawn to fit and please.

But what Louis Napoleon best understood was the sociological and hygienic condition of modern civilization. The Napoleonic dynasty always maintained that it was born of the Revolution, and that its chief function was to accelerate that movement. Napoleon III. appreciated fully all the utilities for which the Revolution stood. He had before him a city in which much had been planned, but little accomplished. It was still an old mediaeval town, to which a magnificent modern population was trying to accommodate itself. The sympathetic duty was forced upon him of making a suitable home for these people. As Prince-President and as Emperor before the coming of Haussmann he labored diligently toward the performance of his task, but the instrument which he required was not at hand. The excellent Berger, who then held the office of Préfet de la Seine, was utterly unable to grasp the ensemble of the Paris map, and Haussmann appeared at the right moment to replace him.

We have shown in previous articles that in all its larger lines the plan of Paris had already been carefully studied. This study, however, fine as it was, and important, was largely that of the drafting-board and library. Even the serious work of the first Napoleon and Louis Phillipe made little impression upon the vast, incoherent mass of the city. In his Mémoires, Haussmann draws an interesting picture of the situation in 1853. The general appearance of Paris at that time is well shown by the etchings of Martial, a superb record of the disappearing town, several of which we reproduce in the illustrations.

The Civic Center of Paris.

A curious phase of the situation at the beginning of the Second Empire was the fact that the center of gravity of Paris was drifting rapidly toward the northwest. The true port of Paris is at Saint-Denis, and the commercial forces are constantly pulling the city in that direction. In 1853 the center had reached a point a little to the west of the present location of the Opéra. In any American city a fact like this would have dominated every consideration. The civic center would have been placed as near as possible to the actual center of forces. Not so in Paris. The sympathetic French mind would not tolerate a cold-blooded commercial solution of the problem. The historic center of Paris is the Ile de la Cité, and this must also be the monumental civic center.

Even the engineers and bankers who built the great railways between 1842 and 1848 bowed before this sentiment, and placed their original stations in a circle, the center of which was, approximately, in the Ile de la Cité.

This determination to retain the civic center of Paris in the Ile de la Cité is the key to the scheme for the transformation accomplished under the Second Empire.

The Grande Croissée.

If, in the plan of Paris, one assumes that the old Roman Cité is still the center of the modern metropolis, the next and logical step is to the consideration of the Grande Croissée; and that step Louis Napoleon, Haussmann and the people of Paris took with true French directness. The two great trade routes, following closely the old Roman roads, and crossing approximately at the Ile de la Cité, were recognized, enlarged and restored to their normal function in the city. An American student or architect, accustomed to the brutal civics of our land, finds it difficult to conceive a vast metropolis entering upon a period of transformation on historic lines, and in the face of conflicting commercial considerations; but that is precisely what happened in Paris, and that is, for our present purpose, quite the most significant and characteristic fact to be noted in the administration of the Grand Préfet.

The Réseaux.

In the transformation of Paris the term réseau was adopted for administrative purposes, and is not necessarily topographical in its significance; at the same time the three systems or réseaux in which the work was arranged did correspond in a general way with the topography. The Premier Réseau officially included simply the improvement provided for by the law of 1855, appropriating sixty million francs for the Rue de Rivoli, the Boulevard de Sébastopol and the region surrounding the Hôtel de Ville, Tour de Saint-Jacques and the Place du Châtelet. As this includes the

greater part of the Grande Croissée, it may be permitted, for our present purpose, to consider the Premier Réseau as loosely identical with the Grande Croissée, although the later part of the work was included in the appropriations for the Deuxième and Troisième Réseaux.

The Rue de Rivoli.

In the old maps, and historically, the east and west arms of the Grande Croissée were composed of the Rue de Saint-Honoré on the west and the Rue de Saint-Antoine on the east, united through the center of the city by an extraordinary network of narrow and tortuous streets, well shown in section 5 of the map of Verniquet, printed in our second article. Passage by this route was always difficult, and the necessity for improvement must often have suggested itself. As we have several times noted, it seems quite probable that the people who designed the Place du Thrône and the Place de l'Etoile intended to create some monumental connection between them. Nothing, however, was done until the time of Napoléon Bonaparte, when the first section of the Rue de Rivoli, opposite the Tuileries gardens, was built. The plan of Percier and Fontaine for this section, which we reproduce, draws the street to the Palais Royal. The section parallel with the garden was opened in 1802.

Something had already been done in the way of clearing out the adjacent city when Haussmann's operations on the Rue de Rivoli began. They proceeded in four sections, which it is not necessary to describe here in detail, from the Palais Royal to the old Place Birague, where union with the Rue de Saint-Antoine was practicable.

Cutting a rather irregular street 22 mètres wide through an old city was a simple matter. In the transformation of Paris, however, the making of a street carried with it the entire reconstruction of the region through which it ran. The continuation of the Rue de Rivoli to the Rue du Louvre, and the construction of the Rue du Louvre itself were part of the scheme for the completion of the Tuileries and Louvre palaces. Into an

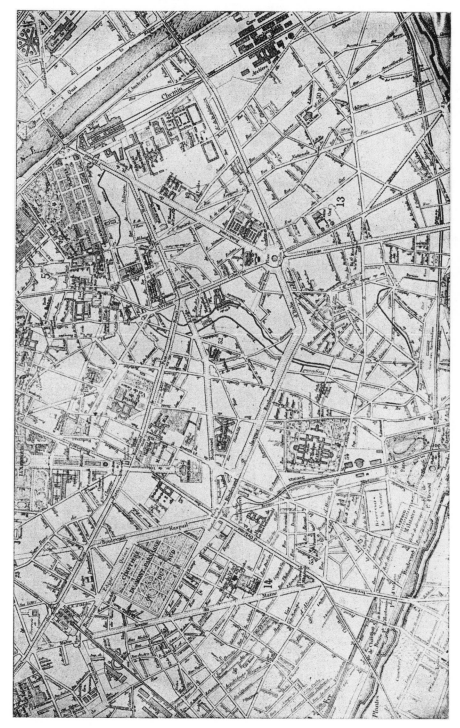

MAP OF THE CENTRAL REGION OF PARIS, AFFECTED BY THE OPERATIONS OF THE PREMIER RESEAU.

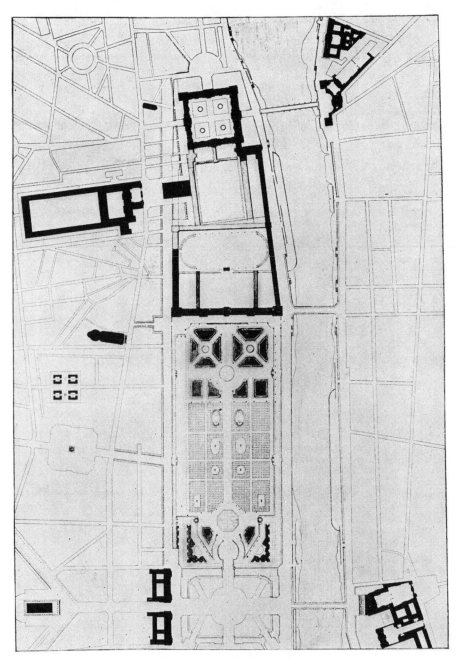

SCHEME OF THE FIRST NAPOLEON FOR RUE DE RIVOLI.
From Percier and Fontaine Monuments de Paris.

THE CHURCH OF SAINT GERMAIN AUXERROIS, THE MAIRIE OF THE FIRST ARRONDISSEMENT AND THE NEW TOWER.
(From lithograph.)

PLACE DU CARROUSEL IN 1849.
(From etching by Martial.)

RUE DE JEAN PAIN MOLLET IN 1847.   (From etching by Martial.)

account of this great architectural undertaking we cannot at present enter. The work was national, paid from the civil list, and did not directly concern the city of Paris and Haussmann.

Rue de la Vieille Lanterne in 1854, Showing
Fountain of the Place du Châtelet.
(From etching by Martial.)

The condition of the region within and without the quadrangle of palaces, however, did concern Haussmann very much.

The original Place du Carrousel of Louis XIV. occupied only a small part of the interior space. With the exception of three small courts in front of the Tuileries, the rest of the region was filled with a dense mass of old houses, which extended to and enveloped the Palais Royal. More disgraceful than the condition within the line of palaces was the condition without. The Louvre quadrangle was completely surrounded by old buildings; even within the shadow of the Colonnade itself. Haussmann cleared all this away, and created the greater Place du Carrousel and Place du Louvre as we see them to-day.

It was characteristic of Haussmann to respect the old church of Saint-Germain-l'Auxerrois, which he was urged to destroy, and to arrange a monumental mass about it which should have some importance in contrast with the Louvre. He was not especially pleased with the manner in which the architect Hittorff performed his part of the task in the Mairie of the First Arrondissement, considering it a much too literal copy of the old church. The tower by Ballu was more successful, although as seen over the roof of the Louvre it has the curious effect of accentuating the slight deflection in the axis of the palace.

Another interesting monument which lay in the course of this improvement was the fine tower of Saint-Jacques-la-Boucherie, which dates from 1508. The church itself was destroyed early in the Revolution. The tower stood on an eminence, and, as the new street passed at a lower level, Haussmann, not wishing to disturb it, supported the entire mass, and placed under it a new basement, a famous piece of engineering in those days. The Square Saint-Jacques gave it proper isolation and vista.

The Grande Châtelet, at first a fortress and afterwards the municipal prison of Paris, was destroyed in 1802. In the square which replaced it the Fontaine du Palmier was built by Napoleon in 1808 from the design of the architect de Bralle. Situated near the actual point of intersection of the two arms of the Grande Croissée, the Place du Châtelet became a point of strategic importance in

Haussmann's scheme, and a difficult matter to arrange satisfactorily on account of the entire lack of symmetry in the relation of the Pont au Change to the several intersecting avenues; due to a lack of study on the part of the original designers of the Boulevard du Centre. In order to give the ensemble a dignified center, it was necessary to move the Fontaine du Palmier twelve mètres toward the west into the axis of the Pont du Change. It was at the same time raised four mètres. The change was made April 1, 1858, by Alphand and Davioud.

The Rue de Rivoli improvement carried with it the reconstruction of the Halles Centrales and the completion of the Square des Innocents.

From the earliest times there had been a market-place in this region. This old agora became in the middle ages one of the most important marts in Europe. It was, like all mediaeval markets, a wretched complex of crooked streets and unwholesome rookeries, and retained this general character to the moment of the inception of the Second Empire, when Napoleon III. undertook its entire reconstruction to meet the requirements of modern civilization. The Emperor was much attracted by the iron train shed which had been built for the station of the Chemin-de-fer de l'Est, and after a long struggle against the prejudices of the architect Baltard, Haussmann secured from him the present convenient and monumental market of Paris in the same style of construction. The creation of the Halles Centrales carried with it the opening of two large streets to the river—the Rue du Pont-Neuf and the Rue des Halles—and, of course, the complete renovation of the included and adjacent spaces.

The region between the Châtelet and the Hôtel de Ville was the bottomless pit of old Paris. In this unwholesome network of crooked lanes the Rue de Saint Honoré and the Rue de Saint-Antoine tailed off and connected through the Rues de la Tixeranderie, de la Coutellerie, Jean Pain Mollet, des Ecrivains, de la Beaumerie, de la Tableterie, des Fourneurs and des Déchargeurs. The appalling state of things in this vicinity

Haussmann describes at length. He was much amused by the condition of an old rookery in the Rue des Teinturiers, which tried to fall and could not. It simply leaned against the house on the opposite side of the street. "Et quelle population habitait la."

The Hôtel de Ville had been completed in the reign of Louis Phillipe, but the region about it remained essentially in its mediaeval condition. The Place de Grève looked much as it did when it was the common execution-place of the city. Haussmann rectified the place and quai, and drew the Avenue Victoria in the axis of the Hôtel de Ville through the Place du Châtelet. The Pont Nôtre Dame was reconstructed to lower the grade. Haussmann has been blamed for the loss of much picturesqueness in this region; but this has been more than compensated for by the quiet dignity of the result. The Rue de Rivoli was completed to its intersection with the Rue François Myron, where it was continued by the Rue de Saint-Antoine. The Place de la Bastille is so largely a creation of the reigns of Napoleon and Louis Phillipe that it need not be considered here.

The strategic importance of the Rue de Rivoli is obvious.

The Rue de Rivoli is not a fine street, as compared with many of Haussmann's later productions. Its form was predetermined and forced upon him by a certain historic necessity. The construction of the street, however, and the improvements which went with it, disemboweled old Paris and forced the lower classes into the faubourgs. The disengagement of fine monuments which it accomplished more than compensated for the rather uninteresting character of the street itself.

The Boulevard de Sebastopol.

The placing of the great railway stations in a circle about the old center of Paris brought the administration into contact with the problem of providing for them proper avenues of approach. Before the time of Haussmann, a beginning was made with the Gare de l'Est as the starting-point for a great "Boulevard

RUE DE LA TIXERANDERIE IN 1848.
(From Martial.)

du Centre," which should develop the north and south arms of the Grande Croissée; this street, 30 mètres wide, was finished as far the Boulevard de Saint-Denis in 1852, and took the name Boulevard de Strasbourg.

The continuation of the "Boulevard du Centre" to the river was taken up by Haussmann under the provision for the Premier Réseau, and was opened with great éclat April 5, 1858. It was named Boulevard de Sébastopol, from the Crimean victory of September 9, 1855.

This fine street is essentially a continuation of the Boulevard de Strasbourg, constructed by Louis Napoleon before the appointment of Haussmann. It is a true French avenue of the type brought to perfection in the reign of Louis XIV., composed of a roadway, trottoirs and lines of trees, carefully profiled. Haussmann approved it on general principles. It was definitely better to build a new street through the blocks than to widen either of the old streets, the Rue Saint-Denis and the Rue Saint-Martin, with its continuation of the Rue des Arcis. In this way, without disturbance of traffic, three large parallel streets were secured, which have proved none too much for the requirements of the situation. Haussmann was, h o w e v e r, much distressed by a lack of care on the part of the engineers who designed the Boulevard de Strasbourg. A minute deviation at the Gare de l'Est would have brought the axis of the Boulevard du Centre into line with the dome of the Sorbonne, giving vista to that monument. At Haussmann's suggestion the architect Bailly afterwards designed the Tribunal de Commerce in such a manner as to supply this defect.

RUE DES CARCAISONS IN 1851.
(From etching by Martial.)

DUE DE RIVOLI AND TOUR DE SAINT-JACQUES LA BOUCHERIE, SHOWING HAUSSMANN'S
FAVORITE METHOD OF GIVING VISTA TO A MONUMENT.

BOULEVARD DE SÉBASTOPOL.

PROFILE OF THE BOULEVARD DE SEBASTOPOL,

THE COMPLETELY "HAUSSMANNIZED" NEW PLACE SAINT-MICHEL.

The construction of the Boulevard de Sébastopol carried with it that of several important intersecting streets; the Rue Réaumur continued by the Rue du Quatre-Septembre to the Opéra, the Rue de Turbigo from the Church of Saint-Eustache to the future Place de la République, and the Rue Etienne Marcel to the Place des Victoires.

The Boulevard du Palais.

The continuation of the Boulevard du Centre (Strasbourg and Sébastopol) made necessary the replacement of the old Rues de Saint-Barthélemy and de la Barillerie, leading across the island from the Pont au Change to the Pont Saint-Michel, by an avenue of the first class which took the name Boulevard du Palais and became part of the general scheme for the rehabilitation of the Ile de la Cité. To make the Cité again the civic center was fundamental to the entire scheme for the transformation of Paris. The consideration of the great buildings which took the place of the original slums of the island must be postponed to another article, where the entire subject of the Parisian architecture of the Second Empire will be taken up.

The Boulevard Saint-Michel.

Technically, the Premier Réseau stopped with the river. The continuation of the improvements on the south side (Rive Gauche) came under the provision for the Deuxième and Troisième Réseaux, but as the Boulevards Saint-Michel and Saint-Germain are topographically connected with the Grande Croissée, they should be considered here.

The old route from Orléans came to the river through the line of the Rue de Saint-Jacques, where portions of the Roman pavement have been found. As that line was too far eastward for the continuation of the Boulevard du Centre, which took the name Boulevard Saint-Michel, Haussmann used instead the old Rue de la Harpe as far as the old Place Saint-Michel at the Rue Soufflo. From this point to the Carrefour de l'Observatoire, the new street followed the old Rue d'Enfer. In order to clear the Lycée Saint-Louis and the Thermes with the Hôtel Cluny, he was obliged to curve the

Boulevard Saint-Michel. He took advantage of this to bring its axis into line with the spire of the Saint-Chapelle.

Boulevard Saint-Germain.

Before Haussmann's appearance in Paris the Emperor had seen the necessity for a large street running east and west on the southern side, and had begun the Rue des Ecoles to do this work. When he had studied this situation, Haussmann saw clearly that this street was badly conceived. It lay upon the northern declivity of the Hill of Saint-Geneviève, began nowhere, led no whither, and had no organic connection with the plan of Paris. He saw that a much broader solution of the problem was required, that the Rive Gauche, as well as the Rive Droite, should have a large connection between the Place de la Bastille and the Place de la Concorde. He conceived the splendid Boulevard Saint-Germain, with its extension by the Pont Sully and the Boulevard Henri IV. This street, finished in 1882, was built under the conditions of the Troisième Réseau, but its intersection with the Boulevard Saint-Michel determined its character and obliges us to consider it as a part of the general scheme for the rectification of the Grande Croissée.

The Boulevard Saint-Germain is a street of the true Haussmann type. Its profile resembles that of an avenue designed in the time of Louis XIV., but it has not the rigidity characteristic of that period. Its direction adapts itself gracefully to the work which it is called upon to do, and to the emplacement of two fine old monuments, the Church of Saint-Germain des Prés and the Hôtel de Cluny. The most characteristic part of the scheme was its completion to the Place de la Bastille by way of the Pont Sully and Boulevard Henri IV.

The Boulevard Henri IV. was so designed that the Colonne de Juillet and the dome of the Panthéon should be in its axis, giving vista to both monuments. To carry out this plan it was necessary to build the Pont Sully diagonally across the river, and to this the Emperor earnestly objected, holding back the entire project for several years. "A Londres," he said to Haussmann, "on ne s'occupe que de satisfaire le mieux possible aux besoins de la circulation." "Sire," said Haussmann, "les Parisiens ne sont pas des Anglais; il leur faut davantage."

The result of Haussmann's Premier Réseau and the improvements which grew out of it were universally approved. Even the serious opponents of the Empire, led by Thiers, were obliged to admit the splendid and useful accomplishment. The Deuxième and Troisième Réseaux were not so fortunate.

Edward R. Smith.
Reference Librarian Avery Architectural Library, Columbia University.

BIBLIOGRAPHY.

Revue générale de l'Architecture et des Travaux Publics; Journal des architectes, des ingénieurs, des archéologues, des industriels et des propriétaires, 1840-90. Small fol. vols. 1-45.

Encyclopédie d'architecture, Journal mensuel. Paris, 1851-62; vols. 1-12.

Haussmann, Georges Eugène, baron: Mémoires. Paris, 1890-93; 3 vols. 8°.

Hoffbauer, F. Paris à travers les ages; aspects successifs des monuments et quartiers historiques de Paris depuis le XIII Siècle jusqu'a nos jours; d'après les documents authentiques. Paris, 1885; 3 vols. fol. 92 pls.

Société Centrale des Architectes; Manuel des lois du Bâtiment, deuxième édition, revue et augmentée. Paris, 1879; 2 vols. in 5.8°.

Dulaure, Jacques-Antoine. Histoire de Paris et de ses Monuments; nouvelle édition refondue et completée jusqu'à nos jours par L, Batissier. Paris, 1846; 1 vol. 4°.

Baltard, Victor, and Callet, F. E.: monographie des Halles Centrales de Paris construites sous le règne de Napoléon III et sous l'Administration de Baron Haussmann. Paris, 1863; 1 vol. fol.

Potémont, Adolphe Martial (called Martial): Ancien Paris, Paris, 1866; 3 vols. fol. 300 pls.

Paris dans sa splendeur; monuments, vues, scènes historiques, descriptions et historie. Paris, 1861; 3 vols. fol.

Guédy, H. Le Palais du Louvre, extérieur et intérieur; Architecture, sculpture, decoration, ensembles et details. Paris, 1905; 1 vol. fol.

Charcoal Drawing.

THE BUDAPEST PARLIAMENTARY BUILDINGS.

Impressions of Budapest

Although certain sections of Budapest built by the Romans are still in existence, there is left little trace of the Roman regime. The dirt and filth which accumulated through centuries of indifference, and for which the capital of Hungary was notorious twenty-five years ago, have disappeared with a celerity that marks an epoch in Hungarian enlightenment. Whether one comes from Venice through southeastern Austria to the Dèli-vasùt in Buda, the older and more northerly section, or direct from Vienna by boat down the Danube, or by train to the West-vasùt in the center of Pest, one is impressed by the modern, progressive atmosphere of the new city. Clanging tram cars and the harsh cries of the cabbies and taxi drivers greet the traveler as he steps from the railroad station, while the bustle and confusion savor of Charing Cross or the Gare du Nord. As the steamer from Vienna ties up at the dock, along the waterfront rows of extensive buildings, quays teeming with people, the Parliament houses, similarly situated to those of England on the Thames, greet the eye, and as one walks through the city squares adorned with imposing statues and playing fountains are met here and there. One feels an indescribable charm at the ever-hurrying current of the Danube and the pleasant features of the people. A bet-ter situation for the city could hardly be imagined—on one side the mountains, on the other a vast plain, through which the river flows. The streets are clean and well paved, and all the comforts of a Western city can be had for the asking. In these respects Budapest is little different from many other cities, but the Magyar people in whose veins still flows the rich Eastern blood give it a touch with their isolated language that is like paprika to the sterlet.

In the past two decades the city has been practically rebuilt upon an economic and sanitary basis, entailing the wholesale destruction of the old disease-filled buildings and so-called public works which had been slumbering in filth while Western Europe had already learned the advantages of a thorough housecleaning. At the same time, an attempt has been made to develop Hungarian architecture, which had long lain dormant, and as a result, Budapest is to-day one of the most modern cities of Europe. Its subway was built before New York had broken ground for her system, and her telephone service is as unique as it is perfect. By paying a reasonable subscription, the reports of the Stock Exchange, foreign and local news, concerts and grand opera can be heard by simply removing the receiver from the hook—at the side of one's bed, if need be,—and properly directing the central operator, a great boon to the invalid and the lazy. The business streets—Lipot-Korùt, Váczi-Korùt and Andrassy Utcza—are lined with up-to-date shops, whose windows are dressed with a keen, artistic sense for position and display that even an American can see is inborn and not developed by a course in a correspondence school. Whoever has been to Budapest knows the delights of the cafés, cafés in the true sense of the word, where delicious coffee, ices and cool wine are served, while boys bring the morning or Hungarian orchestras play; in some, the Bosnian bands; while now and then the larger cafés delight with the wild Hungarian Czárdas, a dance which thrills with its gay *abandon*. The dancers are controlled by the leader of the orchestra, who sways and directs them as he draws now a slow, almost pathetic strain, now a fierce, passionate burst of music from the orchestra. It is to the cafés that the business and professional man resorts between the hours of 12.30 and 3, and 5 and 7. He gets to his office before 9 and works until 12.30, when he goes to his

WAITZNER RING.

afternoon papers. And the newspapers to be obtained are not confined to Hungarian journals, but French, German, Italian, Turkish and English are there for the asking. Writing paper, pen and ink are always convenient, and to spend an hour or two over one cup of coffee is not only expected, but encouraged. The cafés are more numerous than the "pubs" in England, but how different! All are practically out of doors, either with their chairs and tables on the sidewalk, as in Paris, or in gardens surrounding a playing fountain. In many, favorite café for coffee or a snack, reads the news of the day, or perhaps plays a game of cards or chess, and at three returns to his office, perhaps only for an hour, but generally until five, when he again returns to the café. At this hour the fashionable place is the quay along the Pest bank of the Danube, where gaily dressed women, with a coquetry which *ne laisse rien à désirer,* or, if you prefer it, *laisse tout à désirer,* accompanied by more gaily uniformed officers with clanking swords and spurs promenade back and forth, or sit in the cafés

THE EASTERN RAILWAY TERMINAL AND ZAROSS MONUMENT.

WESTERN RAILWAY TERMINAL.

while the less energetic or perhaps more penurious pay a penny for a seat along the quay to watch the lively picture. Along the quay, too, are the large hotels, whose cafés afford a beautiful view of the surrounding mountains and the ruins of the old fortress on the hill commanding Buda.

In Buda are the few monuments of the Roman period. Császar Fürdo and Lukacs Fürdo were famous as medicinal baths in Nero's day, and they are just as famous in Hungary now, and probably more popular. The sulphur springs

lost souls of Dante's Inferno. This system of bathing in one promiscuous mass is now prohibited, and like many other of the old Magyar customs, has been swept away before the onward march of civilization.

With the Danube between them, Buda and Pest are similar in situation to Brooklyn and New York, while the relation between them is identically the same. A number of beautiful bridges span the river, and with ferries and frequent trolley service make Buda accessible.

ANDRASSY STREET.

on Margarethen Insel are a source of great luxury to the people, while the charming surroundings of the vast park, with its walks and playgrounds, increase the popularity of the baths. Not many years ago a great public bath was provided by the city for the poorer people, where all ages and sexes, after having been cupped by an attendant, according to an almost superstitious faith in blood-letting, wallowed together practically naked in a common pool of steaming sulphur water, where they lingered for hours, a veritable melting pot for the

One of the most interesting sights in Budapest is the fruit market. In the early morning the peasants, many in their native costumes, bring in the fruit from their farms. Peaches, pears, plums and watermelons grow in great abundance in the rich loam of that section which the Danube waters. Displayed in large baskets or heaped high on carts, the fruit is first inspected by the police, who walk about with long, sharp sticks picking out the decayed and over-ripe, the authorities knowing well the dangers of spreading disease from bad fruit.

CHAIN SUSPENSION BRIDGE.

THE ELIZABETH BRIDGE.
The first bridge designed and built entirely by Magyar engineers.

Fruit-growing is only another instance of the progressive policy of the present government, and evidence of enlightenment and social advancement. The Hungarian government, with seat in Budapest, in 1897, started its now large system of planting state roads on both sides with fruit trees, especially in those sections of the country where there was a deficiency, owing to the unfavorable soil and climate. At the present time over 800,000 fruit trees have been planted along 6,000 miles of road, the main purpose of the trees being to make their

of young trees are apportioned to the several communities, and to priests and school masters at a nominal cost. In the past ten years more than 60,000,000 fruit trees have been so distributed, and grafting stems are supplied at one-fifth of a cent a piece. The management of these parish orchards is in the hands of the parish priests and school masters, who have qualified by attending classes in which the study of fruit culture is taught. Prizes are presented each year to the most successful in grafting stems and in the general management of the

THE LEOPOLD RING AND LUSTSPIEL THEATER.

produce pay for maintaining the roads, which novel idea is realized with the maturity of the trees. In addition to the state roads, an act of Parliament requires that all suitable country and parish roads shall be planted, and that a public orchard shall be planted in every parish. The state again comes to the aid of the parishes by establishing twenty-five large nurseries in order to lessen the task of stocking the parish orchards, and from which the needs of the different districts may be supplied at a low rate. From these, every year large numbers

orchards. The largest part of this system feeds into Budapest.

In Budapest, of the 750,000 inhabitants, about 500,000 are Magyar or pure Hungarian, but in the parish districts, where imigration has changed the whole character of the country, the ratio is about one Magyar to four of other nationalities. As the governing body, they are, of course, the leaders, physically and intellectually, but as the years go on the ingress of the other peoples is leaving fewer of the pure blood, and little now remains but the pride of the

ST. STEPHENS CHURCH.

THE FISCHER BASTILLE.

Magyar race. In the dark days of frequent fighting, when the frontier was beset on all sides by invading hordes, it was this pride which dominated the people and kept them together, and it is their best present asset in their effort to place themselves with the civilized nations and win back what has been lost in intellectual and political position in their long strife against Mohammedan and Slav.

The Magyars are justly proud of their capital and bitterly jealous of their Austrian compatriots. They resent Golden Bull, as it is called, obtained in 1222, is in force to-day. Strange as it may seem, Austria owes its constitutional rights to Hungary. In 1867, when it was proposed to join the two states, the Hungarians objected on the ground that they did not want to be connected with a nation which lacked the political freedom of their own state, and so a constitution was granted Austria in order to put the two states upon an equal basis.

Budapest is extremely curious to study from an architectural standpoint. It is,

THE MUSEUM RING.

strongly the statement that Vienna is the capital of Austria-Hungary. It is not an uncommon thing for Hungary to be referred to in newspapers and magazines as a province of Austria, classifying her with Croatia and Moravia, a statement as absurd as it is injudicious. Budapest, insists the Hungarian, is the capital of Hungary, and Vienna of Austria. While he bows to the architectural beauty of Vienna, he inwardly vows to make Budapest its equal. Hungary is the second oldest constitutional monarchy of Europe. Its magna charta, or in fact, interesting to see what the genius of a modern people, very intelligent, evidently artistic, who have no traditions, is able to produce; who have always had intimate relations with the older races among whom were born the arts; who have gathered together immense resources and wish to build a capital worthy of their ambitions, original, if possible, or at least avoiding any too direct influence of other cities. One must take careful account of the ambition of Budapest, unable to repudiate completely all artistic influence of

THE ST. LUKE'S BATHS.

TYPICAL APARTMENT HOUSE IN BUDAPEST—WITH INTERIOR COURT AS DESCRIBED.

Munich and Vienna, its rival capitals and centers of art, to hold essentially to its complete self-government, its perfect independence in art as in politics. But although it is not given to any modern nation to develop an architecture without extraneous influences, yet at Budapest, where they could not wait even for the effect of accumulated years of sluggishness to pass away, there is to be seen the result of a very remarkable effort. In order not to appear dependent upon any one influence exclusively, the Hungarian architecture has accepted

separated by a river, the Danube, the only power which comes between them. The main bridge across the river on the Buda side enters a long tunnel cut through the hill, back of which lies the greater part of the city, and on whose side has been built the magnificent palace for Emperor Joseph, which he seldom uses. At the entrance to the tunnel there is presented an architectural aspect in which one readily distinguishes the pure classic origin of an art as it is understood at Munich and Vienna. When one emerges

CUSTOM HOUSE RING AND PUBLIC MARKET.

them all, carefully adapting the composite to its particular needs. It is precisely this conflict of traditions, of education and training that has resulted in the most diverse and picturesquely bizarre, though very often very beautiful, architectural creations. One is not surprised, in view of her restless past, that in the present period of great prosperity, Hungary is not possessed of secular traditions, which permit a national art to develop peaceably.

As has already been said, Buda and Pest, like New York and Brooklyn, are

from the *Gare Centrale* and turns about in order to look at the vast, sumptuous façade of this monument, for a moment one has the illusion that the late *Palais des Champs-Elysées* has not completely exchanged this over-material world for one of mere memory. One is almost justified in believing that, stone for stone, that edifice has been transported from Paris to this faraway quarter of Europe. The squares, too, and the streets leading from the Gare Centrale have a Parisian atmosphere that is unmistakable. Among the other foreign influences, German, Italian and sometimes English, there is always the Viennese, which the Hungarians have not been able to disregard completely, try as they would.

In leaving the Gare Centrale, one naturally follows the Kérépesi Utcza, a long avenue, which has not the rectilinear perfection of the Andrassy Utcza, but it is none the less interesting for its amplitude, its animation and the variety of the constructions along its sides. In passing up this street, one again thinks of Paris and finds the Kérépesi Utcza

sale, creating an atmosphere of commercial activity which in no way appears to preoccupy itself with the nearness of a statue of Luther, although the whole would be built practically under the same roof.

In Vienna the houses are usually four stories high, while in Budapest one seldom sees them over two or three, and the further one goes into the provinces from the Hungarian capital the more the height diminishes, going down to two and then to one story. But everywhere is found the same *luxe de façade* ob-

EMPEROR FRANCIS JOSEPH'S PALACE.

strikingly like the famous Boulevard Strasbourg, but in one point having a marked advantage, namely, the diversity of aspect. While on the former one can admire only the constructions in the "*Haussmannesque*" style, in Budapest one passes with prodigious rapidity from Gothic to Renaissance, from Italian to German, then to a classic style intermingled with Arabic, the whole adorned with virulent colors along the borders and copings of the buildings. Then round about are grouped shops, displaying an abundance of goods for

tained without too much dependence on foreign influence by the ingenious and practical process that has already been mentioned. Nor have the windows and doors in Budapest any one particular style. The variety of styles is great, but there is nothing disagreeable in the composition.

The interior distribution of this plan is also particularly interesting to note. There is in the Hungarian, as in Spanish houses, an interior court, forming a patio, with a balcony running around on each floor. This balcony very often gives the effect of a cloister. One can conceive, without much explanation, the resulting commodiousness of the interior distribution. As the court is frequently converted into a sort of covered garden, in the provincial regions this disposition gives a most pleasing aspect, and during the fair season becomes a huge dining-room. In the large houses, the Hungarian makes little use of our wall paper and tapestry for interior decoration. The stucco-like mortar which replaces our plaster is painted and decorated with patterns of simple but often very effective designs. As the operation is not costly, the decorations of an apartment house interior are often changed to suit new tenants.

One cannot speak of Budapest without mentioning the beautiful Varos Liget, which is certainly the most beautiful spot in the whole capital. Imagine a wild wood in the center of a great city! Such was the Varos Liget ten years ago, but to-day finds it the setting for the buildings of the Agricultural Museum, the work of the State Architect Alpár. In the center of the wood is a lake about which many of the buildings are grouped. The museum is reached by any one of the broad, shady streets which stretch out into the city, and it is but a step to the most brilliant and animated part of the capital.

In this brief sketch, it only remains to turn back towards the Danube. There are quiet streets, almost deserted, the seat of the majority of the old state buildings, bureaus of administration and commerce, great, solemn apartments. Owing to the effect of the climate on the decorations, these buildings give the effect of having very plain, common façades, but though the opposite is the fact they are simply shields for the more ornate interiors of characteristic depth. This section of the city is always peaceful and quiet, in contrast to the clamorous streets not far away. Passing straight on to the river, one reaches the newest official buildings where but a few years ago was a neglected quarter. Here are found the houses of Parliament, Gothic from one end to the other, and the pride of the Magyar people; directly opposite on the Buda side, the palace, a Classical structure of colossal dimensions. In Buda, as everywhere, we see the old replaced by the new, a stirring activity, dormant for so many years, infused in their Magyar blood, impetuous at times, adorned here and there with tinsel perhaps, but we need a little to keep alive. And all the world knows it is far better to be a simple potter living than an Achilles dead.

Schuyler M. Meyer.

THE WEST SIDE, RESIDENCE OF H. C. MERCER, ESQ., AT DOYLESTOWN, PA.
"He was building from the inside outward....and risked being responsible for a house which might terrorize the whole neighborhood."

"PERSONAL ARCHITECTVRE"

THE EVOLVTION OF AN IDEA IN THE HOVSE OF H.C. MERCER. ESQ.. DOYLESTOWN.PA.

By W.T. TAYLOR

DEFINITION in matters architectural is often dangerous—more so, perhaps, than in any others of the fine arts. It is very apt to be both unsafe, unfair and stupid to say "this building is bad" or "that building is good," and the reason for this is not far to seek. One may present admirable general proportions, but be unfortunate in its detail, and another, upon which exquisite detail has been lavished may be an utter failure in the matter of proportion. Neither should be summarily and comprehensively condemned, nor should either be accepted. All architectural values can only be determined by discriminating analytical study, and often one perfect doorway or the profile of

a cornice may go far to offset much else that is ill-studied and unpleasing.

In the case of the great concrete country house at Doyleston, Pennsylvania, recently conceived, designed and built by Mr. Henry C. Mercer, it would be obviously dangerous to hail it with unqualified praise. In many points it flies defiantly in the face of all precedent, but in an equal number of points its growth is from stronger and better based convictions than govern the greater part of our more widely accepted American architecture.

Here is a "personal" architecture—a building which will stand ever as a monument to the individual tastes and

205

THE RESIDENCE OF H. C. MERCER, ESQ., DOYLESTOWN,
PA. THE TOWER TERRACE, WITH CHIMNEYS AND STAIR
HOOD, PHOTOGRAPHED FROM THE WEST TERRACE.

"In many points it flies defiantly in the face of all precedent"—
it is not "good architecture" but it is the outgrowth of good architectural ideas.

beliefs of its builder. He has followed no "school" or "style" with the blind and futile energy of the copyists of today, nor has he launched a thing wholly new. Back of it all is a clearly visualized composite of impressions of Mediaevalism, rendered in an essentially modern type of construction and further brought to date by the introduction of every necessary modern convenience.

The size and peculiarity of the house impress the casual observer at once even if its architectural interest is not appreciated at its own unique values. Mr. Mercer has designed and built a large, far-from-ordinary country house comprising sixty-five rooms, and his friends who have seen it talk to others and arouse their curiosity to such an extent that the maids have to respond to frequent ringings of the doorbell.

The house has an individuality as insistent as Mr. Mercer's and as entertaining.

The architecture, particularly the ex-

THE ALCOVE AND STAIRWAY LEADING TO THE BREAKFAST ROOM.
"A composite of impressions of Mediaevalism."

THE RUSSIAN STOVE IN THE BREAKFAST ROOM.
Note the reproduction of one of the workmen's hands in the ceiling above the stove.

terior, has been criticized for its inconsistency, but this perturbs its owner not at all. He built the house for himself and in his own manner, and considers these to constitute complete reason and justification for its apparent vagaries. It is a direct and sincere expression of his architectural impressions gathered from many sources. A charge of inconsistency of design can only be applied to the building because of its mixture of the architectural schools; for there is a consistent looseness in the adaptation of various styles and periods. Mr. Mercer's reverence for the romance and charm of the old castles on the Danube and the architecture of the older countries led him to build a house which would, in his own words, "Combine the poetry of the past with the convenience of the present."

The thing that age had done to the buildings of the old lands Mr. Mercer determined to have in his house in Doylestown. To merely reproduce the style of the buildings without represent-

A SKETCH OF A TYPICAL CORNER—RESIDENCE
OF H. C. MERCER, ESQ., DOYLESTOWN, PA.
"The house has an individuality......"

a suite was finished in clay they were set together with regard for the relation of the floor-levels. When all of the rooms were made and arranged in suites, the suites were composed to the best advantage. Large stairways were avoided for economy of space and irregular stairways and passages made to conform with the arrangement of the suites. The roof was modelled when the suites and stairways were complete, its shape being determined by the disposition of the rooms and the chimneys. Garret space was avoided by flattening the roof for terraces wherever possible. The lines of the exterior were developed when the model had reached this stage of its growth, the outside appearance being a minor consideration to the arrangement of the interior. The clay model when completed was reproduced to scale and a plaster cast made to be placed on the ground and serve as a working model.

Before deciding on the placement of his house, Mr. Mercer spent several days in Boston for the study of the

THE FRONT DOOR.

"A fine piece of craftsmanship in itself, made of heavy timber, studded with large-headed nails."

ing the irregularities of form and surface caused by age would be to lose the full charm of the old architecture. The Doylestown house must have the patina of the antique without sacrifice of modern comfort.

With a memory stored with pictures of buildings studied during protracted travel in Austria, Holland, Egypt, Turkey, Italy, Germany, Spain and France, Mr. Mercer commenced the designing of his house. A keen appreciation of drawings by Adrian Ostad, Dürer, Gerard Dow, and Rembrandt prompted an effort to secure a play of light and shade in the ceilings of the house similar to that of the drawings by the old masters. One drawing was made for each wall of the sixty-five rooms, and from these drawings the rooms were modelled separately in clay. When a sufficient number of rooms for

THE GALLERY STAIRS.

The back of the balustrade in the salon appears through the opening.

houses in the north part of the city. The twisted streets gave him the desired opportunity for observation of the sunlight on the differently placed houses. With the aid of a compass he decided on the best way to place his house so as to secure the greatest amount of sunlight.

The building of the house presented many problems and resulted in the invention of some novel methods.

In order to have the work done in his own way Mr. Mercer employed day-laborers for all of the construction work. The skilled mechanic was banned and the

A CORNER OF THE BREAKFAST ROOM.

THE DOOR OF THE BAY ROOM OPENING ON THE WEST TERRACE.

The wall of the passage is treated with a mosaic of tiles.

plumb-line scorned except for the putting in of window-frames.

Concrete was selected for the material for several reasons. It could be handled in a free manner, and its variations of color and texture used to advantage in the interior. Old boards with cracks and holes were purposely used to give the face of the concrete an unevenness.

Very little measuring was done. Seeking only "a reasonably straight line" Mr. Mercer relied upon his eye for the erection of walls and columns.

The concrete was fully reinforced with iron rods and screens, but the building does not rely on this reinforcement for its strength. To avoid the dependence of beam-construction upon iron, the ceilings are, in nearly every case, vaulted. The great variety of vault-formation employed was secured in a most ingenious manner. Instead of the complicated carpentry which would have been required to erect centering and patterns of the usual kind, a platform was placed at the base of the intended vault; the platform was surmounted with grass and earth mounded into shape and covered with fine yellow sand. The concrete was then moulded from above.

The ceiling of the room for which the

THE EAST ROOM.

The bathroom is placed nearer the ceiling than the floor, and the ceiling is typically irregular.

doned and a mansard roof, modified by the chimneys and the hood of the staircase, built for the sake of obtaining a high terrace commanding a fine view of rolling country and woods.

Mr. Mercer was offered much friendly criticism and advice. The small model with its irregularity had been generally approved but the aberrant form of the huge building, bristling with scaffolds, startled the neighbors. And even Mr. Mercer became a little bit uneasy in his own mind. Still he held firmly to the determination he started with, not to "construct any decoration" nor to build merely to look "pretty." He was building from the inside outward, and possessing the courage of his conviction, he risked being responsible for a house which might terrorize the whole neighborhood.

vault was constructed and the floor of the room immediately above were made simultaneously. Elliptical and irregular vaults, which would have been impossible in stone, were easily made and the flat vault was generally adopted to avoid garret space and minimize the thrust, while the mound method also permitted the free use of groined vaults.

During the construction of the house some variations from the model were made, and if they affected the outside appearance, the model was altered to retain a suggestion of what the completed house would look like. Here, certainly, is an illustration of designing "from the inside outward." The tower of the model was pointed; this was aban-

The house was made much larger than necessary for the purpose of working out problems with concrete and tile. The tile decoration with which the house is lavishly embellished throughout was part of the construction work and came from Mr. Mercer's own works. The ceilings, with their intricate designs, required on an average only a few hours' work. If the same ceilings had been put together in the usual manner by imposing the tiles after the concrete of the ceiling had set, each

A SUGGESTION OF THE CONCRETE VAULTING.

ceiling would have required about two weeks' time. The mound method of making the vaults made possible this great saving of time and expense.

When the platform had been erected, the mound of grass and earth shaped, and the yellow sand distributed over the mound with a depth of two inches, the tiles were placed face downward in the

PASSAGE SHOWING DOOR OF THE EAST ROOM.
A corner of the stairway to the West Terrace appears at the left.

sand with one-eighth of an inch projecting upward to be seized by the concrete. None of the concrete flowed over the face of the tiles, and when the mound was removed the ceiling with its decoration was complete.

The first view of the house from the public road excites one's interest immediately. The upper part of the tower, with its curiously formed chimneys and dull-red tile roofs, which harmonize well

THE STAIRWAY TO THE CRYPT.
This was the first piece of construction—the crypt has the appearance of the Roman Catacombs.

with the warm gray of the concrete, is all that is seen till the visitor enters the gate. Two concrete bridges, one for each of the two roadways which cross a stream about fifty yards in front of the building, add to the impression the tower first gives, of finding an old-world castle. The view of the exterior from the roadway does not do more than excite curiosity and more or less piqued conjecture.

But when the door with its broad, rounded steps is reached, the interior absorbs one's interest just as it did Mr. Mercer's. The irregular arch over the entrance and the beautifully arranged tiles in the risers of the steps are suggestive of what is to be found inside. The door itself is a fine piece of craftsmanship, made of heavy timber, studded with large-headed nails. The lock is an antique, but the electric button gives the touch of modern convenience.

The hall has a rich, warm hue, obtained by the use of brown sand for the concrete, and reddish brown tile for the floor. An occasional tile in the cross-vaulted ceiling introduces notes of other color. The columns have tiled capitals.

drawings of old masters. The large windows have cemented frames, and admit a strong light, but by the use of dark sands the ceiling holds a curious air of mystery. Its odd beam-arrangement is enhanced by the shadowy forms to be seen over the balustrade of the gallery stairs.

The library, which is entered from the salon, is also of good size. It has a balcony built of concrete and a large fireplace. The tiles used in the ceiling have a high relief, giving them a play of light

A PORTION OF THE LIBRARY CEILING.
A good example of the tile treatment of vaulting and capitals.

tained by the use of brown sand for the concrete, and reddish brown tile for the floor. An occasional tile in the cross-vaulted ceiling introduces notes of other color. The columns have tiled capitals.

The kitchen and domestic workrooms occupy the rear of the lower floor.

The salon occupies the ground floor of the tower. Its large proportions give ample space for two large fireplaces; tall pillars carry the eye to the ceiling, which justifies Mr. Mercer in his claim to a relationship between his ceilings and the

and shade in addition to their color—this being true of nearly all the ceilings throughout.

In wandering about the house one finds sometimes obscurely, the origin of the architecture of this curious house—in ceilings which suggest the crypts of cathedrals, in winding staircases which are memory replicas of staircases of ancient castles in lower Austria, in window-shapes from Constantinople, balustrades suggestive of Venice, and roofs reminiscent of Turkey and Germany.

THE STAIR TO THE WEST TERRACE.
The risers are inlaid with tiles, usually spelling a
motto or legend.

big Saint Bernard, walked up, leaving his footprints clearly defined in the concrete; "Rollo's Stair" was lettered in the risers, and the footprints will outlive Rollo.

The passages are well lighted by many windows and their peculiarities do not make them dangerous. The risers of all important stairs have tile decoration, either purely decorative or with quaintly lettered mottoes and legends.

Large open fireplaces are in all the living rooms, each one with individual design and proportions, and in addition to these there is a beautiful Russian stove of tile in the breakfast room, and another built in the wall between the kitchen dining-room and the sewing room. The breakfast-room stove is shown in one of the illustrations. The door shown at the end of the stove opens the end of the flue which folds in the manner of a steam or hot-water radiator. A wood fire is built inside the flue near the door and kept burning actively till the stove becomes heated; the flue is then closed at the mouth of the chimney; the stove retains its heat for hours and as it radiates from a large area it provides economical heat. The stove in the kitchen dining-room and sewing-room wall is operated in the same way as the other. The wall is extra thick with the flue built in the cen-

The stairways and passages have many twists caused by their adaptation to the various floor-levels and the arrangement of the suites, and an additional complication exists because of the building being placed on a slope and the floors of the rooms in the lower side of the house having lower level.

The suites are entirely isolated so that several families could live in the house without seeing each other.

When the stairs to the Belvedere were still moist and impressionable, Rollo, a

AMONG THE ROOFS.
A curious concrete gutter designed to throw the rain water, through a drain, to the terrace, and away from a door below.

THE SALON, SHOWING GALLERY STAIRS AND
DOOR TO HALL.
This is the largest room. The ceiling is supported by a
number of tall pillars, varying in diameter like tree-trunks.

ter; the stove heats the entire wall. Both rooms have the stove-wall covered with tile. The stove door is in the doorway connecting the rooms.

The fuel for the fireplaces and stoves is cut from the woods which are on Mr. Mercer's property, and faggots are piled in convenient places throughout the house. This inspires the gushing lady, who has been awarded the palm for foolish remarks regarding the house, to applaud Mr. Mercer for using the picturesque "Italian faggots."

The sixty-five rooms include ten bathrooms equipped with modern plumbing, to the disappointment of occasional over-sentimental visitors, and seven extra large bedrooms with modern brass beds. No two of these rooms are in the least similar in design. The East Room has one of the most irregular vaults in the house. There are also nine chambers, seven kitchen bedrooms, and three roof-rooms, included in the total.

The "Wind Room" near the top of the tower is untiled and stands just as it came from the mounds. It has a groined vaulted ceiling with corbels modelled to represent the heads of the Winds from Virgil. Another interesting room in the tower contains the water-tank, which is built in the floor, having the appearance of a pool in a grotto. The concrete was successfully treated to prevent leakage.

Tiles have been Mr. Mercer's study for years, and their use in the building displays a great variety of kind and arrangement. The key-note of the work is Spanish, but in some of the rooms, pictures composed of silhouetted tile possess the quaintness and oddity of German decoration.

The tile-work in the "Columbus Room" is extremely elaborate; its color harmony and balance of design make it much more than a mere novelty. How Columbus sailed from Spain and discovered America is conveyed by pictures and lettering in the form of mosaics on both floor and ceiling, the silhouetting of the tiles—letting the concrete separate each tile—permitted the fitting of the pictures

THE WEST SIDE—RESIDENCE OF H. C. MERCER, ESQ.—DOYLESTOWN, PA.

"Here is a 'personal' architecture—a building which will stand ever as a monument to the individual tastes and beliefs of its builder."

to the various shapes. The relief of the tiles varies, the sails of the ships and the waves having a realistic high relief.

Other rooms, such as the Smoking Room, Morning, East and West Rooms, and the Alcove have appropriate decoration. The tile-decoration of the Bay Room vault illustrates Mexican themes, Mosaics of fish, sea-monsters and ships give the "Green Room" its title. Mottoes in tile decorate the fireplaces.

An old stone farmhouse built in the year 1742 stands encased in the building, and the "Forty-Two Room" is its commemoration.

A CORNER IN THE LIBRARY.
Concrete and tile are virtually the sole materials used in the house.

furniture for its beauty. The variety of tone in the concrete walls, secured by the use of different sands, and the rich color of the tiles, give the whole interior a harmonious warmth.

The roof with all its peculiarities has no unnecessary features. Heavy cornices were avoided and no gutters applied to the roof, with the exception of one or two places where the drain happened over the doorways below. The seven roof terraces are all fairly large, the west terrace being reached by a lift

Mr. Mercer has collected antiques of many kinds, and his house is full of objects interesting for their beauty, oddity and historic significance: antique chairs, old engravings, and frames either old or of old design, time-worn chests, antique stove-plates, andirons, cooking utensils, old locks, and many such things add to the fascination of the house. But the house does not depend on remarkable and intended for use as an eating place during the summer.

The unusual character of his house does not interest Mr. Mercer. He simply devoted considerable time and money to the making of a house to meet his own desire and fancy, even if he sees in it nothing more than the house of his dreams, still he has erected a monument to certain saliently sincere architectural ideals, which may grow to find a wide and significant acceptance.

THE CAMPANILE OF ST. MARK'S AT VENICE.

An Authentic Account of the Circumstances That Led to Its Fall.

THE construction of the Campanile of St. Mark's at Venice, which was built between the tenth and twelfth centuries, was influenced by the crude methods of that period. The walls were composed of large bricks of unequal size, which were obtained by the destruction of ancient monuments. The visible surfaces of the walls were composed of bricks which were laid in fairly regular fashion; but, in the interior of the walls, the bricks were placed irregularly and bound with inferior mortar.

This fact was established by the downfall in which the edifice subsided into a mound of small fragments, from which rose a gigantic cloud of dust.

The tower had undergone repairs on several occasions, in the course of centuries; but these, for the most part, had been limited to the bell room, whose final form was of the style of the Renaissance. According to the information obtained from chronicles, it appears that the body of the tower never had had more than partial repairs before the eighteenth century. It had, however, been stuccoed in color, in imitation of brick, which covering was, in recent years, only visible in spots.

It was about the middle of the century in question, and exactly in 1745, that serious fissures had been caused by lightning, on the side above the Loggetta of Sansovino, and that this side had to be repaired completely.

The work was carried out under the direction of the celebrated Bernadino Zendrini, the engineer of the Republic, and cost 6,800 ducats, a very considerable sum for those times. This restoration, it should be carefully noted, consisted of an exterior wall of brick masonry similar to that used in our own time, laid with a mortar of lime and pozzolana in such fashion that this side of the tower presented a very modern appearance. However, inasmuch as the bricks of the new exterior wall could not be fastened to the older ones of the inner (ancient) wall, large square blocks of stone were set in, to unite the two. The white exterior surfaces of these were visible, scattered over the surface of the wall and set in its angles.

This outer masonry had remained in good condition until 1898, and then only had need of some slight repairs in the upper portion, which were called for by unimportant fissures, which did not affect the general stability of the tower. Thus the Campanile of St. Mark's might have stood for many centuries, if the hand of man had not intervened to cause its ruin.

*　　*　　*　　*　　*　　*

In the month of last June the Ufficio Regionale for the preservation of the monuments in Venetian territory, which had charge of the repairs of the Loggetta, undertook to replace the lead covering of the roof of this little monument.*

Since the Loggetta was built against the side of the tower, the roof leaned upon its wall, and at the line of union there was built into this wall a projecting and sloping coping, which kept the rain from entering the joint between the leaden covering and the surface of the wall.

Those who were directing this work, being under the necessity of renewing the leaden plates, had the unfortunate idea to remove the projecting coping, with the intention of replacing it immediately, and in order to do this they cut into the wall of the Campanile horizontally for more than two-thirds of its breadth. In this manner they seriously weakened the base of the outer wall, which had been built by Zendrini, as above explained. It must be remarked that at this height the outer wall was thinner than above, because a much more considerable thickness had been given to the outer wall above—that is to say, at the points where the lightning had caused the largest fissures in the old wall—whereas, a thinner wall had served the purpose lower down. But this was also the portion subjected to the greatest strain, as having to support, to a large extent, the whole weight of the upper wall.

To give the last touch to this misfortune, it happened that in cutting through the outer wall the inner one was injured at certain points and this cutting caused the downfall of a considerable amount of debris, thus making a hollow space within, reaching upward, which could not be filled in.

In this fashion, either as a result of the horizontal cutting, which was left open for several days, or as a result of the cavity which had been caused in the interior of the wall, the outer wall of 1745 was thrown out of plumb and perceptible movements began to show themselves in the interior of the tower.

During this time the engineer, Saccardo, architect in charge of the Basilica of St. Mark's, was ill and no one had mentioned to him that the work was going on. Notwithstanding this, as soon as the Ufficio Regionale invited him to visit the tower on Thursday, the 10th of July, he did so, in spite of his illness, but he immediately perceived that any attempt at repair would be useless;

---

*Under the direction of its Associated Architect, Signor Domenico Rupolo.

and that the only thing that could be hoped for, was that when the cutting had been filled in, the outer wall might regain its stability.

It must, however, be remarked that, although the architect of the Basilica had been advised of the cutting into of the exterior wall, he had not been told of the interior cavity, so that his hopes were justified, as far as his knowledge went.

It is also important to notice that, up to the given date, no obvious signs of danger had appeared in the exterior walls. It was not until Sunday, the 13th of July, that fissures began to appear at the northeast corner of the tower, of such a menacing character, that the architect, Saccardo, although still ill, was obliged to make immediate arrangements, of thorough-going character, for the public safety. In fact, on the following Monday, at five minutes before ten o'clock in the morning the Campanile fell.

In the manner of this fall evidence was given that the immediate and only cause of the catastrophe was the cutting into the outer wall of 1745, and the damage caused in the ancient interior masonry by this cutting, for the collapse began with the total downfall of the aforesaid outer wall, which preceded by several seconds the complete ruin of the monument.

*   *   *   *   *   *

We may thank Providence that we have not had to lament the sacrifice of any human victim, and that the Basilica of St. Mark's, although only a few metres distant from the Campanile, was not injured at any point by its ruin. It must be added, however, that there was a victim, and this victim was Signor Pietro Saccardo architect of the Basilica, who having labored in years past to repair the Campanile, had had the pain of seeing his undertaking interrupted by the plots of envious adversaries. On this last occasion, he was removed from office with enormous injustice, even though temporarily; in spite of the patent evidence of his complete innocence and without regard to his age, to his forty years of service, and to his infirm health; while the real culprit of the catastrophy still tranquilly retains his position. *Cherchez la femme—La Politique.*

An investigation is, however, pending, through which one may hope that justice will be done, if there is still an atom of justice to be had in this world. And if, against all evidence, that justice should not be done, it is not only the architect, Saccardo, who will have been injured, but also his host of friends, who within a few months had presented him a gold medal for his services to the Basilica of St. Mark's.

Pietro Saccardo.
Formerly Architect in charge of the Basilica of St. Mark's.

NOTES
AND
COMMENTS

Champ Clark's suggestion that the people of the United States be asked to decide regarding the location of the proposed Lincoln memorial in Washington, has been accepted by the Washington Chamber of Commerce. A committee has been formed, consisting of about seventy-five prominent men and women—few of them holders of public office—to inform the people and get their judgment. Glenn Brown, the secretary of the American Institute of Architects, is chairman of the committee, and he has issued an illustrated pamphlet giving information concerning the three plans which are before Congress, and presenting the arguments in favor of the Newlands bill, which is in behalf of the site proposed by the expert commission. The other bills are the McCall bill, for a structure on the ground adjoining the Union Station, and the Lafean bill, for a highway from Washington to Gettysburg. Of the first, Mr. Brown says: "The McCall bill offers neither a definite design nor site. The memorial is to be somewhere and of some form, on an irregular forty acre tract. Among the schemes favorably under consideration was a peristyle encircling the plaza of the Union Station; in the center of this is to be the Columbus memorial. Thus the memorial to Lincoln becomes a part of the station, a vestibule guiding to the great structure, and forms a background to the Columbus memorial—an admirable embellishment for the station but lacking the individuality and distinction necessary to commemorate Abraham Lincoln. A suggested colonade on Delaware avenue was another effort to attain an approach to the station and call it a memorial to Lincoln. A further plan is a great triumphal arch. Such arches remind us of triumphal processions, commemorating great battles, troops of warriors with their captives chained to their chariots, all pomp and ceremony, certainly not a fitting form for a tribute to our simple American." Concerning the Lafean bill, he remarks that a highway is not a tangible memorial, that it suggests nothing of the character or work of Lincoln, that it would cost an enormous sum for construction and for maintenance, and that if lined with memorials to other people its commemorative value as regards Lincoln would be confused. Concerning the bill of Senator Newlands, Mr. Brown expresses the opinion that this gives the ideal site and form of memorial. He says: "This site should appeal to the artist, the business man, and to the sentiment of the community. To the artist it appeals because of its beauty and fitness, because it is a focal point of interest, because of its harmonious relation to the great plan, its orderly relation to the Capitol and the Washington Monument, because it is so separated as to be independent of and still equal in importance with these great monuments. The suggestion of a great classic portico as the character of the design gives an opportunity for the most simple and refined treatment, —so typical of Lincoln's life and expressing forcibly the dignity shown in his character and the grandeur of his accomplishments. The river hills of Virginia, and proposed planting of the landscape, providing beautiful landscape vistas, noble lagoons and approaches as indicated in the Park Commission's plan, will make more imposing this important memorial."

It will be remembered that Congress has already, in its recent session, made the appropriation of two million dollars for the memorial, and that a committee composed of seven members, who are President Taft, Senator Cullom of Illinois, Wetmore of Rhode Island, and Money of Mississippi, and representatives Cannon of Illinois, McCall of Massachusetts and Clark of Missouri, have the matter in charge. President Taft is stated to be in favor of the park commission plan. This, it may be further explained, surrounds the proposed portico with terraces, gardens and fountains on the east bank of the Potomac, extending in a straight line, the axis of the Capitol and the Washington monument. Mr. Cannon is known to be in favor of the railroad station site. Wetmore and McCall are believed to favor the Potomac. The other members of the committee have not yet publicly expressed their preference.

ARCHITECTURAL ABERRATIONS.*

No. 7.—THE FAGIN BUILDING, ST. LOUIS.

N eminent sculptor has been heard, home returning from Philadelphia, soothly to swear that it was something to have seen the worst in any kind, and that in Philadelphia h e had seen the exactly worst piece of architecture in existence, in the *Record* building. It may be worth while to reverse Matthew Arnold's maxim and in the interest of culture to know the worst that has been done in the world, but one is always prone to puff himself up with the belief that he knows it when in fact he does not. We have already dealt in this series with the *Record* building and we shall not be suspected of entertaining any mawkish tenderness for that structure. But if the sculptor we have quoted had been confronted, just after delivering his judgment with the Fagin building of St. Louis, how would he have deplored his temerity !

"Ah ! where shall we go then for pastime,
If the worst that can be has been done."

It may be apprehended that there will be a good deal of fun hereafter in Philadelphian architecture, even though the *Record* building " has been done,"

and perhaps some future architect of St. Louis may exceed the absurdity of the Fagin building. We cannot say that it is the worst that can be, but can anybody indicate anything quite so bad that has been? If so, he will confer a favor by sending a photograph of the object in question to join the collection of yet unpublished aberrations.

In such a structure as this (if there be on the whole planet another such) the psychological problem early arises: What can have been in the man's mind when he did it? What did he think he thought? An architect in Baltimore, upon whose work we had occasion to comment not long ago, delivered himself into our hand, though we refrained from administering further justice upon him, with the defense that it was necessary to make a commercial building conspicuous and to arrest the attention of the passer. This intention to " collar the eye" is visible in all the aberrations of our architecture. Whether it proceed from personal vanity on the part of the designer or from deference to the requirements of his clients, it is essentially a vulgar motive and cannot have other than a vulgar result. When complicated with ignorance sufficiently dense, or with unsoundness of mind, it produces architectural aberrations. It is plain enough that the designer of the Fagin

---

* We are making a collection of " Aberrations," and shall present one to our readers in each number of THE ARCHITECTURAL RECORD.

THE FAGIN BUILDING, ST. LOUIS, MO.

building meant to make people look at his work, and so far he has been successful. Nobody but a blind man who should pass it could possibly escape it. But there is novelty in the method by which he has sought his result. Apparently his notion was, after sacrificing to practicality by making a front that is nothing but a sash-frame, to produce an architectural work by making the sash-front look massive. The thing is impossible, of course. Although by skillful treatment an architect may mitigate his misfortunes and make the utmost of inadequate dimensions, a massive sash-frame is beyond his powers, and a cyclopean sash-frame, such as the architect of the Fagin building has attempted, is beyond his dreams.

An architect, if for his sins he had to design a front with such a proportion of voids to solids, would have made his basement as solid as possible, have tied his front together with emphatic horizontal lines, and have tried for an expression of lightness and grace, an expression of mass and solidity being out of the question. The designer of the Fagin building, instead of dissembling the unfortunate weakness and tenuity of his supports, has called attention to it by every means in his power. He has projected them from the plane of the front, he has not crossed them with a single horizontal band from the sidewalk to the roof, he has diminished them into shafts at the bottom and left them as boulders above, and he has treated them with the utmost rudeness, as if rudeness and vigor were the same thing, and slovenliness, profanity and profuse expectoration signs of force of character. The comparison is not inapt, for protruding rough stones and leaving capitals and bases off from columns is analogous to going about in one's shirt sleeves and with unblackened boots. It is a disregard of elementary decencies, and such a disregard characterizes the whole design of the Fagin building so that the predominant expression is not so much of crudity or rudeness or mere ignorance, as of impudent rowdyism.

It does not attain its purpose, for it

cannot possibly frighten anybody. In fact, all the efforts to make it look vigorous betray and enhance its pitiable weakness. Six completely independent piers, running through from top to bottom, divide the front into five vertical slices, none borrowing any strength from any other, and all consequently seeming in imminent danger of toppling down. To look at it one would say that a healthy child would have no trouble in kicking it over. Our swashbuckler, so far from being formidable, is "staggering drunk." The apparent instability of equilibrium that would be in any case produced by the erection of the front in vertical slices and without horizontal lines, is aggravated by the fact that the stilts that support it are grievously overloaded at the top. Not only does this top over-weight the substructure, but the things of which it is made up are even more outrageous than the detail of the sub-structure, which one would say was impossible if he saw only the sub-structure. The huge cornice of the central slice, the things that support it, the thing it supports, the imitation in the side gables of logs of wood in masonry, the difference between these gables—has the heart of man ever conceived such atrocities elsewhere or before?

Up to date, and so far as we know, the Fagin building is the most discreditable piece of architecture in the United States. In spite of our caution about the superlative degree we are compelled to employ it. This has all the vices and crudities that we call "western," though in fact the geography has nothing to do with them. As we have before remarked, the commercial architecture of Philadelphia is, upon the whole, more western than anything in the West, though there is nothing quite so outrageous in Philadelphia itself as this building in St. Louis. But it is significant, we fear, of the same lack of anything that can fairly be called a public from which Philadelphia suffers that such a defiance of common sense and common decency should be offered to the people of St. Louis as has been offered them in the Fagin building.

The Pennsylvania's New York Station

It were useless and superfluous to advertise the new station of the Pennsylvania road. No project since the Chicago Fair has been more industriously and effectually "boomed." It would sadden the members of the Pennsylvania's Department of Publicity and Promotion to learn that there was any adult within the reach of the "system" who could read or even who could look at pictures and who did not already know that there was such a thing, and that it was such a big thing. Infinitesimal must be the basis for such a regret. It would not be exact to say that this thing was not done in a corner. In fact it was. The excavations and the edifications have been made in a neglected quarter of Manhattan which not one Manhattanite in a thousand has occasion to visit from year's end to year's end. That, in fact, from a civic point of view, is one of the interesting points about the undertaking, that it is a project of reclamation as well as of "réclame." One of our chief civic needs is that of multiplying and scattering "centres." To establish a new centre which shall serve to divert traffic from the old ones and relieve their congestion, which shall create or enhance values in a neglected and derelict neighborhood is a civic benefaction, even though the enterprise was entirely selfish on the part of its promoters. The successful establishment of a new centre pays for itself very speedily, in so great and growing a city as New York, in the "unearned increment" of the value of the surrounding land. The success of this establishment may be already assumed. The terminal and the post office together insure the creation of

what may fairly be called a new city on the shore of the North River.

Doubtless this aspect of the improvement has been or will be dwelt upon sufficiently by the Pennsylvania's Press Bureau. It is only the strictly architectural aspects of the project that invite and indeed compel illustration and comment from an "Architectural Record." Probably no larger and costlier building than the station has been under construction concurrently with it. Certainly no larger. There are other buildings of greater cubical contents contemporaneous with this, notably the Metropolitan Life in New York, and very many superior in altitude have been going on at the same time. In fact it is the lowest big building of recent years, only the New York Public Library, of buildings in the same city, having so little height in proportion to its area. But the area of the station is enormous. The frontage, from Seventh to Eighth Avenue, is almost exactly the same as that of the Capitol of the United States, including the wings. There is nothing in New York anywhere near as long, excepting the front of the Museum of Natural History, which one supposes to be about the same. The Metropolitan Life, indeed, occupies a block front each way. But the block from Madison to Fourth is, of course, only half a "long block," half the distance from Fourth to Fifth Aves., the other half being occupied by Madison Square, whereas the new station occupies the whole space from Seventh Avenue to Eighth. And the other dimension is equally exceptional. The closing of Thirty-second street west of Seventh Avenue gives the shorter fronts the unequalled length of 430 feet. The area is thus not far from 300,000 square feet, half as much again as that of St. Peter's, nearly three times that of Milan. Doubtless we are dealing with a "big thing." To find an American building of as great area as the new station, we should have to recur to the temporary and occasional architecture of the fairs of Chicago and St. Louis.

The lowness is of course an architectural advantage in the sense and in the degree that it emphasizes the horizontal extent of these walls. Excepting the emergence of the roof of the great concourse at the centre in what is virtually a sort of transept, though it is not carried out to the street-fronts, the enormous spread of the structure has a height of only three moderate stories and a moderate attic. The level line of the cornice, unbroken except by the moderate projection of the portico at the centre of each front, stretches away interminably to an undeniably impressive effect which might, it seems, have been enhanced by a more pronounced and emphatic base-moulding. Everything, indeed, concurred to enable the architects to emphasize this "horizontal extension" which, according to Freeman, is the character of "classic" as vertical extension is of Gothic, and as "rest," or immobility, is of Romanesque. No doubt the classic effect is attained, especially in the most elaborated and "important" front, the Eastern, which contains the main entrance, and carries a colonnade along its whole extent—

As where, from Pluto's garden Palatine
Mulciber's columns gleam in far piazzian line.

Another adventitious advantage, especially for a strictly classic treatment, the architects had in the comparative blankness of the walls, at least of the most conspicuous walls. An American architect in the days of the old Greek revival incurred some just enough ridicule by saying that modern architecture would not be so difficult if it were not for the windows. In other words, if men would be content to live and do business behind blank walls, their claims would not conflict with those of the buildings which they foolishly imagined to be meant for their accommodation, holding that architecture was made for man, not man for architecture. Of course the retort upon the foolish architect was obvious that if classic architecture did not allow for the admission of necessary light, it was his business to find or make some architecture that did. All the same, the foolish man was right enough from his point of view. In the Greek and Greco-Roman templar architecture, the portico, the colonnade, which is to say the architecture,

was relieved against the absolutely blank wall of the cella, and doubtless it was much more effective with that relief than with any form of opening whatsoever in the intercolumniations. When the Romans undertook "miscere utile dulci," to unite the practically necessary with the architecturally agreeable, they used the order which was the entire construction of the temple as a kind of trellis to overlay a construction of arches, so that the Roman building involved a contradiction which was never reconciled until what Freeman calls "the classical or transitional Roman" had ceased for some centuries to be built. Even now, an architect who starts out to make his architecture out of the "orders" is very lucky if he can ignore the openings and produce a building

Where the blank windows blind the wall
From pedestal to pedestal.

That good luck has befallen the architects of the Pennsylvania station in unusual measure. It results from the lowness, the perspective shows, that the interiors can almost all, or almost all on the conspicuous and "architecturesque" fronts, be lighted from above, or from courts, and that the walls can be treated as mere backgrounds or foils for the colonnade. That is conspicuously the case on the principal or eastern front. And nearly half way down the side, or until you come to the central portico of the entrance, the order, here subdued from columns to pilasters, is relieved against a wall virtually blank, to the great enhancement of the architectural effect. The western front is apparently the "business end" of the structure. It accordingly contains four tiers of practicable windows. The architects have hardly attempted to bestow more abundant comeliness upon these more uncomely parts. They have simply carried through the order, in the form of pilasters, and made the openings mere rectangular holes, not "treated" architecturally at all, but recognized perforce as an ugly necessity. This, you will observe, is precisely the method adopted in the public architecture of Washington, in the Treasury and the Patent Office, by the Greek revivalists of half a century ago. It is hard to see what better could be done, given the primary commitment to strictly classic architecture. It is true that one cannot exactly see a Greek architect resorting to such a confession of impotency. But still less can one see a Greek architect resorting to the hybrid construction of the Imperial Romans. If not what a Greek architect would have done, it is exactly what Isaiah Rogers and Thomas U. Walter and Robert Mills and Ammi B.

7th to 8th Avenue, 31st to 33d Street, N. Y. City.   THE PENNSYLVANIA RAILROAD STATION.   McKim, Mead & White, Architects.

Young would have done, if they had had all this money to spend and all these dimensions over which to spread themselves. It is what they would have done for it, it is what they did. In fact the exterior of the Pennsylvania station, with one notable exception, is what would have been done in this country seventy years ago. It has no trace of the later inculcations of the Beaux Arts. There is no more taint of "modernism" about it than about a Papal allocution. This must not be taken as dispraise of the architecture. Quite the contrary. Given Greek architecture, the absence of anything "smart" or modish, or modern, is an advantage as an adherence to the type that has "pleased many and pleased long."

Doubtless the structure has the defects of its qualities, and also of its conditions. The lowness, the massiveness, the solidity and the blankness make for gloom as well as for dignity. The poet may be right in saying that

Stone walls do not a prison make.

But these stone walls do. A stranger set down before this Seventh Avenue front, out of sight of the emerging mass at the centre, and told to guess what it was all about, would be apt to guess it a good substantial jail, a place of detention and punishment of which the inmates were not intended to have a good time. The simplicity of arrangement and detail furthers this impression. The plain unfluted Roman Doric of the order, of which this is an impressive example, is the most "serious" of the orders, as serious as the Greek Doric in the modern, not the Greek use, in which it is not relieved and enlivened by sculpture or by color, and more so than the sprightly Corinthian, or even than the Ionic, of which the voluted capital has an interest in itself to which the Roman derivative Doric does not pretend. The carving of the porticoes, excellent as it is in adjustment in scale and in execution, by no means suffices to relieve the sadness of the interminable fronts. The architecture raises one or two questions which it does not answer. Why should the central intercolumniations of the porticoes be wider than the others? And particularly why should the otherwise unbroken horizontality of the design be subjected to the single exception of the projected pediments of the terminal pavilions on the Seventh Avenue front, when the pediment does not reappear at the centre, nor on the sides of the same pavilions, nor anywhere else throughout the vast structure? It has undoubtedly an anomalous air. If it be meant to denote and signalize the corridor to

which the portals under the pediment give access, it is manifest that this purpose would be equally secured by a reduced reproduction of the central portico, in the same plane with it, and like it crowned with a pedestal instead of a pediment, relieved against the flat attic. If it be an attempt to enliven the architecture, and to relieve it of monotony, the attempt has plainly miscarried. And in fact, the monotony of the building, the interminable sequence of "magnitude, uniformity and succession" is not only connected with its artistic quality, but is its artistic quality. It seems a mistake to have disturbed it, most of all to have disturbed it in one solitary instance. For the impressiveness of the building is very great. Whatever abatements and qualifications we may be moved to make, it is securely one of our public possessions, and liberal owners and sensitive and skilful designers are entitled to the public gratitude for so great and grave an example of classic architecture.

Much of the interior work is of the same grave and simple character as the exterior, and here we may perhaps expect that, in the fulness of time, the gravity and simplicity will be relieved, without being disturbed, by mural decoration. The tympana in the loggia of the entrance seem to have been reserved expressly for such an enrichment. One may walk for long distances in the interior, as he may inspect the entire exterior, without once being reminded that "we live in times unknown to the ancients." The most emphatic recognition of that fact is in the treatment of the great hall, or "concourse," both inside and out. "Modernism" and Gallicism are unmistakably indicated from the outside by the emerging mass of the transverse roof, with the three heavily mullioned arches, each decorated with a protruding keystone, and covered with its own low gable. Within, an enormous and lofty shed of iron and glass is an architectural feature for which no classic precedent exists, since no Greek architect or Roman engineer ever had occasion to treat such a construction. Originality, or at least modernism, is here enforced. The architectural treatment is constructional and straightforward, with as much, perhaps, as the case admits, of the gravity and simplicity of the abundantly precedented design of the exterior, but with necessarily much less of the impressiveness of massiveness, and of the monotony which the massiveness here entails. But of the design, classic or modern, in masonry or metal, one has to own that its dignity everywhere escapes frivolity. In the language of Mr. Edmund Sparkler, there is no nonsense about it.

THE NEW GRAND CENTRAL RAILROAD TERMINAL, APPROACHED FROM A
BRIDGE OVER 42ND ST., AT PARK AVE. REED AND STEM,
WARREN AND WETMORE, ARCHITECTS.

"THE CROSSWAY," CIVIC IMPROVEMENT FOR NEW YORK CITY.

It is understood that the projected diagonal avenue between the terminal station of the Pennsylvania and Grand Central Railroads proposed by Henry Rutgers Marshall, architect, is under consideration for definite action. Inasmuch as such a project may be said to affect the development of the city in many ways, it is interesting to print herewith the memorandum presented by the architect, together with a plan and other drawings relating to the proposal:

"It is evident that the public convenience would be greatly served, and the districts involved greatly benefited, if a diagonal avenue were cut to connect the southwest and northeast parts of the city at some point below Central Park.

"THE CROSSWAY." It is proposed to construct such an avenue from Fortieth Street and Fifth Avenue to Seventh Avenue and Thirty-first Street. This location is suggested:

1st. Because it would meet the demand for a connnection of the Pennsylvania Railroad Station, the commercial district adjacent thereto, and the ocean steamer and freight piers on the North River south of Thirty-first Street; with the Grand Central Railroad Station, and the rapidly developing region north of the same; a demand which is certain to be permanent.

2nd. Because, if cut on a curved line, as per the plan suggested, it can be constructed at a minimum cost. It would cross Broadway and Sixth Avenue at their intersections with Thirty-seventh and Thirty-eighth streets respectively, and if constructed at once would avoid all expensive modern buildings, except the Knox building at Fortieth Street and Fifth Avenue. Any diagonal avenue cutting into Fifth Avenue must of necessity involve the taking of valuable property on that avenue; but at this point, because of the open ground at the south of the Public Library only one building need be taken.

3rd. It would not be necessary to carry the new street east of Fifth Avenue, for the new viaduct over Fortieth Street, connecting upper and lower Park Avenue, ends at Fortieth Street; and by narrowing the sidewalks, and widening the roadway, in Fortieth Street from Park to Fifth avenues, the cross connection would be completed.

It is proposed to make the width of the roadway 60 feet, 5 feet wider than that of Fifth Avenue. Part of this extra width, in the middle of the road, would be used for cab stands; and part for ventilation openings to the sub-surface road referred to below.

THE SUB-SURFACE ROAD. It is proposed to construct a sub-surface road under "The Crossway" and Fortieth Street to Lexington Avenue, which at that point is about on the level with the tunnel under

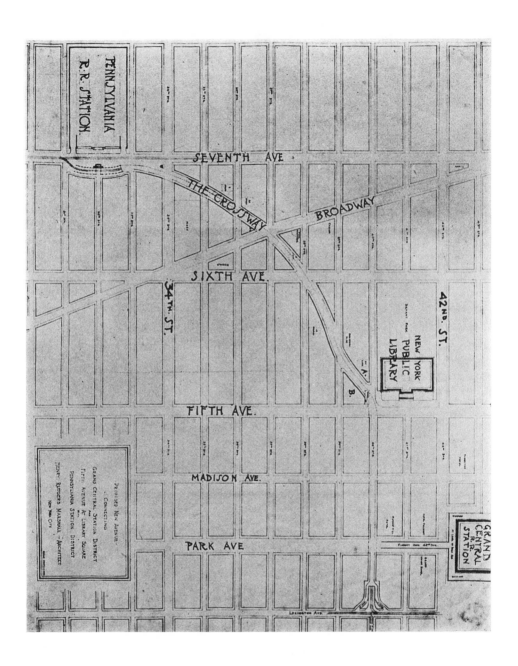

STREET PLAN FOR "THE CROSSWAY," THE PRO-
POSED NEW STREET FOR NEW YORK CITY.
HENRY RUTGERS MARSHALL,   ARCHITECT.

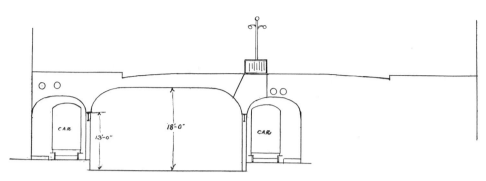

GENERAL SECTION THROUGH SUB-SURFACE ROAD
UNDER "THE CROSSWAY" LOOKING WEST.

Henry Rutgers Marshall, Architect.

Park Avenue, carrying the car tracks of the Fourth Avenue line. At the south end this sub-surface road would rise to the level of Seventh Avenue by a gentle grade between Thirty-first and Thirty-third streets on a plaza in front of the Pennsylvania Station. Thirty-second Street at Seventh Avenue would be bridged for foot passengers over this sub-surface road, and vehicular traffic at this point would be carried down an easy grade north and south, reaching the level of Seventh Avenue opposite the carriage entrances of the railroad station.

An entrance to this sub-surface road by an easy grade would be made at Sixth Avenue and Thirty-eighth Street. The easterly outlet at Lexington Avenue would also be reached by an easy grade. A vast proportion of the slow moving cross town traffic which is now forced to pass through Forty-second Street would be thus diverted.

The width of this sub-surface road would be 50 feet, sufficiently wide to accommodate two lines of trolley tracks and four lines of vehicles. It would be brilliantly lighted by electric light, and ventilated by openings in the middle of "The Crossway" over it, as above referred to.

The trolley tracks would carry the Lex-

ington Avenue line directly to Seventh Avenue at the Pennsylvania Station, connecting there with the station of the Rapid Transit line, and at Fortieth Street and Park Avenue with the Madison Avenue trolley line. There would be stairways to the streets at important points.

As this sub-surface roadway would be protected from the weather, and unobstructed by cross streets, it would attract slow moving traffic, and would thus materially reduce the congestion on Fifth and Sixth avenues, which is mainly due to the obstruction caused by slow moving cross town traffic.

The immense convenience to the public of the sub-surface trolley connection between Lexington and Seventh avenues would itself warrant its construction.

If this double roadway is constructed at once it can be done very economically. As laid out only one expensive modern building would be taken on the whole line, most of the buildings to be condemned being old structures not over five stories high.

Its cost would be offset by the added values given to the property adjacent to it; for it would open up a large district for valuable improvement west of Fifth Avenue;

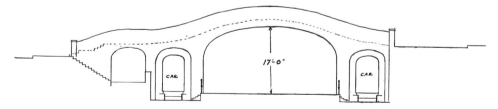

32ND STREET FOOT BRIDGE
ACROSS "THE CROSSWAY."
AT 7TH AVENUE.

Henry Rutgers Marshall, Architect.

and, as it would tend to concentrate attention upon the region of Fifth Avenue itself, would be of advantage to property on this notable thoroughfare.

The aesthetic advantages of the proposed scheme are self-evident; and civic beauty is an important asset to a city.

The curved avenue would break most agreeably the monotony of our gridiron city plan; thus adding to the interest of the parts of the city directly affected. The view down "The Crossway" from Fifth Avenue at the Library Plaza would add much to the artistic value of this centre of interest, and would emphasize the importance of Fifth Avenue itself. The crossing at Broadway would become a new centre of interest, especially in the fact that from this point a fine view would be obtained of the monumental Pennsylvania Railroad Station, which itself would gain greatly in value by the construction of the plaza in front of it, as indicated on the plan."

Among architects who have signed a letter to the Hon. George McAneny, advocating the carrying out of the project are Messrs. A. W. Brunner, Grosvenor Atterbury, Henry Bacon, W. A. Boring, J. Cleveland Cady, Cass Gilbert, Thomas Hastings, C. Grant LaFarge, William R. Mead and George B. Post. Sculptors and painters are represented among the signatures by Messrs. Daniel C. French, Karl Bitter, Herbert Adams, J. W. Alexander, E. H. Blashfield, C. W. Turner and the late F. D. Miller.

Upon consideration of the plan it would seem highly desirable to park the points marked "A" and "B" on the plan, affording a more adequate setting for the Public Library, as well as an oasis midway between Madison Square and the Plaza. A semi-monumental treatment of these spaces, with well-studied planting, would also form an effective portal at this end of "The Crossway," and might well warrant the additional cost involved.

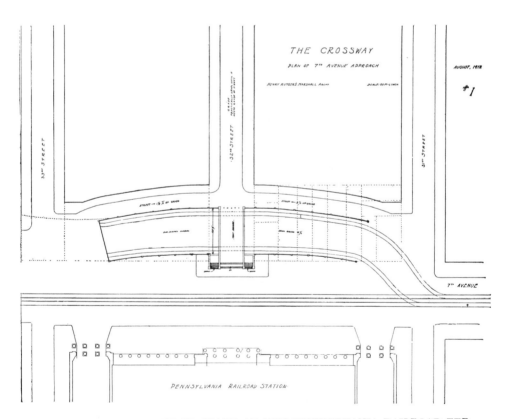

PROPOSED ADJUSTMENT OF GRADE AT THE PENNSYLVANIA RAILROAD TERMINAL, "THE CROSSWAY." HENRY RUTGERS MARSHALL, ACHITECT.

The "Flatiron" or Fuller Building.

ARCHITECTURAL APPRECIATIONS.—NO. II.

IT seemed that there was nothing left to be done in New York, in the way of architectural altitude, which would attract much attention, after the way in which for years we have been piling Pelion upon Ossa. But the architect of the Flatiron, bounded by Broadway, Fifth Avenue and Twenty-third Street, has succeeded in accomplishing that difficult feat. His building is at present quite the most notorious thing in New York, and attracts more attention than all the other buildings now going up put together.

It follows from this extreme conspicuousness and notoriety of the work that it excites more comment, in exciting more attention, than any other recent building. "He who builds by the wayside," says the proverb, "has many judges." And certainly nobody else is building so obviously "by the wayside" as the author of the structure of which the public has thus far refused to accept the official title of "Fuller," preferring the homelier and more graphic designation of the "Flatiron." The corners furnished by the intersection of Broadway with the rectilinear reticulation imposed upon Manhattan island by the Street Commissioners of 1807 are not only the most conspicuous, but really the only conspicuous sites for building, the only sites on which the occupying buildings can be seen all around, can be seen all at once, can be seen from a distance that allows them to be taken in by the eye as wholes. In a civilized municipality these so advantageous spots would have been reserved for public uses, would have been the sites of public and monumental buildings. They are besides so few:

> Oh, it was pitiful
> In a whole cityful,

that those misguided men should have left only half a dozen sites for public buildings, outside, it is true, of those which face public squares. Let us count: This present corner, and the corresponding corner at Twenty-sixth, facing southward, at the intersection of Broadway and Fifth Avenue. At the intersection of Sixth Avenue the truncated triangle, largely spoiled, for the purposes of monumental building, by the intrusion of the elevated road, but set back a block by the reservation of Greeley Square, and the corresponding trapezoid on the north, wisely seized upon, years ago, for the uses of the New York Herald, and occupied effectively by the enlarged or at least elongated reproduction of the pretty palazzo of Verona, a building which compels attention by its modest altitude,

THE "FLATIRON" OR FULLER BUILDING.

Broadway and 23d Street, New York City.

permitting the owner to stand chronically and increasingly astonished at his own moderation, and has, in addition to its intrinsic attractiveness, the interest of lighting up, on one of the most valuable street corners in Manhattan, the "Lamp of Sacrifice," no matter at how queer a shrine. At the intersection of Seventh Avenue, the triangle, also truncated by the recession from Forty-third into a trapezoid, of which the base is now occupied by the new ruin of the Hotel Pabst, and the residue by a hole in the ground for the uses of the subway, and the corresponding and broader trapezoid at the north end of Longacre, at Forty-seventh. At the intersection of Eighth Avenue, the highly irregular space formed by the laying out on the gridiron of the street system of the "Circle" now such a scene of chaos, but at some early day, it is to be hoped, to be converted into something cosmical by the adoption of Mr. Lamb's plan, or some equivalent, and at which early date it is to be hoped the buildings which now line the segment and constitute the "improvement" of the Circle may in their turn be improved off the face of the earth; and at the north end the very eligible triangle lately occupied by Durland's riding school. Beyond this, westward and northward to the intersection of Ninth Avenue, it is not necessary now to extend our inquiries. Thus far, and in the heart of middle Manhattan, we have found just five sites for noble buildings, for we leave out of view the concave frontage of the circle at Fifty-eighth Street. Just one of these sites is thus far occupied by a modern tall building, which is the Flatiron. The building is thus unique, built not by one wayside alone, but by four waysides, and each of its three frontages far seen from the quarter it respectively confronts, and the Broadway front visible and apprehensible from the east side of Fifth Avenue almost up to the entrance to Central Park. No wonder that the architect should have found "many judges," no wonder that his building should have acted as a challenge, and goaded to architectural criticism those who never architecturally criticised before, while those who are victims to the habit of architectural criticism criticise all the more. With apologies to Catullus for dislocating his metre, one may say:

> Hic judicet qui nunquam judicavit;
> Quique judicavit, hic judicet.

It is the first condition of a sane criticism to take account of the conditions. "The sculptor cannot set his own free thought before us, but his thought as he could translate it into the stone that was given, with the tools that were given." And, if this be true of the sculptor, how much truer of the architect, whose work must be "modified at every turn by circumstance and concession." We have been saying that the architect of the Flatiron had a unique opportunity. But also he had to labor with corresponding disadvantages, mainly, of course, the shape of the area he was to cover. This is recognized in the popular name of his building, the long triangle which is called the Flatiron but which has been as graphically described as "a stingy piece of pie." The thoughtless public seems to impute this disadvantage to the architect, by way of criticism as a fault, instead of condoling with him upon it as a misfortune. In fact, the popular judgment upon buildings as works of art is mostly vitiated by the thoughtless habit of ascribing to the architect his advantages as merits, and correspondingly imputing his disadvantages to him as faults. Criticism must keep clear of this confusion.

The main, indeed, the only advantage the architect of the Flatiron had, was the comparative magnitude, the complete detachment, and the consequent conspicuousness of his work, and that is an advantage or not accordingly as the result is or is not successful enough to justify the conspicuousness. The problem in this case was how to make the most of the advantages of detachment, magnitude, altitude, and conspicuousness, and at the same time to min- imize the disadvantages of the awkward shape of the plot, and to do these things without any the least sacrifice of the strictly utilitarian purposes of the structure. For to sacrifice the money getting possibilities of such a site in such a quarter to the monumental aspect of the building would have been as much a mistake in art as in "business." The point was to utilize the site to the very utmost, multiplying as many times as possible, as Paul Bourget has it about the tall buildings of Chicago, "the value of the bit of ground at the base," and yet to make as expressive, harmonious and beautiful a building as the conditions admitted. A candid inquiry into how far such a result has been attained in the actual erection ought to have interest and value.

Foremost among the practical advantages of the site is the fact that the designer did not have to trouble himself in the least about the lighting of his building. Even if we can imagine it confronted on three sides, across Twenty-second Street, across Broadway, and across Fifth Avenue, by buildings as tall as itself, it would be better lighted than many, than most, of the downtown office buildings of comparable altitude. The base is of nearly one hundred feet, but the straight side of the triangle must be nearly, and the hypothenuse on Broadway rather more than two hundred. There is thus no reason why every room on the base of the triangle, or at least of every suite of offices, should not receive light from one of the sides which receives its light from the great area to the north, from which the light cannot be intercepted, the comparatively dark middle of the southern front being backed against an included and counterparting triangle devoted to the service of the building, in which less illumination than in the rentable parts, or even an illumination entirely artificial, is entirely admissible. And then the problem would become, how to get rid of the architectural awkwardness and the practical ineligibility of the thin edge of the wedge, of the apex of the triangle, to get rid, in fact, of the "edge," which, in the expressive language of the street, must "queer" the whole structure if it be allowed to assert itself. We say this edge is practically ineligible, and shall presently point out that fact more in detail. But the architectural intolerableness of it might be expected to appeal first and most powerfully to an architect who was not only a prudent and frugal planner, in the interest of his employer, but also an artist. He would have devoted himself, one would say, to circumventing this awkwardness. Doubtless he would have tried many experimental devices to that end, "proving" them by their practical and their architectural results, and holding fast at last to that which was good, or best. Let us imagine, for example, that, instead of rounding his edge at the bottom, he had truncated the angle to the width of a decent doorway, and had continued this truncation to the top of the architectural basement, including the fourth story, treating his doorway as massively as possible with the dimension he had allowed himself, and, above the doorway, emphasizing the solidity of the truncated wall by leaving a single slit at the centre, which should serve for a lookout to the northward. Then suppose he had terraced the superstructure emphatically back, until the truncation amounted to, say, fifteen or twenty feet, enough to present something that could be called a face of wall, rather than a mere edge, and carried this through the "shaft." Above the shaft, suppose he had still more boldly and emphatically "refused" the superstructure by another terrace, leaving only a trapezoidal tower of, say, half the length, and two-thirds the area of the whole triangle, and carried this tower high enough to include all the rentable area he had omitted below. If this had been sensitively, that is to say artistically done, would not his building have shown more logic, more organization, more form and comeliness, more variety in a higher unity, than it shows now? And could he have been accused of sacrificing his clients to his architecture, if he had provided them with the same area of rentable apartments of which he had deprived them, at no greater cost, in a more eligible shape, and had even added to the altitude which is the distinction of the existing building, and which he might then, without offense, on such a site, have extended even to "the record," or "the limit," whatever the limit may be.

Of course, this is only a suggestion of one solution. Doubtless there are others, which would commend themselves to an architect buckling down in earnest to such a problem. To convert difficulties into opportunities, out of this nettle, a difficult ground plan, to evoke this flower, architectural beauty, is the work of an architectural artist of high degree. Comparisons are odious. But compare the Flatiron with the John Wolfe Building at William Street and Maiden Lane, where the area was quite as awkward a base for a skyscraper as this present plot, and which was moreover entirely without the advantages of isolation and conspicuousness which constitute this present opportunity. How have the awkwardnesses there been circumvented and overruled to expressiveness and beauty which here have been left entirely undisguised, and without even an attempt to disguise them, if they have not even been aggravated, by the treatment. That is, in fact, the peculiarity and the misfortune of the present erection, the fact that the problem does not seem to have presented itself to the architect as a problem. It is not his solution which we have to discuss, and with which we have to quarrel, but his failure to offer any solution. Having an awkward triangle as a site, he has not recognized its awkwardness, nor its triangularity, nor the fact that his building was to be seen in perspective and from various points of view. He has simply drawn three elevations of its three fronts, and apparently seen it, certainly studied it, in elevation only. If, architecturally, the "Flatiron" were simply a street front, like so many other skyscrapers, it might very well pass as "ower bad for blessing and ower good for banning." Let us assume that either of the long fronts is the elevation of such a building, visible, or meant to be seen, like the paper elevation, only from a point in front of it. In that case, we should find it respectable but not interesting. Like Dante, we should not speak, but look only and pass, having, in truth, nothing to say. It is the conventional skyscraper, and shows that the architect is aware what is doing in skyscrapers. We should have to acknowledge that his general dispositions are according to the best authorities, that his three, or four, story basement is in accepted relations to his four-story attic and his twelve-story shaft, and that the eight-story hanging oriels which diversify his front are so spaced as on the one hand not visibly to destroy their own purpose of gaining sidelong views out of certain favored offices, and, on the other, as agreeably to diversify the monotony of the wall without impairing the effect of the repetition of its equable fenestration. Indeed, whether from accident or from design, these oriels have a happy effect in perspective, when the front from which they are projected is seen at a sharp angle, and they take on the appearance of plain piers, bordered above and below by fretted walls. The attic irresistibly recalls that of the Broadway Chambers, from which it seems to be immediately derived. To have improved on the original would have justified the imitation. But it is neither so successful and well adjusted as a crowning member, nor so effectively detailed, nor is it so effective in either respect as the crown of the St. Paul, in which building the architect was no more successful than the architect of the Flatiron in overcoming or dissembling the difficulties of his site, but of which the crowning feature is in itself most effective and even impressive. The variety of color which makes so much of the charm of the crown of the Broadway Chambers is here expressly renounced.

We have, however, to congratulate the designer upon the effectiveness of his material. "There is safety in monochrome," and monochrome cannot be too monochromatic. In this case, the manufacturer has managed exactly to match the warm yellow-gray of the limestone base in the tint of the terra cotta above. Moreover, we have to congratulate the architect upon the success of his detail, especially upon that which answers the purpose, by means of a surface enrichment, of giving appropriate texture to his walls. The frequent failures in this show that it is more of an achievement than the uninitiated might suppose. In a front of hewn stone, this texture is given by means of the various modes of dressing the surface which are employed. In terra cotta it is, or should be, given by ornament. A designer who should confine himself in terra cotta to the limited range of variety available in stone work, and seek appropriate texture simply by roughening the surface according to the distance from the eye, and to the other relevant considerations, would show that he was not alive to the capabilities of his material, to the one point in which terra cotta has an actual advantage over masonry, and that is the facility with which its surface may be moulded into ornament. Systems of ornament, calculated in scale and density to effect the same varieties of texture attained, by cruder means, through the use of the hammer or the chisel, are here imperatively "indicated." And in this respect the architect of the Flatiron has attained a result which is not only satisfactory but exemplary. Whatever its value as ornament, the scale and character of the surface enrichment are throughout such as to make it acceptable as a representation of texture. And, strictly as ornament, none of it is distinctly bad, and some of it is distinctly good. The frieze of the fourth story is effective in itself and particularly effective as denoting and emphasizing a transitional member of the composition. And the detail of the attic, especially of its bounding stories above and below, indeed, the whole feature, even if excessive, and even if inferior to its original, is well adjusted in scale, and the detail well adapted to its altitude.

But this praise, which one can honestly bestow, is all limited to the assumption, which the architect inscrutably chose to make, that

he was designing elevations and not a building. Either of the principal elevations, taken in conjunction with the edge upon which they
converge, has not the aspect of an enclosing wall, so much as of a
huge screen, a vast theatrical "wing," which conceivably rests upon
Titanic castors and is meant to be pushed about, instead of being
rooted to the spot. Nor, when one takes the point of view from
which both fronts can be partly made out at once, the point opposite the thin end of the wedge, is the case at all bettered. To continue the spacing of the fenestration equally whether the space the
windows are supposed to light is a hundred feet across, as at the
south end of the Flatiron, or five, as at the north, is to invite criticism, even from the utilitarian point of view. The openings which
are merely adequate to light an apartment say of thirty feet in depth,
would evidently be excessive to light one with an extreme depth
of fifteen, even if there were a dead wall opposite them. But to re-
open the dead wall with a similar row of windows, and even to carry
them across the five-foot end, in a double opening with the minimum of sash frame, is to denote want of thought. It is to provide
a mere bird-cage for your tenant. As one looks through the bars
of the cage, one pities the poor man. He can, perhaps, find wall
space within for one roll-top desk without overlapping the windows,
with light close in front of him and close behind him and close on
one side of him. But suppose he needed a bookcase? Undoubtedly
he has a highly eligible place from which to view processions. But
for the transaction of business? And the æsthetic effect is even
more depressing. The wedge is blunted, by being rounded, to a
width of five or six feet—possibly ten. But it might as well have
been produced to the actual point, nay, better, if the angle had been
devoted to broadening the piers. For the treatment of the tip is an
additional and seems a wanton aggravation of the inherent awkwardness of the situation. The narrowness of the tip and the high
lanky columns wherewith the designer has seen fit to flank the
entrance, give this feature a meanness of aspect and elongates the
columns to an almost intolerable lankiness. And as the eye travels
upward, past sash frame after sash frame, which takes away all aspect of massiveness from the point which most of all should seem,
as it were, spiked to the ground, the possibility of repose is increasingly removed. And, finally, when, at the very top, one finds the
gauntness of the bottom repeated and even enhanced, by the inser-
tion in the narrow tip of another pair of columns running through
an attic higher than two average stories of the substructure, he
must say to himself that it is a great pity that the architect should
have chosen to build on this very odd site an ordinary tall building,
"built to the limit" in every dimenson, and thus have produced a
very commonplace and conventional skyscraper, as the solution

of a very unusual and a very interesting problem which clamored for an original and unconventional solution.   Such a spectator is bound to admit that

> Evil is wrought by want of thought
> As well as want of heart,

and that the altitude of this five-foot tip is really a "productio ad absurdum."

The Dorilton.

A T the corner of Seventy-first Street and Broadway, in the city of New York, stands a most questionable and question-provoking edifice in the guise of an apartment house. It not merely solicits but demands attention. It yells "Come and look at me" so loud that the preoccupied or even the color-blind passenger cannot choose but hear. And the effect of it on the passer is unusual. It is very infrequently that a building goads to such a pitch of animosity mild men, not especially interested in architecture, insomuch that they can scarcely express themselves about it in parliamentary language. "I don't know what it is about that man," observed Stevenson; "but he excites in me passions that would disgrace hell." Let us, then, institute a candid inquiry into "what it is" about this edifice that produces this effect.

Mere description would not take us far. In fact without the "ocular proof" of the photograph, or, still better, of the building itself, the impartial outsider would wonder, from the mere enumeration of the items of the aggregation "what it was" that made the man who experienced it so "hot," when he himself, the impartial outsider, would have only to be planted opposite the main front in order to fall to swearing also. The general scheme is harmless, current, and plausible. A central court, opening to the south, of fairly liberal dimensions for its purpose of light and air, certainly not obnoxious to the common reproach of being a mere slot, is flanked by two masses of building each somewhat wider than itself. If these wings could be further separated by widening the court, doubtless the effect of the disposition would be better, or if the building were half as high, six stories instead of twelve, in which case the court would be architecturally as well as practically ample. But one allows and must allow for these exigencies of the New York apartment house, and if the reservation of space for light and air is not liberal, as little is it mean. It is true that there is no sense in bridging the court at the level of the main cornice with an arch which at midday darkens two stories with its shadow. But distinctly the lateral composition of this front is not "what it is." Neither is it the lateral composition of the Broadway front, which shows a centre, marked by a five-story oriel in sheet metal, and ends forming the returns of the southern walls, and combining with them to form a pavilion, unmarked in the basement, but marked in the field of the wall by wide and emphatic quoining, and in the high Mansard by a projecton of the roof. It is true that both on the side and in the front the triple divisions are

THE DORILTON APARTMENT HOUSE.
Broadway and 71st Street, New York City.

too nearly equal for the best effect, or even for a good effect, but there is nothing necessarily infuriating about the arrangement.

Neither is there anything necessarily infuriating about the vertical composition. This also is triple. The precept of the excellent Aristotle is scrupulously and emphatically observed. The work has a beginning, a middle and an end—a beginning of limestone; a middle of ditto and brick; an end of slate and copper. These divisions also are more nearly equal than is customary, the middle the shaft, occupying just about half the total height and comprising six stories, while the basement has three and the roof three. Perhaps an addition to the shaft of two stories, taking one from the bottom and one from the top, would have much ameliorated the effect. That Irishman, celebrated by Joseph Miller, who, finding that his bed sheet, while it came comfortably up to his chin, did not cover his feet, cut a strip from the top and sewed it on to the bottom, has always passed for an example of fatuity. But if that Irishman had been an architect, he might have deserved praise instead of ridicule. Nevertheless, the somewhat high-waisted and somewhat low-shouldered look which this edifice derives from the disposition of its parts, would not account for the emotions which it excites.

Neither, entirely, would the material, though here we approach the heart of the mystery. A basement of light limestone, a superstructure of red brick, a roof of black slate and copper, there is nothing maddening about that. Moreover, the setting off of a single story at the top of the base and another at the top of the shaft, and striping it with the two main materials, as a transitional member, is a sensible and not too trite device, especially when, as here, each of the transitional stories carries a strong projection, in one case a row of balconies, in the other the main cornice, and the corbels of the projection are continued downward through the story. But the contrast of color is made violent by the peculiarly vivid redness of the red brick. A milder and mellower tint, or a less staring uniformity of tint, would have helped much the looks of things. We may do an injustice to mere pressed brick, but the fronts seem to have been painted. On the sides, which are "treated" only provisionally, this is still more apparent. The owner and the architect are entitled to credit for endeavoring to make presentable what is only casually visible, and for trying to bestow comeliness upon the more shameful parts. By employing a cheaper, rougher and less uniformly colored red brick upon these subordinate walls, they have made them much more agreeable objects than the smooth expanse of fierce red that burns upon the main front. In fact, the view of the lower part of the flank the spectator sees from the eastward along Seventy-first Street is very

agreeable, so far as the color and texture of the field of wall
goes. It would be altogether agreeable, with the return of the
striped story at the level of the main cornice, and with the other
indications of the treatment of the front, but for some grievous
drawbacks. The ugliest of these is the edging of the pavilion with
a convex curve of sheet metal in absurd imitation of ashlar. Another is the fact that above the cornice line, a corbel course is projected in white brick, and to account for its projection not only the
chimney but also the window frames are set in the advanced plane,
while, worst of all, the brickwork here, where it is sure to be seen,
has the same painted look as that of the main fronts, showing the
insensibility of the designer to the merits of his rough and mottled
wall below.

Doubtless this violent contrast of color is productive of base
passions and is partly "what it is." One detail of it, which has a singularly exasperating effect is the glaring red of the terra cotta
vases which have been placed upon the intermediate pedestals of
the balustrade of the balconies above the third story, the terminal
pedestals being surmounted with vases in cut stone, or sheet metal
painted to that effect. (N. B.—The red vases are backed by the
limestone quoining, but so for that matter are the gray ones.) At
any rate, the fiery tint of the vases which seems to be meant to
match that of the brickwork, is just far enough from doing so to
set the sensitive spectator's teeth on edge.

Next to the violent contrast of color which is the most conspicuous fact about the building, one is inclined to note as most in-
flammatory the gross excess of scale throughout, the wild yell
with which the fronts exclaim "Look at me," as if somebody were
going to miss seeing a building of this area, twelve stories high!
Regard a little those stone balls on the gate posts of the entrance,
two feet in diameter, left there for Titans to roll at ten pins.
Only less are those which surmount the pedestals of the railing,
though these are so transfixed with metal handrails that the Titans
could not get at them. Consider the stone-cutting of the basement, the enormous rolls and the deep recesses that attest the
architect's insistence upon that kind of emphasis which the French
call "emphase." Contemplate the flat arches of the basement, in
which five of the round rolls do duty as voussoirs, the central one
being prolonged to the floor line above and flattened on the face.
Reflect upon that arched opening which runs through two stories
at the centre of each wing, sustaining the three-story oriel in sheet
metal. Mark the scale of the corbels at the top of the basement
and under the main cornice. Most of all, inwardly digest that
huge cartouche above the archway of the court. See the width of

the quoining.   How everything shrieks to drown out everything else!

Above the cornice line the riot is even less restrained. Nay, it is possible that a big quiet mass of roof, broken only by the necessary openings reduced to their lowest terms might have done much to bring even what is below to some sort of unity and subordination.   But violent buildings come to a violent end.   The architectural basis of this three-story roof is twofold—the necessity of "building to the limit," and the cheapness of sheet metal.   It is really, this roof, under pretence of being a roof, three full stories in tinware, including the parapet story, ostensibly of brick and stone, with scarcely any reduction in area from its substructure, and the fact would give it a squeezed and skintight look, no matter how it was treated in detail.   But it is treated with extreme cruelty. What a wonderful feature is that accumulation, on either front, of central dormers, in the plane of the wall below, but thanks to the cornice seeming to impend threateningly over and beyond it in place of crowning it!   And then there is always or at least so often, the suspicion of fraudulency.   What between the architect's frequent introduction of sheet metal in imitation of masonry, and his frequent introduction of masonry in imitation of sheet metal, that is to say, with that bloatedness and inflation of design which belong to the cheaper material, he "keeps us guessing" in a manner truly infuriating.   "At least that is costly," you say of one detail which you take to be cut stone, or "at least that is cheap," of some other which you take to be of tin, but with no certainty, when the object is beyond the reach of ocular certainty in the case of either, that it is not the other praise to which it is really entitled.   And this is unsettling to the intellect as well as embittering to the heart. The grand cartouche of the central arch "ought to be" of sheet metal.   The outlying cartouches with the elongated shields, that drip down the piers are of sheet metal confessed, as much as the oriels.   But even the corbelling of the balconies are under suspicion of malleability, though in a position where an imposture should be easy to detect.

The incendiary qualities of the edifice may then be referred, first to violence of color, then to violence of scale, then to violence of "thinginess," to the multiplicity and the importunity of the details.   It would not be fair to pass without noting how thoroughly the sculptor has "worked in harmony" with architect, and caught the detestable spirit that reigns throughout.   Remark, if you please, the cherubs, carved with some blunt instrument, that sprawl above the central gate.   Remark, also, the allegorical figures that flank the base of the tin oriel at the centre of the side,

denoting—well, what? Peace and Plenty? Flora and Pomona?
Nonsense. Gambrina and Bologna.

It is something to have abounded thus exceptionally in the
sense in which so much of our current building abounds, to have
put up an edifice which cannot be regarded with apathy, at sight of
which, on the contrary, strong men swear, and weak women shrink
affrighted. As Carlyle says of the London statues: "That all men
should see this; innocent young creatures, still in arms, be taught
to think this beautiful; and perhaps, women in an interesting situation look up to it as they pass? I put it to your religious feeling,
to your principles as men and fathers of families!"

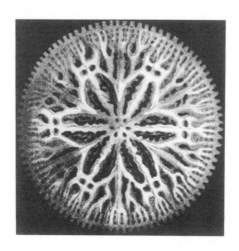

A Conversation with Henry Janeway Hardenbergh

A quiet interior, a harmony of deep reds and browns, frugal but elegant equipment and a subdued light effect, this was the first impression I received. Then out of the window a glimpse of the colossal Waldorf-Astoria, one of the architect's most notable achievements. The architect himself, Napoleonic in stature, but of wiry build, with a shrewd, worldly-wise expression in his eyes, at his office desk on an elevated platform that runs along the window, and I on a leather chair below, which obliged me to look up to him.

The first moments in contact with a new personality are always decisive with me, and, in this instance, I had not only to reckon with the personality of the architect, but also a sample of interior decoration, and a successful specimen of his work to judge from. It was like hearing a pianist play the theme of the variations which he is going to perform. "This man knows what he is about," I thought to myself; "I am sure he deserves the reputation he has of *having a roof on every house he builds.*"

We at once settled down to serious business, to an interview, one of those old-fashioned, matter-of-fact interviews that have really taken place, and are in no way masked with inadequate ornamentation.

"I believe you studied with one of the old New York architects, Detlef Lienau by name?" was my first turn of the key.

"Yes, he was a remarkable man for his time," and Mr. Hardenbergh's face was lit up for a moment as with pleasant recollection. "Of course, building—I entered Lienau's office in '63—had not yet reached such dimensions in New York, as it did in the following decades. But he did good, solid work, notably in the French Renaissance. I do not remember at this moment all he did. One of the best specimens is that old residential dwelling, Tenth Street and Fifth Avenue."

"You never studied abroad?"

"No, I never got to Europe until after quite a number of years of active practice."

"Then your case seems to prove that a man can become an architect without studying abroad?"

"Emphatically, yes," he exclaimed with peculiar emphasis, that did not solely betray conviction, but also pride in what he himself had accomplished. "It only depends on how one studies. For that matter, one could live at the seashore, and become a good architect. Of course, there were drawbacks; books and photographs were scarce at that time. The facilities for reproductions were still slight. I remember how delighted I was when I got my first collection of Parisian buildings; I thought it a rare treasure."

"But are you not of the opinion that there are too many publications nowadays?"

"Decidedly so. The young men rely too much on their assistance. They go from one book to the other, and get a little bit here, and a little bit there; but do not understand how to put them together."

"I suppose you served a real German apprenticeship at Lienau's?"

"Yes, it was a true apprenticeship. Conditions were different. He had never more than six men in his office. He could really devote some time to them. Now, many offices have forty to fifty men on their pay-roll."

"I know of one firm which, several years ago, had as many as ninety-three draftsmen in their employ. This, I suppose, makes personal instruction impossible in these days?" I interpolated.

"Absolutely! I have not more than ten minutes a day to give to the younger men—but they learn from the older draftsmen," he said, after some reflection. "Yet without arrogance, only with due respect to my way of doing things, I can say that I have done my work with a

HENRY JANEWAY HARDENBERGH.

smaller clerical force than most offices. If you have too large a force, you have to depend too much on other men. You lose touch with your own work. The individuality of one's style is apt to suffer thereby."

"You are particularly interested in municipal art?"

"Yes, I was one of the founders of the Municipal Art Society."

"And if I am not mistaken, you individually have also helped matters along on that line?"

"Yes, I have always regarded mural decoration a part of architecture, and always tried to persuade my clients that there was a necessity for such a thing. At the Waldorf-Astoria we simply gave out the work. I had made up my mind to have Blashfield, and insisted until I got him. At the Manhattan, in order to avoid what might look like favoritism, I managed to arrange a competition with a thousand dollars in prizes. Five artists competed."

"How did the painters adapt themselves to the work?"

"Of course, it was a new experiment with them. They all 'paint' a trifle too much. They do not seem to be able to adapt themselves to their environment, to any particular style. There are hardly any of them who understand ornament. Simmons seems to get nearer to the real thing than any of them. And even he is still too much of an easel painter. Look, for instance, at this little panel," and he pointed to a canvas by Shean, over the mantelpiece, representing "The Architect and His Client," in mediaeval costume and surroundings. "It is very nice, well painted, but hardly mural in feeling."

"You seem to have made a specialty of hotels?" I asked, remembering that we owe to this architect the popular structures of the Waldorf-Astoria, the Manhattan, the Dakota, and others.

"Yes, it seems to have been my fatality that things have come that way. I have built a large number of them. But I have also done a good deal in apartment houses, and lately in office buildings. To show you how eclectic an architect really has to be: One of my first commissions

was a Gothic chapel for Rutger's College, in New Brunswick, my native town. Soon after came a row of Ohio limestone dwellings. About the same time I constructed a Turkish bath in the private house of a gentleman. It was done all in the Pompeian style. I had the entrée to the Neo-Grec through Lienau. Lienau was a pupil of Labrouste, the architect of the St. Geneviève Library, in Paris, and the Hospital at Lausanne, who effected a successful combination of the modern French and Neo-Grec. You will notice in all the works of the French architect a certain simplicity and severity of detail."

Labrouste was one of the first who succeeded in the employment of modern building materials, thoroughly in accordance with beautiful form and original ideas. Through Lienau his skill and cultivated taste has descended upon Hardenbergh, who thereby was prepared to avoid the reefs on which so many of our modern architects have suffered shipwreck. My remarks gave Mr. Hardenbergh an opportunity to express his views on the modern French.

"I have always been charged, though unjustly, of being opposed to the modern French. This objection applies only to later work in the style. They can't go much further. It is all for sensational effect, and will end in sheer brutality. Their ornaments," and he made a descriptive gesture, "are crude and clumsy. There would be no objection if they would stick to the fine examples of the past, but this way——"

"Do you think the New York architects set the taste for the whole country?"

"I think so. When Richardson had built his Trinity Church, you saw bad Richardsons cropping up all over the country. For instance, in Chicago, it was simply awful. Of course, we all do incongruous things in our time. They lately tore down a building of mine, of which I felt very proud at the time it was built; but I was really delighted when it was gone."

"Do you think we will arrive at more uniformity of style?"

"Possibly," he remarked rather drily.

"Conditions and needs will bring it about. But elements of new formations must necessarily be based on reminiscences of those already existing."

"And at present these reminiscences seem to be all modern French," I insinuated.

"Not entirely; the classic movement is very strong. Nearly everything that some of our leading architects build of late has the characteristic columns and the tympanum on top. I myself am very fond of the German Renaissance. Not when it was loud, overloaded with ornaments, but modified. I also have a liking for the Dutch Renaissance," and he showed me a sketch of the New York Club. In its elegant simplicity it reminded me slightly of the building of the Fine Arts Society, which I consider one of Hardenbergh's masterpieces.

"Yes, that was really a work of love," he explained. "If it only could have been placed differently. The apartment house next to it spoils much of the effect. The model for it was a Francois I., in the Court de la Reine, Paris. I only saw it two years ago, long after the New York building was finished. I had been in Paris before, but had missed it. And when I at last made it my object to see it, I was highly delighted."

"How is it with more utilitarian buildings? Do not the difficulties of the internal arrangement take so much thought and time, that there is comparatively little left for the consideration of the art element?"

"Not in the least," he said most decisively. "You see, the laying out of the plans of lighting, heating, etc., one has, after all, to leave largely to the engineers. No man can do that all by himself."

"You try to make the interior correspond as much as possible with the outside; it seems to me that the latter is often merely a shell."

"Yes, that is a fault that I find with many buildings. But I always try to bring everything into a certain harmony. Of course, in a hotel all tastes have to be satisfied, and one must know pretty well how the space is going to be utilized before one can realize the artistic vision of the outward appearance of a building."

The architect has to deal with three factors, all of equal importance, first, the artistic element; second, construction, and third, interior decoration. It is just as in music, a certain *Leitmotif* should run through everything. Otherwise, it would be merely a collection of miscellaneous details, as you have correctly said, a husk, a shell. The trouble is, that we are always in such a hurry in this country. At times, this may prove a stimulant. One simply has to go work and do it. But if it comes to details of ornamentation, or interior decoration, it is deplorable. The outside of a building should always indicate what is inside. Look, for instance, at those big windows over there," and he pointed at the Waldorf-Astoria as an object lesson. "You feel that there is a big assembly hall behind them, and so it is with everything. The windows of the various parlors are still large in comparison with those of the ordinary rooms, but much smaller than those of the ballroom."

This emphasized a trite architectural truth, that the outside forms must be characteristic of the aim and object of the interiors, which they hide from view.

"How do you think our architecture compares with the European; do you think we have as much claim to originality?"

"I am certain of it. And that is said without any conceit or partiality. In England they are not handicapped by space, as we are here, and they have quite a number of beautiful buildings to their credit; but they are not more frequent than on this side. L'Art Nouveau in France was a failure. The rest is entirely under the influence of the modern French. In Italy they live largely on classic traditions."

"Have you been at Cologne? There they seem to have produced a great variety of forms."

"Yes, but that is Belgian influence. The Dutch Renaissance is very adequate."

"It always seemed to me that the new Court House in Brussels is a very fine specimen of modern architecture."

"Very impressive. The combination

of Assyrian and classic styles shows very much ingenuity; but one can hardly call it good architecture. No, I think we are fully awake over here. And in the specialty of residential houses, of office buildings, and hotels, I think we have accomplished what nobody else has. done. We have adapted ourselves to new conditions, both esthetically and in accordance with style."

Our chat, excepting a few telephone interruptions, had run on smoothly. To every ten words I had uttered, Mr. Hardenbergh had, at least, two hundred to his credit. Getting ready to leave, I remarked:

"Have you any special method in following out your theories?"

"My method is really a very simple one. There, for instance, is a sketch of the new Plaza Hotel," and he showed me a sketch of that giant caravansery. There seems to be a striking tendency in this latest of his work, to abandon the picturesqueness and irregularity of his former style, and to arrive at a simpler, and at the same time more pleasing effect. I had involuntarily to smile, however, at what seemed to me interminable rows of windows. He guessed my thought: "None of them is unnecessary. Now, what would be the use of introducing columns, colonnades, as they do. The Greek didn't build buildings of this kind. Edifices of this order have been unknown to past generations. They have no proto-types. All one can do is to take some good model, that served some kind of purpose as a hotel, and enlarge upon it. And then embellish it as well as one can, as for instance, in this case, with the early French Renaissance."

After I left, my first thought recurred to me: He well earns his reputation of never building a house without a roof. I had not been mistaken in my first judgment of him.

For here we have an architect who avoids everything that savors of pretence and unreality. Whatever forms he gives us represent the thing which they really are, and the intentions they express are existent. He gives us the reciprocal relation of the spaces of the interior and the form of the exterior. This is visibly permanent everywhere throughout his structures, and pervades all his work. He offers a further contribution towards a pleasing effect by bringing the various modes of interior decoration into conformity with the construction.

Only by this method, I believe, will we arrive at a period of architectural expression in accordance with our age. And I am convinced that men like Henry Janeway Hardenbergh, in their more utilitarian speciality of apartment houses, office buildings and hotels—which are undoubtedly an improvement upon the old—will materially help to give us buildings of a completer and more harmonious order.

Sadakichi Hartmann.

INTIMATE LETTERS
O F
STANFORD WHITE

CORRESPONDENCE WITH HIS FRIEND
& CO-WORKER AVGVSTVS SAINT-GAVDENS
EDITED BY HOMER SAINT GAVDENS

THIRD INSTALLMENT.

IT IS A CALL of twenty years from 1880 to 1900. Yet throughout these years, as I have explained, the friendship of White and Saint-Gaudens remained unbroken. During the early part of this period letters were few and far between, since White often could be found in the vicinity of Saint-Gaudens' studio where his criticism meant much to the sculptor. Indeed White's advice held so important a place that once when he scored a medallion of himself which Saint-Gaudens was modelling the latter destroyed the work and never attempted a new one. Yet, despite such occasional encounters, the two men for the most part tolerated each other's peculiarities humorously—White sincere in his respect for the sculptor's ability, but anxious to make of him more of a "club man," Saint-Gaudens deep in his admiration for the architect's generosity of effort and high artistic powers, yet hoping to modify the more drastic side of his nature.

By 1897, when Saint-Gaudens went abroad again for his long stay, White still held first place as the rock to fall back upon. But since their personal intimacy had grown somewhat less and since during that especial visit by Saint-Gaudens to France they had little work in common, the correspondence between the two busy men greatly lapsed.

On Saint-Gaudens' return, however, their intimacy revived once more; and then, living in the same land, though White in the city and Saint-Gaudens in the country, their letters became tinged again with the flavor of early days. How

The White-Saint Gaudens letters began in the August issue.

these letters typified the lasting of a friendship of twenty-five years is what I would show in this, the final article.

The first letter is from Saint-Gaudens to White. The Stevenson the sculptor mentions is one which he remodelled for St. Giles Cathedral in Edinburgh, Scotland, and for which White designed the frame. The sculptor writes—

"Windsor, Vermont,
"September 27, 1900.
"Dear Stan:
"I have your telegram. I am getting on very well indeed and, considering that I am as full of holes as a 'porous plas' (as the Italian said), I wonder I am alive. I remain up here until November first when I go to Boston for the secondary operation. I remain there two weeks, and then I come back here to recuperate. If I can stand it, I shall remain up here until well along in the winter, and from what they all say here it is a big sight pleasanter than in summer, and that's saying a great deal. I shall go down to New York, of course, to see about the Sherman site as soon after November twenty-fifth as I can.

"Thank you, very much, old boy, for what you have done about the Stevenson, and here is a reply to your question, although I don't see why I should load you up with this now.

"I should like a light yellowish-bronze patine for the figure of the Stevenson, and the same thing, but much darker, for the inscription. The relief sets in a stone wall. A red Sienna marble is what I wanted; but, if you can think of a better thing, let me know. The surface of the stone frame is to be set out an inch and a half, or thereabouts, from the wall if you think that is right. The frame is to be in four pieces. How have you fixed things, and cannot I attend to it now?

"Is McKim back?

"I had an amusing letter from Garnier describing your trip to Toulouse. He is an amusing chap, isn't he?

"This is the first letter of any length I've written since I left Paris, and it tires me, otherwise I should write reams. You wouldn't know me from my mental state now. I think I was on the verge of insanity in Paris. I roam around the hills in great style and loaf for all I'm worth.

"Needless to tell you that if you should come in this direction you would be mighty welcome.

"Good-by.   Affy.,
      "Gus."

The next letter is from White to Saint-Gaudens. The interest which the architect took in charities, such as the one here referred to, developed from a dominant side of his warm-hearted nature which the sculptor deeply admired. White writes—

     "October 13, 1903.
"Dear Gus:
"* * * We are to have another Portrait Show for the benefit of the Orthopædic Hospital for crippled children. We would like to have any one of your portrait reliefs that you can send— that is, Stevenson's Howells and his daughter, or any new ones that you have done. We of course assume all responsibility as to insurance, expenses, etc.
  "Affy.,   Stanford."

The next letter deals with the last typical attempt White made to hold his friend by him in his many social activities. Saint-Gaudens ultimately, as White wished, joined the Brook Club here mentioned.

     "March 18, 1904.
"My dear Gus:
"You long-nosed farmer you! What 'll do you mean by backing out of The Brook

for? It is not your 'mun' that we want but your name and yourself. That is, we want you as a nest egg and an attraction for a dozen men whom we want in, and I think in the end will come in. What we want to make of the Club is one that is not all society men, like the Knickerbocker, or men of the world, like the Union and Metropolitan, or a Lunch Club, like The Players, or one where mainly actors congregate, like The Lambs, or a Sleepy Hollow, like The Century; but a very quiet, small Club, something like the Beefsteak Club in London, where you will have the freedom of some of the Clubs I have mentioned and the quietness of others, and where you will always be sure, from lunch time to two or three in the morning, to find three or four men you will always be glad to see and no one that you will not be glad to see.

"I think that, once the Club is started, and you have tried it for a year, you will want to stay in it; and I think that McKim and a lot of fellows that you know and like, in addition to those that are already in, will also join it * * * but it will really break my heart if you don't join and at least make the trial.
    "Lovingly,
     "Stanford."

Now the letters turn from recreation to work again, the one to follow referring to White's designs for the extensive architecture for Saint-Gaudens' "Seated Lincoln." The monument has yet to be unveiled as it is to be set up on "made land" still undeveloped in Chicago, Illinois. White writes—

     "September 23, 1904.
"Dear Gustibus:
"I have been making many different studies for the scheme of steps and columns for your new Lincoln; but, as usual, the simple scheme is much the best. The whole thing in fact resolves itself into the proper proportions of the circle and the columns to your figure and to the surroundings; and I think the final studies which I now send you are about as good as I can do. Of course, I do not know how much the Committee have in

AUGUSTUS SAINT GAUDENS' STATUE OF PETER COOPER
—ARCHITECTURE DESIGNED BY STANFORD WHITE.

hand, or are willing to stand, and I really do not know how much this plan will cost. I send it to you, and, if you approve, I will get estimates at once and then we will be able to shave them down if it is found to be necessary.

"Affy.,   Stanford."

Following this comes a letter in a more intimate tone, showing the respect the architect continued to entertain for the sculptor's artistic judgment.

"October 25, 1905.

"Dear Gusty:

"When I was in Syracuse years ago, I was perfectly ravished by a Greek Venus which they have there. I made a lot of drawings of her myself, which I was very proud of, and am still; but I never could find a photograph of her, and I have always regretted that I did not have one made. Lo and behold, however, in the *Sunday Herald* of October 8th they have a photograph of her, and I send it up to you and want to know if you do not think she is the 'most beautifullest' thing that ever was in this world.

"Also, when I was in Paris, I saw, in a little antiquity place, in the back yard, some workmen from the Louvre setting up what seemed to me a wonderful statue which had just been dug up and had come, by underground passage, from Greece. I had a photograph sent me, and I include it. It is life size, of Paros marble, and of the most beautiful color you ever saw, and can be bought for fifteen thousand dollars. It is of course late work, but it does seem to me as if I ought to get somebody to 'nab' it. Please send the photograph back to me and let me know what you think of it.

"Affy.,   Stan."

Next I will take up certain letters dealing with the Brooks Monument, for in the elaborate architecture which surrounds this statue White lent his final aid to the sculptor. It is strange that these two men who first worked together in Trinity Church, Boston, also designed their last composition to go under the shadow of that building. These three

letters between them well explain the single direction of their efforts. The first letter is from Saint-Gaudens to White.

"January 17, 1906.

"Dear Stan:

"I return you the drawings you made for the Brooks years ago. I think I like the plan of No. 4 the best and the style of No. 3, but I leave this entirely to you. I will say, however, that I should greatly like to have it in the character of your Parkhurst Church, which I think great and just in the line I thought of for this. I think you must provide for a bulge out in front as in No. 3 and for the cross to run up as in No. 3 also.

"The statue of Brooks is to be eight feet and four inches in height or thereabouts, and the rest of the group very much as shown in the drawings.

"Gus."

To which White replied—

"New York, March 17, 1906.

"Dear Gus:

"I send you with this a careful drawing for the Phillips Brooks Monument. In your letter to me you ask that I should send drawings for both the square and the circular one, but I am so positive that the square form is infinitely the best, everyone agreeing with me, McKim, Kendall and Phil Richardson, that I beg you to give up the idea of the round one and go ahead with the square one. The round one might look well from the front, but all the other views would be complicated and ugly. * * *

Affy.,   Stanford."

To which the sculptor wrote—

"March 30, 1906.

"Dear Stan:

"Thank you for your note of March 17th and the drawing which came duly to hand.

"When the model is made, I will communicate with you. My objection to the square form, and the reason I preferred the circular, was that the circular covered the group more. You remember some one objected to the Cooper Monument that it was a 'protection that did not protect.' Possibly this scheme could be made deeper.

"Will you have sent to me a tracing of the little drawing I sent you showing the scale of the figures in the monument."

Finally here are the two last letters which passed between the friends. Saint-Gaudens writes—

"May 7, 1906.
"Dear Stan:
"Thank you for the perspective of the Pittsburgh monument. It is all right. I am at work on it, and you will hear from me later on.

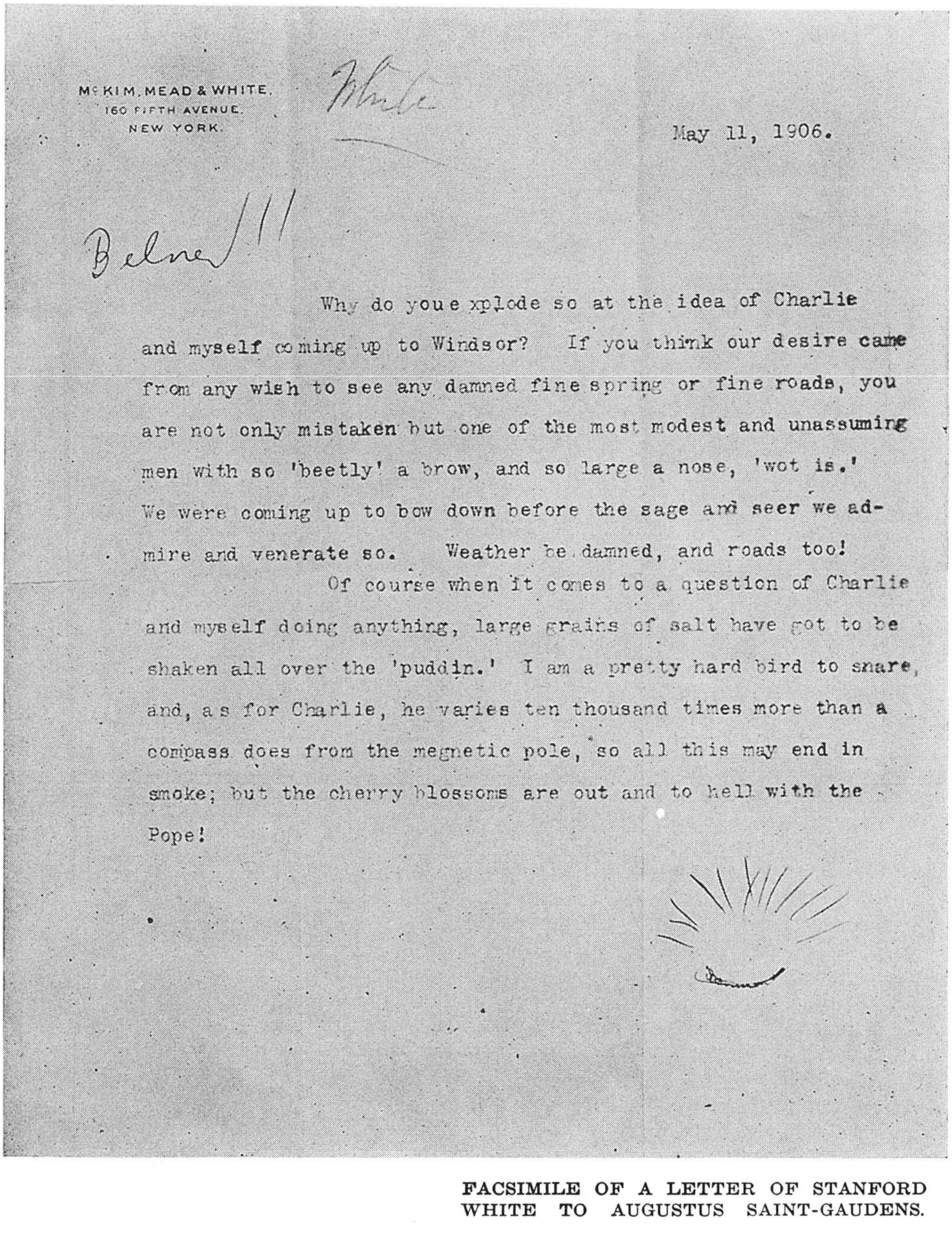

McKIM, MEAD & WHITE.
160 FIFTH AVENUE.
NEW YORK.

White

May 11, 1906.

Belne

Why do you explode so at the idea of Charlie and myself coming up to Windsor? If you think our desire came from any wish to see any damned fine spring or fine roads, you are not only mistaken but one of the most modest and unassuming men with so 'beetly' a brow, and so large a nose, 'wot is.' We were coming up to bow down before the sage and seer we admire and venerate so. Weather be damned, and roads too! Of course when it comes to a question of Charlie and myself doing anything, large grains of salt have got to be shaken all over the 'puddin.' I am a pretty hard bird to snare, and, as for Charlie, he varies ten thousand times more than a compass does from the megnetic pole, so all this may end in smoke; but the cherry blossoms are out and to hell with the Pope!

FACSIMILE OF A LETTER OF STANFORD
WHITE TO AUGUSTUS SAINT-GAUDENS.

Elementary Sketch for Relief of Mrs. White
by Augustus Saint-Gaudens.

of Charlie and myself coming up to Windsor? If you think our desire came from any wish to see any damned fine spring or fine roads you are not only mistaken, but one of the most modest and unassuming men with so 'beetly' a brow and so large a nose 'wot is.' We were coming up to bow down before the sage and seer we admire and venerate. So weather be damned, and roads, too!

"Of course, when it comes to a question of Charlie and myself doing anything, large grains of salt have got to be shaken all over the 'puddin'.' I am

"As to your visit here, I have been trying to get you up here for twenty years and no signs of you and Charles; and now, when we are having the worst spring that ever occurred (the roads are in awful condition), you want to come up in five minutes. Now you hold off a little while and I will let you know, perhaps in a couple of weeks from now.

"Good-by."

(Signed with Saint-Gaudens' caricature.)

To which White replied—

"May 11, 1906.

"Beloved!!!

"Why do you explode so at the idea

Elementary Sketch of Relief Showing the Nature of the Trials Saint-Gaudens Made Before Reaching His Final Composition.

a pretty hard bird to snare; and, as for Charlie, he varies ten thousand times more than a compass does from the magnetic pole; so all this may end in smoke; but the cherry blossoms are out, and to hell with the Pope!"

Such were the relations between the two men at the end of White's life. Therefore it is to be imagined that the news of his death deeply shocked the sculptor. Here is what Saint-Gaudens wrote to his old friend, Alfred Garnier, concerning it.

"6th July, 1906.
"Dear Old Man:
"* * * You have no doubt read in the newspapers of the death of White by an idiot fool who imagined himself wronged, wronged because of a woman. A stupid vengeance, an instantaneous death in a theatre right at the foot of one of his best works! Two revolver shots in the head and one in the arm! An idiot that shoots a man of great genius for a woman with the face of an angel and a heart of a snake!"

Naturally, then, when later Saint-Gaudens was asked by others intimate with White to write a word of his feelings towards the architect, the sculptor longed to do so. Here is the draft of the attempt—

"In a close friendship with Stanford White for about thirty years one thing stands out through the troubles, triumphs and the inextricable complications and entanglements of life, and that is his unfaltering friendship and devotion underlying the occasional asperities of a highly strung temperament of a man pushed and pressed on all sides by the obligations of his profession and the thousand and one not of his profession, which in his exuberant generosity he was constantly taking to himself. Those who really knew him were aware of this steady undercurrent of sincerity and generosity, and this very quality has led to much misrepresentation of his acts. A man who held the love of so many

friends must also have possessed big characteristics, and their number is a reply to the enlargements of his faults or mistakes.

"As to his rôle as an artist, it seems unnecessary to speak. He was a constant incentive to the highest endeavor in all of us who surrounded him. Besides, his achievement has left an extraordinary stamp on our city, the examples of which, whatever their weakness may have been, are all of a distinct and elevating nature that makes one feel the rare thrill that comes when one is in the presence of a work that has the undefinable something that is in the production of genius.* * *"

These words were not published, as they did not satisfy Saint-Gaudens, who at the time was too ill to be able to work over them. Finally, however, a masterly article upon White by Richard Harding Davis which appeared in *Collier's* drew from the sculptor this public letter, a letter which I feel sure places the best of periods to their long and affectionate intimacy. Saint-Gaudens wrote—

"August 6, 1906.
"The Editors of Collier's Weekly,
"420 West 13th St., New York City.
"Dear Sirs:
"I thank you for the remarkable article by Richard Harding Davis about Stanford White in your issue of August 4th. It is, to those who knew him, the living portrait of the man, his character and his life. As the weeks pass, the horror of the miserable taking away of this big friend looms up more and more. It is unbelievable that we shall never see him again going about among us with his astonishing vitality, enthusiasm and force. In the thirty years that the friendship between him and me endured, his almost feminine tenderness to his friends in suffering and his generosity to those in trouble or want stand out most prominently. That such a man should be taken away in such a manner in the full flush of his extraordinary power is pitiable beyond measure.
"Sincerely yours,
"Augustus Saint-Gaudens."

AUGUSTUS SAINT-GAUDENS' MEDALLION OF MRS. STAN-
FORD WHITE AT THE TIME OF HER WEDDING IN 1884.

The Wild Men of Paris

Sculpture by Matisse.

I had scarcely entered the Salon des Indépendants when I heard shrieks of laughter coming from an adjoining wing. I hurried along from room to room under the huge canvas roof, crunching the g r a v e l underfoot as I went, u n t i l I c a m e upon a party of well-dressed Parisians in a paroxysm o f merriment, gazing, through weeping eyes, at a picture. Even in my haste I had noticed other spectators lurching hysterically in and out of the galleries; I had caught sight of paintings that had made me gasp. But here I stopped in amazement. It was a thing to startle even Paris. I realized for the first time that my views on art needed a radical reconstruction. Suddenly I had entered a new world, a universe of ugliness. And, ever since, I have been mentally standing on my head in the endeavor to get a new point of view on beauty so as to understand and appreciate this new movement in art.

"Une Soirée dans le Désert" was a fearful initiation. It was a painting of a nude female seated on a stretch of sand, devouring her own knee. The gore dripped into a wineglass. A palm tree and two cacti furnished the environment. Two large snakes with target-shaped eyes assisted at the debauch, while two small giraffes hurried away from the scene.

What did it all mean? The drawing was crude past all belief; the color was as atrocious as the subject. Had a new era of art begun? Was ugliness to supersede beauty, technique give way to

naïveté, and vibrant, discordant color, a very patchwork of horrid hues, take the place of subtle, studied nuances of tonality? Was nothing sacred, not even beauty?

If this example of the new art was shocking, there were other paintings at the Salon that were almost as dire. If you can imagine what a particularly sanguinary little girl of eight, half-crazed with gin, would do to a whitewashed wall, if left alone with a box of crayons, then you will come near to fancying what most of this work was like. Or you might take a red-hot poker in your left hand, shut your eyes and etch a landscape upon a door. There were no limits to the audacity and the ugliness of the canvasses. Still-life sketches of round, round apples and yellow, yellow oranges, on square, square tables, seen in impossible perspective; landscapes of squirming trees, with blobs of virgin color gone wrong, fierce greens and coruscating yellows, violent purples, sickening reds and shuddering blues.

But the nudes! They looked like flayed Martians, like pathological charts —hideous old women, patched with gruesome hues, lopsided, with arms like the arms of a Swastika, sprawling on vivid backgrounds, or frozen stiffly upright, glaring through misshapen eyes, with noses or fingers missing. They defied anatomy, physiology, almost geometry itself! They could be likened only to the Lady of the Limerick:

"There was a young girl of Lahore,
  The same shape behind as before;
     And as no one knew where
      To offer a chair,
She had to sit down on the floor!"

But it's no use going on; you will, I am sure, refuse to take me seriously. You will merely think I am trying to be funny. Wherefore, I hired a man, a brave one, too, to photograph a few of these miracles. In line and composition the reproductions will bear me out, per-

TETE D'EXPRESSION.

Matisse.

haps; but, unfortunately (or is it fortunately?), the savagery of color escapes the camera. That color is indescribable. You must believe that such artists as paint such pictures will dare any discord. They have robbed sunsets and rainbows, chopped them up into squares and circles, and hurled them, raw and bleeding, upon their canvases.

Surely, one cannot view such an exhibition calmly. One must inevitably take sides for or against such work. The revolt is too virulent, too frenzied to be ignored. Long ago my father said: "When you see a fool, don't laugh at him, but try to find out why he does so. You may learn something." And so I began to investigate these lunatics. Had they attempted to invent a new form of humor? Were they merely practical jokers? Or must we seriously attempt anew to solve the old question: "What is art?"

It was an affording quest, analyzing such madness as this. I had studied the gargoyles of Oxford and Notre Dame, I had mused over the art of the Niger and of Dahomey, I had gazed at Hindu monstrosities, Aztec mysteries and many other primitive grotesques; and it had come over me that there was a rationale of ugliness as there was a rationale of beauty; that, perhaps, one was but the negative of the other, an image reversed, which might have its own value and esoteric meaning. Men had painted and carved grim and obscene things when the world was young. Was this revival a sign of some second childhood of the race, or a true rebirth of art?

And so I sought to trace it back to its

Soireé dans le Désert.

meaning and to its authors. I quested for the men who dared such Gargantuan jests. Though the school was new to me, it was already an old story in Paris. It had been a nine-days' wonder. Violent discussions had raged over it; it had taken its place as a revolt and held it, despite the fulmination of critics and the contempt of the academicians. The school was increasing in numbers, in importance. By many it was taken seriously. At first, the beginners had been called "The Invertebrates." In the Salon of 1905 they were named "The Incoherents." But by 1906, when they grew more pervid, more audacious, more crazed with theories, they received their present appellation of "Les Fauves"— the Wild Beasts. And so, and so, a-hunting I would go!

Who were the beginners of the movement? Monet, Manet and Cézanne, say most, though their influence is now barely traceable. Cézanne, no doubt; Cézanne, the pathetic bourgeois painter, whose greatest ambition was to wear the ribbon of the Legion of Honor, and to have his pictures exhibited in the old Salon, and who, because his maiden sister disapproved of the use of female models, painted nude women from nude men! Truly, he deserved the red ribbon. But Cézanne, though he experimented with pure color, was still concerned with tonalities. He was but the point of departure for these mad explorers. It was Matisse who took the first step into the undiscovered land of the ugly.

Matisse himself, serious, plaintive, a

conscientious experimenter, whose works are but studies in expression, who is concerned at present with but the working out of the theory of simplicity, denies all responsibility for the excesses of his unwelcome disciples. Poor, patient Matisse, breaking his way through this jungle of art, sees his followers go whooping off in vagrom paths to right and left. He hears his own speculative words distorted, misinterpreted, inciting innumerable vagaries. He may say, perhaps: "To my mind, the equilateral triangle is a symbol and manifestation of the absolute. If one could get that absolute quality into a painting, it would be a work of art." Whereat, little madcap Picasso, keen as a whip, spirited as a devil, mad as a hatter, runs to his studio and contrives a huge nude woman composed entirely of triangles, and presents it in triumph. What wonder Matisse shakes his head and does not smile! He chats thoughtfully of the "harmony of volume" and "architectural values," and wild Braque climbs to his attic and builds an architectural monster which he names Woman, with balanced masses and parts, with openings and columnar legs and cornices. Matisse praises the direct appeal to instinct of the African wood images, and even sober Dérian, a co-experimenter, loses his head, moulds a neolithic man into a solid cube, creates a woman of spheres, stretches a cat out into a cylinder, and paints it red and yellow!

Maître Matisse, if I understand him, which, with my imperfect facility with French, and my slighter knowledge of art, I am afraid I didn't, quite, stands primarily for the solid existence of

La Femme.

things. He paints weight, volume, roundness, color and all the intrinsic physical attributes of the thing itself, and then imbues the whole with sentiment. Oh, yes, his paintings do have life! One can't deny that. They are not merely models posed against a background, like thousands of canvases in the Salons, they are human beings with souls. You turn from his pictures, which have so shockingly defied you, and you demand of other artists at least as much vitality and originality—and you don't find it! He paints with emotion, and inspires you with it. But, alas! when he paints his wife with a broad stripe of green down her nose, though it startlingly suggests her, it is his punishment to have made her appear so to you always. He teaches

Le Moulin de la Galette.   Czobel.

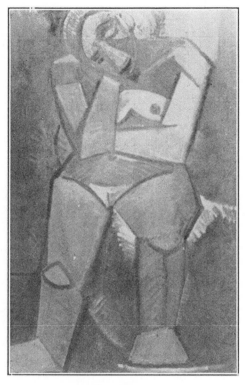

Meditation.

against "mere charm," against accidental aspects of illumination; a return to simplicity, directness, pure color and decorative qualities.

Matisse, being as mild a man as ever tortured the human form or debauched a palette, what of these other Fauves, who had left him out of sight in the runaway from beauty? I picked out seven of the most ferocious and stalked them all over Paris. From Montmartre to Montparnasse I chased, from the stable on the ground floor to the attic on the sixth, through courts, down corridors, up interminable stairs worn to a spoon-like hollowness, in and out of Quartier and Faubourg. And what magnificent chaps I met! All young, all virile, all enthusiastic, all with abundant personality, and all a little mad. But all courteous and cordial, too, patient with my slow-witted attempts to make order out of intellectual chaos. And, after long dialogues on art, on ideals and new orders of beauty, in each studio was a new impossible outrage in color to confute their words. It was amazing in contrast. It was as if some fond mother, after a doting description of her first-born babe, should lift a cloth and show

you to see her in a strange and terrible aspect. He has taught you her body. But, fearful as it is, it is alive—awfully alive!

Painting so, in a burst of emotion, he usually comes to an end of his enthusiasm before he has attained beauty. You point out the fact to him that his painted woman has but three fingers. "Ah, that is true," he says; "but I couldn't put in the other two without throwing the whole out of drawing—it would destroy the composition and the unity of my ideal. Perhaps, some day, I may be able to get what I want of sentiment, of emotional appeal, and, at the same time, draw all five fingers. But the subjective idea is what I am after now; the rest can wait."

Matisse, however, should not be classed amongst the Wild Beasts of this Parisian menagerie. But of him I learned something of the status of the movement, which is a revolt against the subtleties of impressionism. It is a revolt

Portrait d'Homme.

you a diseased, deformed child upon the point of death!

And so, first, to visit Braque, the originator of architectural nudes with square feet, as square as boxes, with right-angled shoulders. Braque's own shoulders were magnificent. He might be a typical American athlete, strong, muscular, handsome, as simple as a child and as modest as a girl of nine. To see him blush when I asked permission to photograph him—and then to turn to the monster on his easel, a female with a balloon-shaped stomach—oh, it was delicious to see big, burly Braque drop his eyes and blush!

It was in a court off the Rue D'Orsel, up I don't know how many flights of stairs. No one could have been kinder than was Braque to the impertinent, ignorant foreigner. He gave me a sketch for his painting entitled "Woman" in the Salon des Indépendants. To portray every physical aspect of such a subject, he said, required three figures, much as the representation of a house requires a plan, an elevation and a section. His chief preoccupation is the search for violence (he spars, too, does Braque), for a primitive emotion. He looks at Nature in order to possess it emotion-

Georges Braque.

ally. In his sketch there is a "harmony of volume," which is a step further than any mere flat decorative effect. It is a spiritual sentiment. Now, gentle reader, look at his drawing! I had to keep my face straight.

"I couldn't portray a woman in all her natural loveliness," says Braque. "I haven't the skill. No one has. I must, therefore, create a new sort of beauty, the beauty that appears to me in terms of volume, of line, of mass, of weight, and through that beauty interpret my subjective impression. Nature is a mere pretext for a decorative composition, plus sentiment. It suggests emotion, and I translate that emotion into art. I want to expose the Absolute, and not merely the factitious woman."

Do you get it? It takes a bit of trying. Let's repeat the dose. Follow me, with Braque leading, to visit Dérain, whom all consider the most intelligent and earnest of the Fauves, an experimenter like Matisse, seeking to find the way for the youngsters to travel.

La Femme.   Braque.

Dérain.

Why, here's Dérain, now, across the street, with his model, a dead-white girl with black hair, dressed in purple and green, Dérain leaves her pouting, and we walk through a strange, crowded bourgeois neighborhood with Dérain, who is a tall, serious-looking young man, with kind brown eyes and a shrill blue tie. We plunge down a narrow lane-like passage, with casts amidst the shrubbery, into a big open studio, with a gallery at the end.

Look at his biggest picture, first, and have your breath taken away! He has been working two years on it. I could do it in two days. So could you, I'm sure. A group of squirmy bathers, some green and some flamingo pink, all, apparently, modeled out of dough, permeate a smoky, vague background. In front sprawls a burly negro, eight feet long. Now notice his African carvings, horrid little black gods and horrid goddesses with conical breasts, deformed, hideous. Then, at Dérain's imitations of them in wood and plaster. Here's the cubical man himself, compressed into geometric proportions, his head between his legs. Beautiful! Dérain's own cat, elongated into a cylinder. Burned and painted wooden cabinets, statues with heads lolling on shoulders, arms anywhere but where they ought to be. A wild place, fit for dreams. But no place for mother.

Dérain, being a quiet man, doesn't care to talk, but he sits obediently for his photograph, holding the cylindrical cat in his arms, as I instruct him. He shows us portfolios of experiments in pure color, geometrical arrangements such as you did yourself in the second grade of the grammar school, tile patterns, sausage rosettes, and such.

But who am I, to laugh at Dérain? Have I not wondered at the Gobelin designs, at the Tibetan goddess of destruction, and sought for occult meanings in the primitive figures of the Mound Builders? Let Dérain talk, if he will be persuaded. What has he learned from the negroes of the Niger? Why does he so affect ugly women?

"Why, what, after all, *is* a pretty woman?" Dérain answers, kindly. "It's

Landscape by Dérain.

a mere subjective impression—what you yourself think of her. That's what I paint, another kind of beauty of my own. There is often more psychic appeal in a so-called ugly woman than there is in a pretty one; and, in my ideal, I reconstruct her to bring that beauty forth in terms of line or volume. A homely woman may please by her grace, by her motion in dancing, for instance. So she may please me by her harmonies of volume. If I paint a girl in the sunlight, it's the sunlight I'm painting, not the real girl; and even for that I should have the sun itself on my palette. I don't care for an accidental effect of light and shade, a thing of 'mere charm.'

"The Japanese see things that way. They don't paint sunlight, they don't cast shadows that perplex one and falsify the true shape of things. The Egyptian figures have simplicity, dignity, directness, unity; they express emotion almost as if by a conventional formula, like writing itself, so direct it is. So I seek a logical method of rendering my idea. These Africans being primitive, uncomplex, uncultured, can express their thought by a direct appeal to the instinct. Their carvings are informed with emotion. So Nature gives me the material with which to construct a world of my own, gov-

Picasso in his Studio.

"La Femme," by Picasso.

erned not by literal limitations, but by instinct and sentiment."

Fine, fine—until one looks again at his paintings to get this appeal to sentiment. Then one is thrown back upon one's reason. Where is that subjective beauty that is his? In the cubical man? In the cylindrical cat? In the doughy bathers? But, as he is only an experimenter, the failure of the experiment does not prove the falsity of the principle involved. So much is already clear, though; these men are not attempting to transcribe the effect Nature makes upon the eye, as do the impressionists. It lies deeper than that.

And now for Picasso, of whom, here and there, one has heard so much. Pi-

Study by Picasso.

casso will not exhibit his paintings. He is too proud, too scornful of the opinions of the *canaille*. But he sells his work, nevertheless. That's the astonishing thing about all of them. Who buys? God knows! Germans, I suppose.

It is the most picturesque spot in Paris, where the wide Rue de Ravignan drops down the hill of Montmartre, breaks into a cascade of stairs and spreads out into a small open space with trees. Picasso comes rolling out of a café, wiping his mouth, clad in a blue American sweater, a cap on his head, a smile on his face.

Picasso is a devil. I use the term in the most complimentary sense, for he's young, fresh, olive-skinned, black eyes and black hair, a Spanish type, with an exhuberant, superfluous ounce of blood in him. I thought of a Yale sophomore who had been out stealing signs, and was on the point of expulsion. When, to this, I add that he is the only one of the crowd with a sense of humor, you will surely fall in love with him at first sight, as I did.

But his studio! If you turn your eyes away from the incredible jumble of junk and dust—from the bottles, rags, paints, palettes, sketches, clothes and food, from the pile of ashes in front of the stove, from the chairs and tables and couches

littered with a pell-mell of rubbish and valuables—they alight upon pictures that raise your hair. Picasso is colossal in his audacity. Picasso is the doubly distilled ultimate. His canvases fairly reek with the insolence of youth; they outrage nature, tradition, decency. They are abominable. You ask him if he uses models, and he turns to you a dancing eye. "Where would I get them?" grins Picasso, as he winks at his ultramarine ogresses.

The terrible pictures loom through the chaos. Monstrous, monolithic women, creatures like Alaskan totem poles, hacked out of solid, brutal colors, frightful, appalling! How little Picasso, with his sense of humor, with his youth and deviltry, seems to glory in his crimes! How he lights up like a torch when he speaks of his work!

I doubt if Picasso ever finishes his paintings. The nightmares are too barbarous to last; to carry out such profanities would be impossible. So we gaze at his pyramidal women, his sub-African caricatures, figures with eyes askew, with contorted legs, and—things unmentionably worse, and patch together whatever idea we may. . . .

Then Picasso, too, talks of values and volumes, of the subjective and of the sentiment of emotion and instinct. *Et pat-à-tie et-pat-à-ta*, as the French say. But he's too fascinating as a man to make one want to take him only as an artist. Is he mad, or the rarest of *blagueurs?* Let others consider his murderous canvases in earnest—I want only to see Picasso grin! Where has he found his ogrillions? Not even in the waters under the earth. . . . Picasso gets drunk on vermillion and cadmium. Absinthe can't tear hard enough to rouse such phantasmagoria! Only the very joy of life could revel in such brutalities.

But, if Picasso is, in life and art, a devil, he at least has brains, and could at one time draw. Not so, I fear, poor Czobel, a young Hungarian, almost a Hun, that is, what's not Vandal in him. He hasn't yet succeeded in getting himself talked about, but he did his worst to achieve infamy at the Salon des Indépendants this year. He even sacrificed himself in the attempt, painting his own

portrait for the enemy to howl at. And
Czobel isn't bad-looking, either. He has
Picasso's verve and courage tamed into
a sort of harmless idiocy. As I waited
for him, at the very end of the Cité Fal-
guière, on the bridge that connects a
row of studios built like primeval lake
dwellings above the level of the gutter,
he appeared, bearing a bunch of hya-
cinths. What a country, where such in-
carnate fiends on canvas appear, flower-
bedecked, to welcome intrusions! I expected at least a vivisectionist, feeding on
fried babies.

Czobel's studio was just behind Picasso's in the race for disorder. But, then,
Czobel has to work and cook and sleep
and hang his clothes and entertain his
friends in his one room. Let's scrape
the yellow ochre off a chair, wipe it with
his shirt, and sit down, while Czobel nervously folds and refolds the black
silk handkerchief about his neck, smil-
ingly explaining that he cannot possibly
explain. He is painfully inarticulate; he
struggles like a dumb beast to express
himself, then boils over into German.

In the center of the room is a revolting
picture of a woman. Did I say woman?

Czobel.

Portrait de Femme.   Czobel.

Let us, in decency, call it a female.
Czobel, no doubt, like Braque, would
prefer to call it Woman. She is naked
and unashamed, if one can judge by her
two large eyes. Others of her ilk lie
about. As a rule, they are aged 89.
They have very purple complexions, enlivened with mustard colored spots and
yolk-yellow throats; they have orange
and blue arms. Sometimes, not often,
they wear bright green skirts.

Czobel himself has a green throat, but
it's only the reflection of his green canvas coat. Back to the plough, poor little
Czobel, say I in English, and Czobel
sweetly smiles.

But there was one picture I really
wanted to buy. It satisfied some shameful, unnamed desire in my breast. It
was called *Le Moulin de la Galette,* and
is supposed (by Czobel) to represent
that lively ball on a gala night. I had
been there myself, but I saw no Aztec

children waltzing; I saw no ladies with eyes like gashes cut with a carving knife. All the figures were outlined with a thick line of color. His men were apparently all brothers—to the ape. But let us not take poor Czobel too seriously. Not even Les Fauves do that.

But Friesz is a man we must take seriously, for Friesz is a serious person, and, if he would, could paint. He is a tall, straight blonde, looking like a musician, with clear-cut features, waving

and out of it another room with many beautiful things. Amongst them, of course,, are African-carved gods and devils of sorts. Since Matisse pointed out their "volumes" all the Fauves have been ransacking the curio shops for negro art. But Friesz has a quaint taste of his own, for, hung across the window panes, like transparencies, are funny old magic-lantern slides, "hand-painted," made in Germany. They might be examples of Matisse's later manner. Friesz

"TRAVAIL A L'AUTOMNE," BY FRIESZ.

hair and an air of gentlemanly prosperity. He is dressed sprucely, except for his rubber overshoes, evidences of the chill, watery Parisian spring. Very gentle, almost winsome. He has huge portfolios of reproductions of Cézanne's pictures, he has many of his own drawings, neatly mounted. He has the work of other painters framed upon his walls. It is evident that he is well-to-do.

His studio is long and wide and high, with ecclesiastical-looking Gothic doors,

is not only exquisitely courteous, he has a mind. He speaks well. Listen. We must not call it any longer a school of Wild Beasts.

"It is a Neo-Classic movement, tending towards the architectural style of Egyptian art, or paralleling it, rather, in development. The modern French impressionism is decadent. In its reaction against the frigidity and insipid arrangements of the Renaissance, it has gone itself to an extreme as bad, and contents itself with fugitive impressions and premature expressions. This newer movement is an attempt to return to simplicity, but not necessarily a return to any primitive art. It is the beginning of a new art. There is a growing feeling for decorative values. It seeks to express this with a certain 'style' of line and volume, with pure color, rather than by tones subtly graded; by contrasts, rather than by modulations; by simple lines and shapes, rather than by complex forms."

We're getting nearer, now, though still the theory is apparently inconsistent with the practice. Friesz is the nearest to Cézanne; he's not yet quite clear of tonality. He has only just begun to go wrong. But let's drop in on Herbin, who paints still life and cafés. He's near at hand.

Barely around the corner, it's true,

Herbin.

Othon Friesz.

but what a contrast to Friesz's elegance and aristocratic surroundings! Herbin lives in a garret higher than Braque's, smaller than Czobel's, but as sweet and neat and clean as an old maid's bedroom. It is, in fact, bedroom as well as studio. A rose-colored hanging conceals his couch. There's but one small window, a skylight in the roof, but the place is pleasant with pots of flowers. A shelf is filled with bright-colored vases. A Chinese slipper holds a bunch of fresh green leaves. But the mark of the Wild Beast is over all the room, for Herbin's own pictures are hung there, and the wall is gaudy with palette scrapings. I back into them and have a green smooch forever afterwards to remember Herbin by.

Herbin is almost sad. Not that, quite, though; not even quite melancholy,

though he is poor and a hermit. He has no friends, and wants none, this small-featured, bright-eyed poet-person, with longish hair and sparse beard, immaculately clean in his dress, scrupulously

"Portrait de Femme" by Herbin.

"Nature Morte" by Herbin.

So, finally, to Metzinger's abode. Now, Metzinger himself, like Friesz, has gone through the impressionistic stage; so he should know about this new idea. It is not as if he never were tame. He once painted that "mere charm," of which, it would seem, we are all overfed. Metzinger once did gorgeous mosaics of pure pigment, each little square of color not quite touching the next, so that an effect of vibrant light should result. He painted exquisite compositions of cloud and cliff and sea; he painted women and made them fair, even as the women upon the boulevards are fair. But now, translated into the idiom of subjective beauty, into this strange Neo-Classic language, those same women, redrawn, appear in stiff, crude, nervous lines in patches of fierce color. Surely, Metzinger should know what such things mean. Picasso never painted a pretty woman, though we have noticed that he likes to associate with them. Czobel sees them through the bars of his cage, and roars out tones of mauve and cinnabar.

polite in his hospitality. It seems unfair to describe him, for his aloofness was noble, yet I must draw my picture of life, as he draws his. He sees nobody, never goes to the cafés, is interested in nothing but himself and his work, and a good book or two. There was a completeness about his attitude that forbade pathos.

Nor can Herbin say much of the "movement," if it is a movement. To his mind, it is individualism, and every man works but for himself. He paints for his own satisfaction, at any rate, and the world may go hang. He paints the roundness and heaviness and curliness and plastic qualities of still life; he paints the thing-in-itself. He does not feel the necessity of drawing every twig on a tree, nor yet to present the mere appeal to the eye. Therefore, draw a curved line connecting all the points on the top of a tree, and you have a simple expression of Nature as it appeals to him.

"I don't distort Nature," he says; "I sacrifice it to a higher form of beauty and of decorative unity." And so we leave Herbin, who should be in the green fields, and not cramped under his scant skylight, and go away not quite knowing whether to envy or pity him.

"Bagneuse" by Metzinger.

Dérain sees them as cones and prisms,
and Braque as if they had been sawn out
of blocks of wood by carpenters' appren-
tices. But Metzinger is more tender
towards the sex. He arranges them as
flowers are arranged on tapestry and wall
paper; he simplifies them to mere patterns, and he carries them gently past the
frontier of Poster Land to the World of
the Ugly so tenderly that they are not
much damaged—only more faint, more
vegetable, more anaemic.

What's Metzinger? A scrupulously
polite, well-dressed gentleman as ever
was, in a scrupulously neat chamber,
with a scrupulously well-ordered mind.
He is as complete as a wax figure, with
long brown eyelashes and a clean-cut
face. He affects no idiosyncracies of
manners or dress. One cannot question
his earnestness and seriousness or sincerity. He is, perhaps, the most articu-

Chabaud and "La Place aux Affiches."

"La Gargotte," by Chabaud.

late of them all. Let us not call him
prim.

"Instead of copying Nature," he says,
"we create a *milieu* of our own, wherein our sentiment can work itself out
through a juxtaposition of colors. It is
hard to explain it, but it may perhaps
be illustrated by analogy with literature
and music. Your own Edgar Poe (he
pronounced it 'Ed Carpoe') did not attempt to reproduce Nature realistically.
Some phase of life suggested an emotion, as that of horror in 'The Fall of
the House of Ushur.' That subjective
idea he translated into art. He made a
composition of it."

"So, music does not attempt to imitate Nature's sounds, but it does interpret and embody emotions awakened by Nature through a convention of its own, in a way to be æsthetically pleasing. In some such way, we, taking our hint from Nature, construct decoratively pleasing harmonies and symphonies of color expression of our sentiment."

I think that there I got nearest to it. Let's regard their art as we regard Debusy's music, and Les Fauves are not so mad, after all; they are only inexperienced with their method. I had proved, at least, that they were not charlatans. They are in earnest and do stand for a serious revolt. Now, a revolt not only starts an action, but a reaction, and these Wild Beasts may yet influence the more conventional schools. Whether right or wrong, there is, moreover, something so virile, so ecstatic about their work that it justifies Nietzsche's definition of an ascendant or renascent art. For it is the product of an overplus of life and energy, not of the degeneracy of stagnant emotions. It is an attempt at expression, rather than satisfaction; it is alive and kicking, not a dead thing,

frozen into a convention. And, as such, it challenges the academicians to show a similar fervor, an equal vitality. It sets one thinking; and anything that does that surely has its place in civilization.

Men must experiment in art and in life. Some may wander east or westward from the beaten track, some reactionaries may even go back southward along the trail of the past. But a few push north, ahead of the rest, blazing out the way of progress for the race. Perhaps these Wild Beasts are really the precursors of a Renaissance, beating down a way for us through the wilderness.

But there's the contrast between their talk and their work! It doesn't quite convince me yet. But, then, I'm not a painter, and perhaps none but a painter can understand. There's my clue! And so, as a last resort, as the best way, too, I've bought a color box and brushes. I am going to try it out practically on canvas. That's the only test. I'm going to be a Wild Beast myself! For, mind you, they do sell their paintings, and I may sell mine. Who knows!

Gelett Burgess.

Andre Dérain.

PARIS SCHOOL DAYS*

How the Student Lives and Works at the Ecole des Beaux Arts

III—The Charrette

GEORGE S. CHAPPELL

PERHAPS THE MOST striking phase in the school life is finishing of a projet, the development, crescendo and culmination of feverish energy known technically as "the charrette." The charrette, in reality, is a harmless and humble push-cart, an errant counter from which the small tradesmen of the quarter sell every conceivable domestic chattel. In this vehicle the student packs his finished drawings for transportation to the judgment seat and its name has grown to cover the final weeks of a school chapter with its many incidents. At no time in his experience will the young American have so ample an opportunity to marvel at the automatic operation of the great school machine which, out of chaos and confusion, whips definite results. The very charrette itself is informal. It has no definite starting point; it steals upon one unawares and its signs augment slowly like snowflakes gradually covering the ground. In the battered atelier, day by day, the working hours are lengthened, the babel of conversation is slightly less animated and, as the light wanes, there is a demand for candles to be stuck in huge iron candle sticks which it is the nouveau's duty to collect from stray corners and to distribute as equitably as possible to young men who cry bitterly that they are working in a profound black! Indeed, the nouveau's existence now becomes one of tribulation. White paper is to be stretched—a perilous operation—and the list of necessaries to be purchased on the morning rounds grows to formidable proportions. Cries

for "Service" resound from every corner, insistent demands from workers who have begun to count the hours which separate them from the "rendu." Later and later burn the candles to the delight of the concierge who furnishes miserable tallow dips at a fifty per cent. profit. She hears the young men stamping on the stairs long after she has crept into her stuffy box for the night. "It is good," she thinks, "I must order some more candles to-morrow."

If the nouveau is industrious and shows interest, he soon finds himself in demand as a "Nigger" to work out some detail for one of the ancients, to cast shadows, "pocher" a plan, ink in some joints or to perform any office within his capabilities. In these opportunities lies much of the most valuable instruction made possible by the flexible mixing-up of students of all grades —a tremendous advantage over the cut-and-dried class system. The beginner is set down among the really strong men of the school who are making the records of the year, potential Grand Prix men; he sees intimately not one projet but thirty and from the constant exchange of criticism, the violent arguments pro and contra every detail of theoretical planning he absorbs knowledge through his very pores. He may not digest it but it is there.

At this juncture it is usual for some constitutionally belated comrade to stroll gravely into the atelier ready to begin his projet, the embodiment of leisure and affluence. It is the Comrade Pigeard, for instance whose eleventh hour appearances always create a pleasant flurry of excitement. He opens the door quietly and stands serious-mouthed,

*This is the third and last article of the series. The first paper appeared in the July issue, 1910, the second in the November issue, 1910.

eyes twinkling on the threshold, survey-
ing the scene of absorption with kindly
interest. The bowed backs of his fellows, the falsetto crooning of Grenier
from his corner, the savage ejaculation
of little Baux whose pencil breaks for
the third time—these are minor elements in the picture. They do not turn
to greet him the comrades; they are

"You have come to 'negrefier' for
me?" asks Grenier excitedly, who
knows not the ways of Pigeard.

"Negrefier for you," repeats the latter
quizzically, "I must have three talented
negres, Moi!" and the atelier roars with
delight. "V'la mon affaire," he continues animately, spreading out a roll of
vague sketches. "There is the parti, my

"IT IS THE COMRADE PIGEARD."

busy, very busy. Pigeard smiles piti-
ingly as he hangs his flat-brimmed top-
hat on a hook.

"Bon jour, Mes amis."

There is a general turning and a bark
of derisive laughter from Baux. "Ah!
te voila, Do-nothing! It is at this hour
that you arrive!—and your projet?
Finished, hein?"

"But you are too early," remonstrates
Jacquard gently, "we have already three
days before the rendu."

friends. A veritable first-mention!
One has but to render it! But where
are the intelligent negres. A Moi!"
He bursts into song—the final peal from
Faust—

"A moi les nouveaux!
A moi les negresses!

Ohe, la bas. Thou, Bouton-d'or, stick
me a sheet of Whatman; and thou, the
Tour Eiffel there" (this to a lanky
American) "mount this plan to scale

at top speed!" And having thus set the wheels of progress in motion he lights a cigarette and pays visits of inspection to the other boards, whence he returns with a collection of tracings, details of plan or façade which he declares are made expressly for his "affair."

sockets only to be replaced by fresh ones; sleep is snatched by the hour face-downward on a drawing board with strict injunctions to some comrade to be sure to wake the sleeper at five! These are hours of tense nerves and violent reactions, and woe to the unhappy seller of prints or vender of

"SACRED NAME OF A NAME!"

This is the beginning of the end, for you may be sure it is late when the Comrade Pigeard takes up his T-square and triangle. From now until the finish is the real charrette. The evenings know no end. Candles gutter in their

books who happens upon the atelier in the days of its desolation. Vengeance is short and swift and the innocent sport of fate is sent cursing forth, his clothes in shocking disarray, his features artistically decorated. But usually the commercial satelites know their school calendar and avoid the storm centres.

The length of the long room, drawings are piled or propped in every stage of completion, here a finished plan wanting only the borders and title, there a half-finished elevation upon which six hands are trying to work at once. There is no stopping now—tomorrow is the "rendu." Every stool is occupied, every place taken. The coat hooks are lost under a mountain of hats and coats, the air thick with tobacco smoke and humanity. Eleven, twelve, one, two, the rusty voiced clock ticks off the midnight hours and the cool ap-

you have blacked in the windows and made the walls transparent!"

Alas, it is too true! The goggle-eyed nouveau to whom has been entrusted the plan of Pigeard, harried and driven by his remorseless master, has committed the unforgiveable crime. The drawing is ruined, hopelessly irretrievably ruined. But the outburst is over; with prompt decision Pigeard rips the offending sheet from the board and tacks a fresh one in its place. No time for moistening, stretching and drying now; the sun has already reached the second window on the old hotel opposite, where geraniums gleam on the iron

"CHARRETTE!"

proaching dawn of morning; now the jutting chimneys and mansards of neighboring houses stand black against the silver sky. Haggard helpers who have snatched a few hours of sleep arrive in nervous haste and are instantly at work. The nouveaux are despatched for coffee and "crescents," warm from the morning's baking, while the more forward toilers dash to the little kitchen at the corner where they gulp down bowls of onion soup—a marvellous restorative. Suddenly, Pigeard, the luxurious, who has been overseeing his slaves, emits a scream of rage. "Sacred name of a name! Imbecile that you are,

balcony and the gray stone is turned to amber. "There, mon vieux," he pats the distracted nouveau on the shoulder, "we will arrive all the same, like the Pope."

To describe the final hours of the charrette is impossible for one who has been really in one. There is nothing tangible to lay hold of, no time, no space, nothing but a maelstrom of paper, paint, paste and profanity, or the Gallic equivalent for it, which is not profanity but an expression of naive intimacy with all supernatural powers. One fact alone stands out in the hurly-burly; at two o'clock, the iron gates on the quai close with a bang. Everything hangs on that. In the meantime, the drawings must be not only finished but also mounted and tastefully decorated with bands of gray and gold paper.

The lower courtyard of the atelier is a whirlpool of activity. Wild-eyed, the comrades rush to and fro, their hands dripping with hot flour paste. The gray bands, the gold bands, a chassis! Where in the name of the devil's dam are the chassis? And the charrette is there, under the archway. Two minutes before they depart. Charrette! charrette! come on everybody. En voiture! Slam bang; pile them in. Allez, pull, you nouveaux! No, wait, here is another— Pigeard rushes across the court with the redrawn plan, wet and glistening.

"Bring the bands!" he howls—and paper and paste-pot go lumbering after

him between two exhausted comrades who complete their work on various street corners along the route. A cheer bursts from the waiting crowd as the pack swings into view.

"Charrette . . . hurry, you snails. Ah! les sales Laloux."

With a last final crash the wheels strike the curb, the drawings are hauled out by the breathless runners and handed over to the guardians. Pouf! . . . . . c'est fini! another projet over, and Thursday the loge for the next one.

The young American tottering with fatigue climbs to his room to sleep. Ah! such a sleep. His muscles relax in delicious languor, his numbed brain rings with distant echoes. Charrette! Charrette! It is finished, yes—but there is a deep underlying satisfaction in the thought—it is never finished.

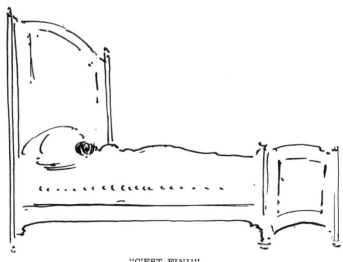

"C'EST FINI!"

The Architect in Recent Fiction

In times past the architect has never apparently been a professional man of sufficiently marked social importance or distinction to figure prominently in the novel. English fiction would be emasculated in case the doctor, the barrister or the clergyman, each clad in the full panoply of his professional position, were omitted. It would even be very much impoverished in case the novelist had been deprived of the wayward and Bohemian artist, as a source of contrast to the respectable business and professional man. But the architect, who is or should be, at once the artist, the professional and the business man, might be cut out of English fiction without the loss of anything of much value. At the moment we cannot recall any character of importance who was described as an architect, except Mr. Pecksniff, and the peculiar qualities for which that gentleman is famous can hardly be attributed to his professional practice or training. The architect appears as the real estate agent might appear—merely as a piece of social or business machinery, which must be lugged in when in the course of imaginary events there is a house to be built. The very combination of artistic, business and professional standards which he represented appeared to rob his personality and his social relations of anything distinctive.

The contemporary English novel is, so far as I know, as little interested in the architect as the classic English novel; but the contemporary American novel has in this respect found new light. There are a number of American novelists to-day who are seeking with varying degrees of success to construct out of their stories a significant comment on American social life. They find more interesting material for fiction in the Boss, the Big Business Man, the Reformer, and the other new Americans than they do in the cleric, the lawyer or the physician; and among the new men which these writers are trying to un-

derstand the architect occupies a respectable, although by no means a dominant, position. At least three novels, all published within the past few years, contain architects among their leading characters; and, what is more to the point, the fact that these characters are supposed to be architects has a decisive bearing either upon the kind of men they are or upon the course of the tale or upon both. This fact is surely a tribute to the position which the American architect has won. He has become a social fact, not quite as conspicuous as the sky-scrapers he sometimes rears, but of such prominence and interest to demand an accounting on the part of our social auditors.

The three recent American novels in which the architect has been recognized as some sort of a social fact, are Edith Wharton's "Sanctuary," Robert Grant's "Unleavened Bread," and Robert Herrick's "The Common Lot." These three writers differ as much as possible in technical methods and in their vision of human nature; but they are all of them seriously interested in modern American city life. Their use of similar material has tempted all of them to seize upon the architect for subject matter, while at the same time their difference in point of view makes the seizures result in very different pictures.

The intrusion of the architect in Mrs. Wharton's pages is, indeed, more or less accidental. Mrs. Wharton's point of view is psychological rather than social; and the appearance of the architect as a conspicuous social fact would not of itself arouse much of her intellectual interest. She does not introduce an architect into her story because he is looming large on the social horizon, but merely as a matter of mechanical convenience. At the same time, the fact that it was mechanically convenient for her to send her heroine's son to the Beaux Arts, and to make him read the Architectural Record (the illustrator has placed a copy of the magazine on his table), testifies to the occurrence of the architect in American life, if to nothing else. It should be added that the situation upon which the culmination of the story turns is suggested by an architectural incident. The professional career and the personal happiness of the young architect both seem to turn upon the winning of a certain competition, and he is sorely tempted to ensure his success by using as his own the superior plans of a dead friend, who had passed these plans on to him to use as he pleased. This situation has little professional interest, and is not intended to have. Mrs. Wharton merely needed to put the architect to a test so as to see whether the vicious temper of his father or the moral influence of his mother would predominate; and the fact that the moral influence of his mother finally conquered, suggests that Mrs. Wharton's imitation of Henry James, of which so much is made, is only superficial. Her longer stories are much more likely to fulfill a moral purpose than are Mr. James'. She shows her fundamental independence by being morally more explicit.

The explicitness of Mrs. Wharton's moral purpose is, however, nothing to that of Mr. Herrick's. I recommend all architects to read his story who feel that the world is too much with them. They will find in it an awful example of the demoralizing effect upon a western architect of worldly ambition. The hero of the "Common Lot," who is also a graduate of the Ecole des Beaux Arts, craves immediate social and pecuniary success, and in order to obtain it, designs anything which will sell. As one of his clients is a dishonest contractor, he finally sells him dishonest drawings, among which are the plans of a hotel which is built in flagrant violation of the law. It is nothing but a fire-trap, and when it burns down in the presence of its designer, the guilty architect is overcome. He sees finally the error of his way, abandons his worldly ambitions, takes a position in a large office, in which his personal work is merged in that of the firm, and so accepts what

Mr. Herrick calls the "Common Lot." The story is conceived and told with sincerity; but I do not find it very interesting or important. It may be considered either as a special instance of moral turpitude, which has little or no bearing upon the conditions under which architects work in this country, or it may be considered as the sort of thing into which a good many architects are tempted and which is in this instance exaggerated for the sake of legitimate effect. In so far as it is merely a special instance, the moral is just the old and respectable one that a man may not with impunity pursue the primrose path, and while I do not dispute that moral, it is a matter for dissertation rather than in clerical homilies than in architectural magazines. On the other hand, in so far as his special instance is supposed to represent prevailing conditions, I do not believe that Mr. Herrick has hit off any very significant truth. A popular architect is doubtless obliged to make a good many compromises with the world; but a high standard of technical integrity has not proved to be incompatible with success in American architecture. The American architect has a right to his place in the world of American life, and will lose much more than he gains by remaining content with the common lot of obscurity. Recognition is the breath of an artist's life. A moral martyr may look for his reward in the approval of the Higher Powers; but the artist who has produced no effect upon his fellow men is a barren artist. And the architect is in this respect a thorough artist. Good American architecture must bring reputation and reward to its makers, or else the American buildings as well as American architects will belong to the "Common Lot."

The architect in Mr. Robert Grant's "Unleavened Bread" is a much more modern and interesting instance. He had, indeed, his troubles with the world, as represented by rich, importunate and ignorant clients, but his worst troubles issue from a troublesome wife. He did not marry a moral paragon, as did Mr. Herrick's hero, but a lady who embodies in a spicy form the old American spirit. Selma believes with all her insistent soul that in a democracy the only qualifications which a specialist needs for his special tasks are untutored enthusiasm, common sense, and a keen eye for the main chance. She stands for the obvious, the practical, the regular and the remunerative thing. The easy critical and personal banter in which her husband's associates pass their hours of social leisure, strikes her earnest intelligence as frivolous; and when her husband throws up a lucrative job because the wife of a client imposes impossible conditions, she stamps him as a weak and ineffective man. It is the old mid-century American point of view of immediate practical achievement at any cost reappearing at a time, when the conditions which gave it vitality and propriety no longer exist. At the same time the reincarnation of this point of view in the jealous and narrow soul of a mercenary and ambitious woman gives the social lesson an individual rendering which makes it vivid without any loss of general significance. Selma White is a very disagreeable but a very convincing character, and she represents the tradition which is the worst enemy of American architecture in American life —the tradition which resents exclusive technical standards and refuses to trust the men who by their thorough training have earned the right authoritatively to represent such standards. It is this tradition which makes so many Americans consider an architect as merely an agent whose business it is to carry out their ignorant ideas, and it is this tradition which gives virtue to the words of a man like Joe Cannon, when he vituperates against the insolent self-assertion of trained architects. It is very much alive to-day, and it was a touch of rare insight on the part of Mr. Grant to individualize it in a form which betrays its real contemporary significance. At the same time, I have some sympathy with Selma White in her attitude towards her architect of a husband. She felt the lack in him of the impulse derived from a well-domesticated tradition which would free his hands and make him build better than he knew, and the lack, which she felt and for which she condemned him, amounted to a genuine and a serious deficiency. Of course, it was not his fault, poor man. A man can acquire training and experience; but a tradition, like a gift, must be given. At the end of another thirty years, perhaps, the American architects will have a sound and popular local tradition given to them by the generation of practitioners who are now struggling along without it.

Herbert Croly.

ARCHITECTURAL RECORD

BIBLIOGRAPHY: July 1891 - September 1914

Articles in bold are reproduced in this collection.

SUBJECT/ARTICLE TITLE	Author	Volume	No.	Month	Year	Pages
ARCHITECTS						
A Conversation with Henry Janeway Hardenbergh	**Sadakichi Hartmann**	**Vol. XIX**	**No. 4**	**May**	**1906**	**pp. 377-380.**
A Pioneer in Apartment House Design: P. G. Hubert	C. Matlack Price	Vol. XXXV	No. 1	July	1914	pp. 74-76.
A. J. Bodker, Architect	C. Matlack Price	Vol. XXXIII	No. 5	May	1913	pp. 381-423.
Alexander C. Eschweiler, Architect	Samuel Ilsley	Vol. XVII	No. 3	March	1905	pp. 209-230.
Baldassare Peruzzi, Architect	M. Stapley	Vol. XXXI	No. 3	March	1912	pp. 226-242.
Barney and Chapman, Architects	Montgomery Schuyler	Vol. XVI.	No. 3	September	1904	pp. 203-296.
Cady, Berg & See, Architects	Montgomery Schuyler	Vol. VI	No. 4	Apr.-June	1897	pp. 517-553.
Carrère and Hastings, Architects		Vol. XXVII	No. 1	January	1910	pp. 1-120.
Charles A. Platt, Architect	Herbert Croly	Vol. XV	No. 3	March	1904	pp. 181-244.
Clinton and Russell, Architects	Russell Sturgis	Vol. VII	No. 2	Oct.-Dec.	1897	pp. 1-61.
Cope and Stewardson, Architects	Ralph Adams Cram	Vol. XVI	No. 5	November	1904	pp. 407-438.
Daniel H. Burnham, Architect		Vol. XXXII	No. 2	August	1912	pp. 175-186.
Donn and Deming, Architects	Leila Mechlin	Vol. XIX	No. 4	April	1906	pp. 245-258.
Dr. William Thornton, Architect	Glenn Brown	Vol. VI	No. 1	July-Sept.	1896	pp. 53-70.
Echo from Evelyn's Diary	William H. Goodyear	Vol. VII	No. 2	Oct.-Dec.	1897	pp. 180-213.
Edgar A. Mathews, Architect	Herbert Croly	Vol. XX	No. 1	July	1906	pp. 47-62.
Ernest Flagg, Architect	H. W. Desmon	Vol. XI	No. 4	April	1902	pp.1-104-
Frank Lloyd Wright	Montgomery Schuyler	Vol. XXXI	No. 4	April	1912	pp. 427-444.
Frank Llyod Wright and his Influence		Vol. XVIII	No. 1	July	1905	pp. 61-66.
Frank Miles Day & Brother, Architects	Ralph Adams Cram	Vol. XV	No. 5	May	1904	pp. 397-421.
Frost and Granger, Architects	H. W. Desmond	Vol. XVIII	No. 2	August	1905	pp. 115-145.
George Edward Harding & Gooch, Architects		Vol. VII	No. 1	July-Sept.	1897	pp. 104-117.
Gram, Goodhue and Ferguson, Architects	Montgomery Schuyler	Vol. XXIX	No. 1	January	1911	pp. 1-112.
Greene and Greene, Architects	A. C. David	Vol. XX	No. 4	October	1906	pp. 306-315.
Henry Janeway Hardenbergh, Architect	Montgomery Schuyler	Vol. VI	No. 3	Jan.-Mar.	1897	pp. 335-375.
Henry Shaw, Architect	C. Matlack Price	Vol. XXXIII	No. 4	April	1913	pp. 285-331.
Herts and Tallant, Architects	Abbot Halstead Moore	Vol. XV	No. 1	January	1904	pp. 55-91.
Holabird & Roche, Architects	Franz Winkler	Vol. XXXI	No. 4	April	1912	pp. 313-388.
Horace Trumbauer, Architect		Vol. XV	No. 2	February	1904	pp. 93-121.
Howard Shaw, Architect	Herbert Croly	Vol. XXII	No. 6	December	1907	pp.421-454.
Hunt and Grey, Architects	Herbert Croly	Vol. XX	No. 4	October	1906	pp. 281-295.
Intimate Letters of Stanford White		Vol. XXX	No. 2	August	1911	pp. 107-116.
Intimate Letters of Stanford White, Part II		Vol. XXX	No. 3	September	1911	pp. 283-298.
Intimate Letters of Stanford White, Part III		**Vol. XXX**	**No. 4**	**October**	**1911**	**pp. 399-406.**
J. Milton Dyer, Architect		Vol. XX	No. 5	November	1906	pp. 385-403.
James Hoban--First U.S. Government Architect	Frederick D. Owen	Vol. XI	No. 2	October	1901	pp. 581-589.
John Russel Pope, Architect	Herbert Croly	Vol. XXIX	No. 6	June	1911	pp. 441-511.
Joseph Twyman, Architect	Frederic E. Dewhurst	Vol. XVIII	No. 6	December	1905	pp. 453-459.
Kilham and Hopkins, Architects	Herbery Croly	Vol. XXXI	No. 2	February	1912	pp. 97-128.
Leopold Eidlitz, Architect	Montgomery Schuyler	Vol. XXIV	No. 3	September	1908	pp. 163-179.
Leopold Eidlitz, Architect, Part II	Montgomery Schuyler	Vol. XXIV	No. 4	October	1908	pp. 277-292.
Leopold Eidlitz, Architect, Part III	Montgomery Schuyler	Vol. XXIV	No. 5	November	1908	pp. 364-378.
Lewis P. Hobart, Architect		Vol. XXVI	No. 4	October	1910	pp. 275-295.
Louis Christian Mullgardt, Architect		Vol. XXX	No. 2	August	1911	pp. 117-136.
M. J. A. Bouvard, Architect	René de Cuers	Vol. X	No. 3	February	1901	pp. 290-312.
M. Nénot, Architect	L. Augé de Lassus	Vol. XII	No. 3	August	1902	pp. 245-269.
McKim, Mead and White, Architects	Desmond and Croly	Vol. XX	No. 3	September	1906	pp. 1-246.

N. LeBrun and Sons, Architects	Montgomery Schuyler	Vol. XXVII	No. 5	May	1910	pp. 364-382.
New Light on Michelangelo	Kenyon Cox	Vol. XIV	No. 5	November	1903	pp. 380-391.
Palladio and his Work	Alfredo Melani	Vol. VII	No. 3	Jan.-Mar.	1898	pp. 241-256.
Palladio and his Work	Alfredo Melani	Vol. VIII	No. 3	Jan.-Mar.	1899	pp. 332-345.
Parker, Thomas and Rice, Architects	Croly and Price	Vol. XXXIV	No. 2	August	1913	pp. 97-184.
Pond and Pond, Architects	Irving K. Pond	Vol. XVIII	No. 2	August	1905	pp. 147-160.
R. H. Robertson, Architect	Montgomery Schuyler	Vol. VI	No. 2	Oct.-Dec.	1896	pp. 184-219.
Richard Morris Hunt	Montgomery Schuyler	Vol. V	No. 2	Oct.-Dec.	1895	pp. 1-180
Rudolph Zahn, Architect	A. C. David	Vol. XXVII	No. 4	April	1910	pp. 299-310.
Rutan and Russell, Architects	Barr Ferree	Vol. XVI.	No. 2	August	1904	pp. 83-115.
Thomas H. Mawson's Civic Architecture	Charles Mulford Robinson	Vol. XXX	No. 5	November	1911	pp. 495-505.
Thomas Jefferson, Architect	M. Stapley	Vol. XXIX	No. 2	February	1911	pp. 178-185.
Walker and Gillette	Alwyn T. Covell	Vol. XXXV	No. 4	April	1914	pp. 277-355.
William Appleton Potter, Architect	Montgomery Schuyler	Vol. XXVI	No. 3	September	1909	pp. 176-196.
William Strickland, Architect	E. Leslie Gilliams	Vol. XXIII	No. 2	February	1908	pp. 123-135.
Willis Polk, Architect	C. Matlack Price	Vol. XXXIV	No. 6	December	1913	pp. 566-583.
Wilson Eyre, Architect	Julian Millard	Vol. XIV	No. 4	October	1903	pp. 279-325.

ALLIED ARTS

A Lost Art Revived--Fresco Buono	M. F. Friederang	Vol. XXXII	No. 6	December	1912	pp. 552-564.
A. A. Weinman	Charles H. Dorr	Vol. XXXIII	No. 6	June	1913	pp. 518-532.
Antique Furniture	K. Warren Clouston	Vol. VIII	No. 2	Oct.-Dec.	1898	pp. 150-167.
Antique Furniture in the Modern House	Alvan C. Nye	Vol. VII	No. 2	Oct.-Dec.	1897	pp. 156-163.
Appreciation of Sculpture	Willaim Walton	Vol. XVII	No. 3	March	1905	pp. 189-200.
Architect in Recent Fiction	**Herbert Croly**	**Vol. XVII**	**No. 2**	**February**	**1905**	**pp. 137-139.**
Architectural Faience	Sturgis Laurence	Vol. XXI	No. 7	January	1907	pp. 62-72.
Architectural Tapestries	George Leland Hunter	Vol. XXXIII	No. 1	January	1913	pp. 1-13.
Architectural Tapestries, Part II	George Leland Hunter	Vol. XXXIII	No. 2	February	1913	pp. 137-151.
Architectural Treatment of Lighting Fixtures	David Crownfield	Vol. XXII	No. 6	December	1907	pp. 476-489.
Arnold Böcklin as a Sculptor of the Grotesque	Herbert Lespinasse	Vol. XIII	No. 2	February	1903	pp. 169-174.
Art Nouveau in Jewelry	Jean Schopfer	Vol. XII	No. 1	May	1902	pp. 67-70.
Art of Stained Glass Windows	Charles H. Dorr	Vol. XXXV	No. 2	February	1914	pp. 162-169.
Art of Whistler	Kenyon Cox	Vol. XV	No. 5	May	1904	pp. 467-484.
Augustus Lukeman, Sculptor	B. MacDonald Furniss	Vol. XXXV	No. 5	May	1914	pp. 414-424.
Bela L. Pratt, Sculptor	Charles Henry Dorr	Vol. XXXV	No. 6	June	1914	pp. 508-518.
Book-Plate and the Architect	Sheldon Cheney	Vol. XXXII	No. 2	August	1912	pp. 141-152.
Ceramics in Architecture	Jean Schopfer	Vol. XI	No. 3	January	1902	pp. 1-7.
Charles Keck, Sculptor	Arthur C. Byne	Vol. XXXII	No. 2	August	1912	pp. 121-128.
Chippendale Furniture	Alvan C. Nye	Vol. VI	No. 4	Apr.-June	1897	pp. 429-438.
Colonial Art and Modern Pianos	J. Burr Tiffany	Vol. IX	No. 3	Jan.-Mar.	1900	pp. 268-272.
Considerations in Painting	Russell Sturgis	Vol. VI	No. 2	Oct.-Dec.	1896	pp. 220-232.
Contemporary French Sculpture	Paul Vitry	Vol. XII	No. 5	October	1902	pp. 472-490.
Cosmati Mosaic	Caryl Coleman	Vol. XII	No. 2	June	1902	pp. 203-220.
Decorative Painting in Mantua, Italy	Alfredo Melani	Vol. XVIII	No. 3	September	1905	pp. 202-210.
Denys Puech--French Scultpure of Today	Frederick Lees	Vol. XII	No. 6	November	1902	pp. 641-648.
Dr. William Rimmer	Edward R. Smith	Vol. XXI	No. 3	March	1907	pp. 187-204.
Dwight H. Perkins, Architect	Peter B. Wight	Vol. XXVII	No. 6	June	1910	pp. 495-512.
English Decoration and Walter Crane	Russell Sturgis	Vol. XII	No. 7	December	1902	pp. 684-691.
European Versus American Color Windows	Joseph Lauber	Vol. XXXI	No. 2	February	1912	pp. 139-152.
Evolution of Architectural Ornament	G. A. T. Middleton	Vol. XXVII	No. 3	March	1910	pp. 258-270.
Evolution of Architectural Ornament, Part II	G. A. T. Middleton	Vol. XXVII	No. 4	April	1910	pp. 321-333.
Evolution of Architectural Ornament, Part III	G. A. T. Middleton	Vol. XXVII	No. 5	May	1910	pp. 415-432.
Evolution of Architectural Ornament, Part IV	G. A. T. Middleton	Vol. XXVII	No. 6	June	1910	pp. 483-494.
Evolution of Architectural Ornament, Part V	G. A. T. Middleton	Vol. XXVIII	No. 1	July	1910	pp. 25-36.
Evolution of Architectural Ornament, Part VI	G. A. T. Middleton	Vol. XXVIII	No. 3	September	1910	pp. 213-226.
Evolution of Architectural Ornament, Part VII	G. A. T. Middleton	Vol. XXVIII	No. 5	November	1910	pp. 365-378.

Evolution of Architectural Ornament, Part VIII	G. A. T. Middleton	Vol. XXVIII	No. 6	September	1910	pp. 443-454.
Evolution of Architectural Ornament, Part IX	G. A. T. Middleton	Vol. XXIX	No. 3	March	1911	pp. 265-276.
Felix Peano--Sculptor as His Own Architect and Builder	Peter B. Wright	Vol. XXVI	No. 1	July	1909	pp. 33-37.
Flemish Painter's Art Treasures	A. J. Wauters	Vol. VI	No. 4	Apr.-June	1897.	pp. 439-445.
Formal and Natural Style of Gardening	George F. Pentecost, Jr.	Vol. XII	No. 2	June	1902	pp. 175-194.
French Sculpture in Wax	Frederic Lees	Vol. XII	No. 4	September	1902	pp. 421-429.
Furniture Exhibition in Paris	A. Hutton	Vol. XIV	No. 2	August	1903	pp. 126-134.
Furniture from the Architectural Viewpoint	Eberlein & McClure	Vol. XXXV	No. 1	January	1914	pp. 33-48.
Furniture from the Architectural Viewpoint, Part II	Ebrlein & McClure	Vol. XXXV	No. 3	March	1914	pp. 202-220.
Furniture form the Architectural Point of View, Part	Eberlein & McClure	Vol. XXXV	No. 5	May	1914	pp. 435-442.
Gargoyles, Grotesques and Chimeras	G. Leland Hunter	Vol. XXXV	No. 2	February	1914	pp. 132-139.
Gargoyles--Old and New	Charles de Kay	Vol. XIX	No. 5	June	1906	pp. 419-424.
Henry Hering, Sculptor	Guy Fène du Bois	Vol. XXXII	No. 6	December	1912	pp. 510-529.
Household Furnishings	Helen Campbell	Vol. VI	No. 2	Oct.-Dec.	1896	pp. 97-104.
Influence of the Early Renaissance on Painting	Banister F. Fletcher	Vol. IV	No. 2	Oct.-Dec.	1894	pp. 157-190.
Jesse Tree	Caryl Coleman	Vol. XXI	No. 5	May	1907	pp. 360370.
Johannes S. Gelert, Sculptor	Charles Henry Dorr	Vol. XXXIII	No. 4	April	1913	pp. 332-338.
John Rogers, Sculptor	Charles Henry Israels	Vol. XVI	No. 5	November	1904	pp. 483-487.
Loïe Fuller as seen by Pierre Roche	J. M. P. Honson	Vol. XIII	No. 1	January	1903	pp. 34-41.
Loïe Fuller in French Sculpture	Claude Anet	Vol. XIII	No. 3	March	1903	pp. 270-278.
Lorado Taft, Sculptor	Robert H. Moulton	Vol. XXXV	No. 1	July	1914	pp. 12-24.
Lorado Taft's Symposium of Adornment with Sculpture	Peter B. Wight	Vol. XXVIII	No. 5	Novemer	1910	pp. 335- 349.
Lorenzo Di Mariano	Alfred H. Gumaer	Vol. XXIII	No. 5	May	1908	pp. 397-408.
M. Emile Wauters as a Painter of Architecture	G. Sérae	Vol. X	No. 2	October	1900	pp. 203-211.
M. Van der Traeten, a Belgian Sculptor	Frederic Lees	Vol. XIII	No. 2	February	1903	pp. 134-143.
Memory of Saint-Gaudens	Kenyon Cox	Vol. XXII	No. 4	October	1907	pp. 249-251.
Modern Decoration	Jean Schopfer	Vol. VI	No. 3	Jan.-Mar.	1897	pp. 243-255.
Modern Mosaics	Isabella de Barbieri	Vol. III	No.1	Jan.-Mar.	1894	pp. 314-324.
Modern Style of Jewelry	Pierre Calmettes	Vol. XiV.	No. 3	September	1903	pp. 205-218.
Mural Paintings and a Word to Architects	Frank Fowler	Vol. XI	No. 1	July	1901	pp. 510-524.
Old Chinese Rugs	Charles de Kay	Vol. XXV	No. 3	March	1909	pp. 203-210.
Portrait Statuettes--a New Fashion in French Sculpture	Frederic Lees	Vol. XIII	No. 3	March	1903	pp. 221-233.
Rationalism in Art	W. Francklyn Paris	Vol. XXXII	No. 1	July	1912	pp. 47-52.
Rembrandt	Kenyon Cox	Vol. XX	No. 6	December	1906	pp. 439-463.
Rockwood Pottery	A. O. Elzner	Vol. XVII	No. 4	April	1905	pp. 295-304.
Rodin	Kenyon Cox	Vol. XVIII	No. 5	November	1905	pp. 327-346.
Roman Art,	Jean Schopfer	Vol. XIX	No. 5	June	1906	pp. 443-458.
Roman Art, Part iI	Jean Schopfer	Vol. XX	No. 1	July	1906	pp. 33-45.
Russell Sturgis' Last Book--Review	John La Forge	Vol. XIX	No. 3	March	1906	pp. 199-206.
Sea of Glass	Caryl Coleman	Vol II	No. 3	Jan.-Mar.	1893	pp. 265-285
Sgraffito--an Ancient Art Revived	Maximilian F. Friederang	Vol. XXXIII	No. 1	January	1913	pp. 22-33.
Some American-Made Fabrics	Margaret Greenleaf	Vol. XVII	No. 6	June	1905	pp. 499-507.
Some Furniture of Other Days	Charles de Kay	Vol. XXIV	No. 3	September	1908	pp. 218-230.
Some House By Howard Shaw	A. C. David	Vol. XIX	No. 2	February	1906	pp. 104-122.
Stage Sets for Romeo and Juliet	Frank Chouteau Brown	Vol. XVIII	No. 3	September	1905	pp. 175-192.
Stained Glass in France	René de Cuers	Vol. IX	No. 2	Oct.-Dec.	1899	pp. 115-141.
Stained Glass in Private Houses	Harry Eldredge Goodhue	Vol. XVIII	No. 5	November	1905	pp. 347-354.
Tapestries and the Hotel	G. Leland Hunter	Vol. XXXV	No. 3	March	1914	pp. 246-261.
Textile Origins in Architecture	Charles DeKay	Vol. XXXIV	No. 5	November	1913	pp. 458-466.
Textile Origins in Architecture,Part II	Charles DeKay	Vol. XXXV	No. 1	January	1914	pp. 70-79.
The Second Spring	Caryl Coleman	Vol. II	No. 4	Apr.-June	1893	pp. 473-492
Vitrail--a Treatise on Stained Glass	Violet-le-Duc	Vol. XXXII	No. 6	December	1912	pp. 496-506.
Wild Men of Paris	**Gelett Burgess**	**Vol. XXVII**	**No. 5**	**May**	**1910**	pp. 400-414.
William B. Van Ingen, Mural Painter	Charles de Kay	Vol. XIII	No. 4	April	1903	pp. 323-334.
Windows of Gouda	Caryl Coleman	Vol. X	No. 3	February	1901	pp. 225-237.

BUILDINGS

"Arbor Lodge"--Morton Residence, Nebraska		Vol. XIX	No. 1	January	1906	pp. 37-47.
"Gordon Hall"--Hanna Residence, Cleveland	Charles Bohassek	Vol. XV	No. 1	January	1904	pp. 19-38
"Haymount"--a Westchester Residence	Harriet Sisson Gillespie	Vol. XXXV	No. 1	July	1914	pp. 49-62.
"Hillair"--Thebaud Residence	William Heming	Vol. XVI	No. 1	July	1904	pp. 1-12.
"Killenworth"--Pratt Residence,	Harriet T. Bottomley	Vol. XXXV	No. 6	June	1914	pp. 558-573.
"Loramoor"--Moore Residence	Charles Bohasseck	Vol. XV	No. 3	March	1904	pp. 261-274.
"Wychwood"--Hutchinson Residence, Wisconsin	John Baptiste Fischer	Vol. XVII	No. 2	February	1905	pp. 127-136.
Aeolian Hall	C. Matlack Price	Vol. XXXII	No. 6	December	1912	pp. 530-551.
An Amusing New York Street Front--West 79th St., NYC		Vol. XIII	No. 1	January	1903	pp. 49-54.
Architecture at the South Kennsington Museum	G. A. T. Middleton	Vol. VIII	No. 4	Apr.-June	1899	pp. 389-406.
Ark of S. Dominic	Caryl Coleman	Vol. XIV	No. 4	October	1903	pp. 255-261.
Arnold Residence, Albany, NY	A. C. David	Vol. XVII	No. 4	April	1905	pp. 305-317.
Avery Library	C. Matlack Price	Vol. XXXIII	No. 6	June	1913	pp. 534-549.
Basilica of Santa Maria Maggiore	William P. P. Longfellow	Vol. II	No.1	July-Sept.	1892	pp. 65-78.
Blair Building, New York City	H. W. Desmond	Vol. XV	No. 3	March	1904	pp. 275-284
Blair Building--a Beaux Arts Skyscraper	H. W. Desmond	Vol. XIV.	No. 6	December	1903	pp. 436-443.
Blicking Hall--A Jacobean Manor House	Russell Sturgis	Vol. XI	No. 2	October	1901	pp. 666-678.
Boston Public Library Addition	Russell Sturgis	Vol. XV	No. 5	May	1904	pp. 423-430.
Brooklyn Plaza and Central Library	H. W. Frohne	Vol. XXIII	No. 2	February	1908	pp. 97-110.
Brown and Wesleyan Univ.; Bowdoin and Trinity Colleges	Montgomery Schuyler	Vol. XXIX	No. 2	February	1911	pp. 145-166.
Building the new Campanile in the Piazza San Marco	A. S. Atkinson	Vol. XIX	No. 3	March	1906	pp. 223-225.
Cabot Residence, Massachusetts	A. C. David	Vol. XVIII	No. 4	October	1905	pp. 263-272.
Campanile of St. Mark's at Venice	**Pietro Saccardo**	**Vol. XII**	**No. 7**	**December**	**1902**	**pp. 723-725.**
Cathedral Church of Liverpool	Wilberforce Horsfield	Vol. XXXI	No. 1	January	1912	pp. 27-44.
Cathedral of the Incarnation		Vol. XXXIII	No. 6	June	1913	pp. 477-491.
Cathedral of Troja	William H. Goodyear	Vol. VIII	No. 3	Jan.-Mar.	1899	pp. 279-296.
Cathedral of Westminster	F. Herbert Mansford	Vol. XXII	No. 5	November	1907	pp. 343-348.
Ceilings in the Galleria Degli Uffizi, Florence	Alfredi Melani	Vol. XXIII	No. 1	January	1908	pp. 39-46.
Chantilly Castle	Jean Schopfer	Vol. XVI	No. 6	December	1904	pp. 499-530.
Chapel of the Intercession	C. Matlack Price	Vol. XXXV	No. 6	June	1914	pp. 526-543.
Chapel of the Queen of All Saints		Vol. XXXV	No. 4	April	1914	pp. 356-374.
Chateau de Champs--Restoration of a French Chateau	André Destailleur	Vol. XIV	No. 1	July	1903	pp. 1-12.
Chateau de Vaux-le-Viscomte	Frederic Lees	Vol. XVIII	No. 6	December	1905	pp. 407-433.
Chateau of Langeais	Frederick Lees	Vol. XVII	No. 5	May	1905	pp. 353-382.
Château Schwab		Vol. XXI	No. 8	February	1907	pp.96-102.
Chateaux of Rochecotte and Reaux	Frederic Lees	Vol. XXIV	No. 5	November	1908	pp. 339-349.
Chicago Auditorium	Dankmar Adler	Vol. I	No. 4	Apr.-June	1892	pp. 415-434.
Chicago Railroad Terminal	Alfred Hoyt Granger	Vol. XXIV	No. 6	December	1908	pp. 401-408.
Church of Our Lady of Lourdes		Vol. XXI	No. 4	April	1907	pp. 295-300.
Col. John Jacob Astor Residence		Vol. XXVII	No. 6	June	1910	pp. 471-482.
College of the City of New York		Vol. XXI	No. 3	March	1907	pp 165-185.
Copenhagen City Hall	Olof Z. Cervin	Vol. XVIII	No. 4	October	1905	pp. 283-299.
Curtis Publishing Company	Scuyler and Nolan	Vol. XXXI	No. 3	March	1912	pp. 275-308.
Curves in the Temple at Cori	William H. Goodyear	Vol. XXI	No. 6	June	1907	pp. 399-419.
Custom House in New York	Montgomery Schuyler	Vol. XX	No. 1	July	1906	pp. 1-14.
Dartmouth College	Montgomery Schuyler	Vol. XXVIII	No. 6	December	1910	pp. 425-442.
Davizzi-Davanzati Palace	Walter Bombe	Vol. XXXI	No. 6	June	1912	pp. 575-590.
Deacon Residence, New York		Vol. XVIII	No. 4	October	1905	pp. 274-282.
Dufayel's--The "Big Store" of Paris	Pierre Calmettes	Vol. XII	No. 4	September	1902	pp. 431-444.
Dülfer's Design for the Proposed Berlin Opera House	Robert Grimshaw	Vol. XXXV	No. 5	May	1914	pp. 450-454.
Ernest Flagg Residence		Vol. XXII	No. 2	September	1907	pp. 177-194.
First Baptist Church, Pittsburgh	Arthur C. Byne	Vol. XXXII	No. 3	September	1912	pp. 193-208.
First Church of the Christian Scientists	Washburn and Cottrell	Vol. XV	No. 2	February	1904	pp. 159-171.
First National Bank of Chicago	A. C. David	Vol. XIX	No. 1	January	1906	pp. 49-58.
Fox Residence, Pennsylvania	H. W. Frohne	Vol. XX	No. 4	October	1906	pp. 316-322.
Fraternity House, Cornell University		Vol. XVIII	No. 3	September	1905	pp. 211-216.

French Garden in the Spanish Mountains	Mildred Stapley	Vol. XXXII	No. 2	August	1912	pp. 97-108.
Galliera Museum--the Newest Art Museum in Paris	Charles Fromentin	Vol. XIII	No. 1	January	1903	pp. 1-18.
Gare de Lyon, Paris		Vol. XII	No. 5	October	1902	pp. 492-497.
Garver Residence	C. Matlack Price	Vol. XXXV	No. 3	March	1914	pp. 181-201.
Gilbert Residence	Shiras Campbell	Vol. XXIX	No. 4	April	1911	pp. 289- 300.
Grammatan Court	Kenneth G. How	Vol. XXXV	No. 2	February	1914	pp. 140-150.
Great Buildings of the World--The Erechtheum	Edwards Gales	Vol. XII	No. 5	October	1902	pp. 498-513.
Griswold Hotel		Vol. XIX	No. 4	May	1906	pp. 345-360.
H. C. Mercer Residence	**W. T. Taylor**	**Vol. XXXIII**	**No. 3**	**March**	**1913**	**pp. 242-254.**
Hall of Records, NYC	Montgomery Schuyler	Vol. XVII	No. 5	May	1905	pp. 383-387.
Hallensee--Pleasure Resort Near Berlin		Vol. XVIII	No. 6	December	1905	pp. 447-452.
Harmonie Club-House	Herbert Croly	Vol. XIX	No. 4	April	1906	pp. 237-243.
Harvard Univeristy	Montgomery Schuyler	Vol. XXVI	No. 4	October	1910	pp. 243-269.
Hoff Residence, Paris	Miss F. Riley	Vol. XIII	No. 2	February	1903	pp. 97-118.
Horizontal Curves in Columbia University	William H. Goodyear	Vol. IX	No. 1	July-Sept.	1899	pp. 82-93.
Hotel Belmont	H. W. Frohne	Vol. XX	No. 1	July	1906	pp. 63-69.
Hotel Biltmore	Montgomery Schuyler	Vol. XXXV	No. 3	March	1914	pp. 222-245
Hotel de Ville, Paris	L. D'Arcy Morrell	Vol. XV	No. 3	March	1904	pp. 245-259.
Hotel McAlpin	David Tarn	Vol. XXXIII	No. 3	March	1913	pp. 231-241.
Humbert de Romans Building--Art Nouveau in Paris	Fernand Mazade	Vol. XII	No. 1	May	1902	pp. 51-60.
Hutcheson Residence, Rhode Isalnd		Vol. XX	No. 4	October	1906	pp. 269-280.
Idyll of the Renaissance--Villa Farnese, Caprarola	Marie Donegan Walsh	Vol. X	No. 2	October	1900	pp. 113-127.
Importers' and Traders' National Bank	H. W. Frohne	Vol. XXIV	No. 5	November	1908	pp. 387-394.
Indianapolis Court House and Post Office	H. W. Frohne	Vol. XIX	No. 5	June	1906	pp. 437-442.
Ingalls Building--the First Concrete Skyscraper	A. O. Elzner	Vol. XV	No. 6	June	1904	pp. 531-544.
Knapp House--an Architectural Experiment	R. A. C.	Vol. VIII	No.1	July-Sept.	1898	pp. 82-91.
Knickerbocker Hotel	Herbert Croly	Vol. XXI	No. 7	January	1907	pp. 1-17.
Knickerbocker Trust Company Building	Montgomery Schuyler	Vci. XV	No. 5	May	1904	pp. 431-444.
Lady Chapel at St. Patrick's Cathedral	A. H. Gumaer	Vol. XXI	No. 6	June	1907	pp. 420-428.
Lawyers' Club of New York City	G. L. H.	Vol. XXXII	No. 5	November	1912	pp. 393-404.
Leader-News Building	Herbert Croly	Vol. XXXIII	No. 6	June	1913	pp. 501-517.
Leaning Tower of Pisa	William H. Goodyear	Vol. VII	No. 3	Jan.-Mar.	1898	pp. 257-294.
Library of Congress	Russell Sturgis	Vol. VII	No. 3	Jan.-Mar.	1898	pp. 295-332.
Louis Sullivan Residence, Mississippi	Lyndon P. Smith	Vol. XVII	No. 6	June	1905	pp. 471-490.
MacKay Residence, Long Island	Herbert Croly	Vol. XVI	No. 6	December	1904	pp. 531-555.
Madlener Residence, Chicago	Russell Sturgis	Vol. XVII	No. 6	June	1905	pp. 491-498.
Maison François Premier, Paris	Bernard St. Lawrence	Vol. XV	No. 6	June	1904	pp. 488-508.
Marquand House, NYC	Russell Sturgis	Vol. XVIII	No. 3	September	1905	pp. 193-201.
Medicean Tombs	Caryl Coleman	Vol. XIII	No. 3	March	1903	pp. 207-220.
Medinah Temple in Chicago	J. E. Murphy	Vol. XXXIII	No. 4	April	1913	pp. 339-349.
Minnesota State Capitol	Kenyon Cox	Vol. XVIII	No. 2	August	1905	pp. 95-113.
Minnesota State Capitol	Russell Sturgis	Vol. XIX	No. 1	January	1906	pp. 31-36.
Mont Saint Michel	Montgomery Schuyler	Vol. XI	No. 3	January	1902	pp. 9-36.
Mortimer Residence, New York	A. C. David	Vol. XVIII	No. 6	December	1905	pp. 461-470.
Mt. Sinai Hospital	Sturgis and Tozier	Vol. XVIII	No. 5	November	1905	pp. 367-383.
Museum of French Art	W. Francklyn Paris	Vol. XXXI	No. 6	June	1912	pp. 621-628.
National Park Bank, NYC	Montgomery Schuyler	Vol. XVII	No. 4	April	1905	pp. 319-328.
Natural History Museum at Paris	Jean Schopfer	Vol. X	No. 1	July	1900	pp. 55-75.
Nela Park--a new Departure in Big Business	Montgomery Schuyler	Vol. XXXV	No. 6	June	1914	pp. 505-507.
Nela Park--a Novel Industrial Park	Florence Dempsey	Vol. XXXV	No. 6	June	1914	pp. 469-504.
Nevill Holt	Maud Cunard	Vol. VII	No. 2	Oct.-Dec.	1897	pp. 143-155
New Cathedral at Westminster	F. Herbert Mansford	Vol. XII	No. 3	August	1902	pp. 317-337.
New Race Course for Parisians	Jean Schopfer	Vol. XXI	No. 5	May	1907	pp. 353-359.
New Stuyvesant Theater	Arthur C. David	Vol. XXIII	No. 2	February	1908	pp. 223-227.
New York Capitol Building	Cuyler Reynolds	Vol. IX	No. 2	Oct.-Dec.	1899	pp. 142-157.
New York Chamber of Commerce	A. C. David	Vol. XIII	No. 1	January	1903	pp. 55-69.
New York City Colleges	Montgomery Schuyler	Vol. XXVII	No. 6	June	1910	pp. 443-470.
New York City Hall	Montgomery Schuyler	Vol. XXIII	No. 5	May	1908	pp. 387-390.

New York Court House and its Site	Montgomery Schuyler	Vol. XXXVI	No. 1	July	1914	pp. 1-11.
New York Public Library	A. C. David	Vol. XXVIII	No. 3	September	1910	pp. 145-172.
New York Stock Exchange	Percy C. Stuart	Vol. XI	No. 1	July	1901	pp. 526-552.
New York Stock Exchange	Montgomery Schuyler	Vol. XII	No. 4	September	1902	pp. 413-420.
New York Stock Exchange	Russell Sturgis	Vol. XVI	No. 5	November	1904	pp. 464-482.
New York Times Building	Montgomery Schuyler	Vol. XIV	No. 5	November	1903	pp. 329-343.
Newborg Residence, NYC		Vol. XVII	No. 5	May	1905	pp. 401-409.
No. 1 East 75th Street--A Fifth Avenue Mansion		Vol. XXVII	No. 5	May	1910	pp. 383-399.
No. 25 West 67th Street--a Cooperative Studio Building	A. C. David	Vol. XIV	No. 4	October	1903	pp. 233-254.
Ottawa Terminal Station and Hotel		Vol. XXIV	No. 4	October	1908	pp. 293-299.
Palace of Fontainbleau	Russell Sturgis	Vol. X	No. 2	October	1900	pp. 129-142.
Palace of the Popes at Avignon	Frederic Lees	Vol. XXX	No. 6	December	1911	pp. 523-537.
Pan American Union Building and Annex	C. Matlack Price	Vol. XXXIV	No. 5	November	1913	pp. 385-457.
Parmelee Residence	Herbert Croly	Vol. XXXV	No. 2	August	1914	pp. 81-97.
Passing of Madison Square Garden		Vol. XXX	No. 6	December	1911	pp. 513-522.
Paul Revere's Old North Church	Willard French	Vol. XIX	No. 3	March	1906	pp. 215-222.
Pavlist Fathers' Church	Charles H. Dorr	Vol. XXXIII	No. 3	March	1913	pp. 187-203.
Pennsylvania Station		**Vol. XXVII**	**No. 6**	**June**	**1910**	**pp. 518-521.**
People's Savings Bank	Montgomery Schuyler	Vol. XXXI	No. 1	January	1912	pp. 45-56.
Plaza Hotel--Designing a Metropolitan Hotel	H. W. Frohne	Vol. XXII	No. 5	November	1907	pp. 349-364.
Princeton University	Montgomery Schuyler	Vol. XXVII	No. 2	February	1910	pp. 129-160.
Princeton University	C. Matlack Price	Vol. XXXV	No. 1	January	1914	pp. 1-27.
Quai D'Orsay Railroad Terminus, Paris	Jean Schopfer	Vol. XI	No. 2	October	1901	pp. 557-580
Renaissance Château of Eastern France	Frederic Lees	Vol. XXV	No. 3	March	1909	pp. 161-168.
Restoration of the Château de Nantes	Frederic Lees	Vol. XXI	No. 8	February	1907	pp. 103-115.
Roman Forum and Concrete Construction	Alfred Hopkins	Vol. XXV	No. 2	February	1909	pp. 95-102.
Royal Polytchnikum at Berlin and Student Life in Germany	Albert F. M. Lange	Vol. V	No. 1	July-Sept.	1895	pp. 65-75
S. Antonio at Padua	Robert W. Carden	Vol. XVI.	No. 3	September	1904	pp. 186-201.
San Ambrogio, Genoa--A Renaissance Leaning Facade	William H. Goodyear	Vol. XII	No. 6	November	1902	pp. 601-619.
Scared Heart Church at Montmartre	Henry Rauline	Vol. III	No.1	July-Sept.	1893	pp. 3-28.
Schlesinger and Meyer Building	Smith and Desmond	Vol. XVI	No. 1	July	1904	pp. 53-67.
Schoenhofen Brewery	Russell Sturgis	Vol. XVII	No. 3	March	1905	pp.201-207.
Sears Roebuck & Co.--a Great Mercantile Plant, Part II	Nimmons and Fellows	Vol. XIX	No. 5	June	1906	pp. 403-412.
Sears Roebuck & Co.--Building a Great Mercantile Plant	Theodore Starrett	Vol. XIX	No. 4	April	1906	pp. 265-274.
Sixty-Sixth St.reet Studio Building	A. C. David	Vol. XXIV	No. 1	July	1908	pp. 1-18.
Spanish Church in New York City	L. R. McCabe	Vol. XXXIII	No. 1	January	1913	pp. 14-21.
St. Ambrose Chapel, Cathedral of St John the Divine	B. G. Mitchell	Vol. XXXV	No. 2	August	1914	pp. 136-141.
St. Anselm's Church, Mayfair, London	F. Robert Mansford	Vol. XIV	No. 5	November	1903	pp. 360-372.
St. Bartholomew's New Portals	Russell Sturgis	Vol. XV	No. 4	April	1904	pp. 293-311.
St. John's Chapel	Rawson W. Haddon	Vol. XXXV	No. 5	May	1914	pp. 389-404.
St. Mark's at Venice--Architectural Refinements	William H. Goodyear	Vol. XIV	No. 5	November	1903	pp. 345-359.
St. Paul's Chapel	Russell Sturgis	Vol. XXI	No. 8	February	1907	pp. 83-95.
St. Regis Hotel	Arthur C. David	Vol. XV	No. 6	June	1904	**pp. 553-?**
St. Thomas' Church	H. L. Bottomley	Vol. XXXV	No. 2	February	1914	pp. 101-131.
Temple of Karnak	Bayard Taylor	Vol. XXIV	No. 2	August	1908	pp. 129-134.
Temple of the Tokugawa at Nikko	C. T. Matthers	Vol. IV	No. 2	Oct.-Dec.	1894	pp. 191-209.
The "Bauernhof" on the Busch Residence	Ernest C. Klipstein	Vol. XXXV	No. 6	June	1914	pp. 544-557.
The Hermitage--An Interesting Skyscraper	Montgomery Schuyler	Vol. XXII	No. 5	November	1907	pp. 365-368.
The Parthenon	Albert C. Phelps	Vol. XXIV	No. 4	October	1908	pp. 306-308.
Thiers Institute--French Academy for Students	Pierre Calmettes	Vol. XIII	No. 3	March	1903	pp. 248-258.
Thomas Music Hall	Russell Sturgis	Vol. XVI.	No. 2	August	1904	pp. 160-164.
Townsend Residence, Washington, D.C.	Percy C. Stuart	Vol. X	No. 4	April	1901	pp. 425-437.
Two Jacobian Houses		Vol. XXI	No. 7	January	1907	pp. 32-42.
Two Rochester Banks		Vol. XXI	No. 7	January	1907	pp. 18-31.
Union, Hamilton, Hobart, Cornell and Syracuse	Montgomery Schuyler	Vol. XXX	No. 6	December	1911	pp. 549-574.
University Club in Chicago		Vol. XXVI	No. 1	July	1909	pp. 1-23.
University of Chicago	Charles E. Jenkins	Vol. IV	No. 2	Oct.-Dec.	1894	pp. 229-246.
University of Pennsylvania	Montgomery Schuyler	Vol. XXVIII	No. 3	September	1910	pp. 183-212.

Unknown Westminster Abbey	W. G. Fitz-Gerald	Vol. XXI	No. 3	March	1907	pp. 205-214.
Vassar, Wellesley and Smith Colleges	Montgomery Schuyler	Vol. XXXI	No. 5	May	1912	pp. 513-538.
Villa Lante	Edward S. Gales	Vol. VIII	No. 2	Oct.-Dec.	1898	pp. 117-124.
Villa Narcissus, Capri	Charles de Kay	Vol. XII	No. 1	May	1902	pp. 71-92.
W. K. Vanderbilt Residence--"Idlehour"		Vol. XIII	No. 5	May	1903	pp. 457-492.
Washington Terminal Station	Theodore Starrett	Vol. XVIII	No. 6	December	1905	pp. 435-446.
West Point	Montgomery Schuyler	Vol. XIV	No. 6	December	1903	pp. 463-492.
Wetmore Residence, Long Island, NY	J. Lawrence Aspinwall	Vol. XIII	No. 3	March	1903	pp. 279-291.
White Enameled Building--Reliance Building, Chicago	Charles Jenkins	Vol. IV	No. 3	Jan.-Mar.	1895	pp. 299-306.
White House in Washington	Montgomery Schuyler	Vol. XIII	No. 4	April	1903	pp. 359-388.
Whitehall Building--an Experiment in Color	Russell Sturgis	Vol. XIV	No. 1	July	1903	pp. 69-73.
Yale University	Montgomery Schuyler	Vol. XXVI	No. 6	December	1910	pp. 393-416.

CITIES

Additions to Chicago's Skyline	Peter B. Wight	Vol. XXVIII	No. 1	July	1910	pp. 15-24.
Along the Harlem River Branch		Vol. XXIV	No. 6	December	1908	pp. 417-429.
An Architectural Oasis--Naugatuck, Connecticut	A. C. David	Vol. XIX	No. 2	February	1906	pp. 135-144.
Architectural Anarchy in Patterson, New Jersey	Criticaster	Vol. XIX	No. 3	March	1906	pp. 207-213.
Architecture in Philadelphia and a Coming Change	Huger Elliot	Vol. XXIII	No. 4	April	1908	pp. 295-310.
Architecture in the Billionaire District of New York	Franz K. Winkler	Vol. XI	No. 2	October	1901	pp. 679-699.
Architecture of Kansas City	Frank M. Howe	Vol. XV	No. 2	February	1904	pp. 135-157.
Architecture of London	Barr Ferree	Vol. V	No. 1	July-Sept.	1895	pp. 1-30.
Architecture of Mexico City	Montgomery Schuyler	Vol. XXXII	No. 3	September	1912	pp. 215-229.
Architecture of Mexico City, Part II	Montgomery Schuyler	Vol. XXXII	No. 5	November	1912	pp. 405-422.
Art Gallery of the New York Streets	Russell Sturgis	Vol. X	No. 1	July	1900	pp. 93-112.
Art in the City--Paris and New York	Jean Schopfer	Vol. XII	No. 6	November	1902	pp. 573-583.
Boston Suburban Architecture	Frank Chouteau Brown	Vol. XXI	No. 4	April	1907	pp. 245-280.
Brick Building in London	D. N. B. Sturgis	Vol. XIV	No. 6	December	1903	pp. 444-452.
Bronxville-a Picturesque American Suburb	Theodore R. Tuttle	Vol. XVI.	No. 3	September	1904	pp. 167-185.
Building in Salt Lake City	Franz K. Winkler	Vol. XXII	No. 1	July	1907	pp. 14-37.
Building of Cincinnati	Montgomery Schuyler	Vol. XXIII	No. 5	May	1908	pp. 337-366.
Building of Seattle	Herbert Croly	Vol. XXXII	No. 1	July	1912	pp. 1-22.
Canberra--the New Australian Capital	J. E. M.	Vol. XXXII	No. 5	November	1912	pp. 423-430.
City Planning Studies for Albany	Rawson W. Haddon	Vol. XXXV	No. 2	August	1914	pp. 170-174.
Colonial Annapolis	T. Henry Randall	Vol. I	No. 3	Jan.-Mar.	1892	pp. 309-343.
Edgartown--Doorways of an Old Whaling Village	Grace Norton Rosé	Vol. XXXIII	No. 1	January	1913	pp. 55-65.
Furnishing of a City--Paris	Jean Schopfer	Vol. XIII	No. 1	January	1903	pp. 42-48.
Hellerau--a German Garden City	John T. Klaber	Vol. XXXV	No. 2	February	1914	pp. 151-161.
How a Rich Man May Live in Paris	Maurice Guillemot	Vol. XIV	No. 2	August	1903	pp. 79-91.
Living in Paris on an Income of $3,000 a Year	Fernand Mazade	Vol. XIII	No. 4	April	1903	pp. 349-357.
How and Where to Live in Paris on $3,000 a Year, Part II	Fernand Mazade	Vol. XIII	No. 5	May	1903	pp. 423-432.
How to Live in Paris on $3,000 a Year, Part III	Fernand Mazade	Vol. XIII	No. 6	June	1903	pp. 548-554.
Impressions of Budapest	**Schuyler M. Meyer**	**Vol. XXVI**	**No. 6**	**December**	**1910**	**pp. 428-447.**
Innovations in the Street Architecture of Paris	A. C. David	Vol. XXIV	No. 2	August	1908	pp. 109-128.
Master Builder of Brabant	Albert H. Michelson	Vol. XXII	No. 2	September	1907	pp. 195-213.
Michigan Boulevard, Chicago	Peter B. Wight	Vol. XXVII	No. 4	April	1910	pp. 285-293.
New Fifth Avenue	A. C. David	Vol. XXII	No. 1	July	1907	pp. 1-13.
New Rochelle, New York		Vol. XXV	No. 4	April	1909	pp. 235-248.
New San Francisco	A. C. David	Vol. XXXI	No. 1	January	1912	pp. 1-26.
New York as the American Metropolis	Herbert Croly	Vol. XIII	No. 3	March	1903	pp. 193-206.
New York Building Law	William J. Fryer, Jr	Vol. I	No. 1	July-Sept.	1891	pp. 69-82.
Nouveautiés de Paris	Montgomery Schuyler	Vol. X	No. 4	April	1901	pp. 361-397.
Old New Orleans	Aymar Embury II	Vol. XXX	No. 1	July	1911	pp. 85-98.
Old Siena	Katherine Budd	Vol. XXIX	No. 5	May	1911	pp. 411-432.
Opening the Center of Denver	Charles Mulford Robinson	Vol. XIX	No. 4	May	1906	pp. 365-367.
Parisian Doorways of the Eighteenth Century	Russell Sturgis	Vol. XIX	No. 2	February	1906	pp. 123-134.

Passy--A Parisian Suburb	Frederic Lees	Vol. XII	No. 7	December	1902	pp. 669-683.
Past Century Charm of New Bedford	Grace Norton Rosé	Vol. XXXIII	No. 5	May	1913	pp. 424-433.
Philadelphia	Brabazon and Fitz-Gibbon	Vol. XXXIV	No. 1	July	1913	pp. 1-88.
Pittsburgh	Montgomery Schuyler	Vol. XXX	No. 3	September	1911	pp. 204-282.
Planning for Seattle's Future	Charles Mulford Robinson	Vol. XXXI	No. 2	February	1912	pp. 165-170.
Portland, Oregon	Herbert Croly	Vol. XXXI	No. 6	June	1912	pp. 591-607.
Promised City of San Francisco	Herbert Croly	Vol. XIX	No. 5	June	1906	pp. 425-436.
Recent Philadelphia Architecture	Thomas Nolan	Vol. XXIX	No. 3	March	1911	pp. 215-264.
Reconstructed Business House Fronts in New York	Alred H. Taylor	Vol. XVI	No. 1	July	1904	pp. 13-25.
Renovation of the New York Brownstone District	Herbert Croly	Vol. XIII	No. 6	June	1903	pp. 555-571.
Round About Los Angeles	Montgomery Schuyler	Vol. XXIV	No. 6	December	1908	pp. 430-440.
Saragossa, Spain	Katherine C. Budd	Vol. XIX	No. 4	May	1906	pp. 327-343.
Stonington, Connecticut	M. W. Pentz	Vol. XXXII	No. 3	September	1912	pp. 230-237.
Suburban Architecture in Philadelphia	Thomas Nolan	Vol. XIX	No. 3	March	1906	pp. 167-193.
Toledo	M. Stapley	Vol. XXX	No. 5	November	1911	pp. 417-431.
Transformation of Paris Under Napoleon III	Edward R. Smith	Vol. XXII	No. 1	August	1907	pp. 121-133.
Transformation of Paris Under Napoleon III, Part II	Edward R. Smith	Vol. XXII	No. 2	September	1907	pp. 227-238.
Transformation of Paris Under Napoleon III, Part III	**Edward R. Smith**	**Vol. XXII**	**No. 5**	**November**	**1907**	pp. 369-385.
Transformation of Paris Under Napoleon III, Part IV	Edward R. Smith	Vol. XXII	No. 6	December	1907	pp. 490-506.
Transformation of paris Under Napoleon III, Part V	Edward R. Smith	Vol. XXIII	No. 1	January	1908	pp. 21-38.
Utilitarian Architecture at Chicago	Peter B. Wight	Vol. XXVII	No. 2	February	1910	pp. 189-198.
Utilitariam Architecture at Chicago, Part II	Peter B. Wight	Vol. XXVII	No. 3	March	1910	pp. 249-257.
Vienna: Development of a Great City	Otto Wagner	Vol. XXXI	No. 5	May	1912	pp. 484-500.
Wonder of Rimini	Claude Bragdon	Vol. XVIII	No. 5	November	1905	pp. 355-366.

EXHIBITIONS

1911 Exhibition of the Architectural League of New York		Vol. XXIX	No. 4	April	1911	pp. 335-346.
Alaska-Yukon-Pacific Exposition		Vol. XXVI	No. 1	July	1909	pp. 24-32.
Architectural League of New York Exhibition		Vol. XXXIII	No. 3	March	1913	pp. 217-230.
Brussels Exposition--1910	Francis S. Swales	Vol. XXVIII	No. 6	December	1910	pp. 405-424.
Chicago Architectural Club Exhibition	Roy A. Lippincott	Vol. XXXIII	No. 6	June	1913	pp. 567-573.
Franco-British Expositions	Robert W. Carden	Vol. XXIV	No. 2	August	1908	pp. 83-97.
French Universal Exposition of 1900	Alphonse de Calonne	Vol. V	No. 3	Jan.-Mar.	1896	pp. 217-226.
German Exhibit of Arts and Crafts	Irving Pond	Vol. XVII	No. 2	February	1905	pp. 119-125.
Last Words about the Worlds' Fair	Montgomery Schuyler	Vol. III	No.1	Jan.-Mar.	1894	pp. 291-301.
Lessons of the Chicago World's Fair	Moore and Burnham	Vol. XXXIII	No. 1	January	1913	pp. 34-44.
Louisiana Purchase Exposition in St. Louis	Franz K. Winkler	Vol. XV	No. 4	April	1904	pp. 337-360.
Milan International Exhibition	Robert C. Carden	Vol. XX	No. 5	November	1906	pp. 353-368.
Pan-American Exposition	Herbert Croly	Vol. XI	No. 2	October	1901	pp. 590-614.
Panama-Pacific Exposition		Vol. XXIX	No. 5	May	1911	pp. 397-400.

GENERAL

Alphabet of Architecture	H. W. Desmond	Vol. III	No.1	July-Sept.	1893	pp. 29-47.
Alphabet of Architecture, Part II	H. W. Desmond	Vol. IV	No. 4	Apr.-June	1895	pp. 477-506.
Appeal to Caesar	C. Francis Osborne	Vol. I	No. 3	Jan.-Mar.	1892	pp. 281-285.
Architect and the Critic	**H. W. Desmond**	**Vol. XIX**	**No. 4**	**April**	**1906**	pp. 279-281.
Architect in History	A. L. Frothingham	Vol. XXV	No. 3	March	1909	pp. 179-192.
Architect in History, Part II	A. L. Frothingham	Vol. XXV	No. 4	April	1909	pp. 281-303.
Architect in History, Part III	A. L. Frothingham	Vol. XXVI	No. 1	July	1909	pp. 55-70.
Architect in History, Part IV	A. L. Frothingham	Vol. XXVI	No. 2	August	1909	pp. 140-152.
Architect's Proper Sphere	W. R. Ware	Vol. XXVII	No. 2	February	1910	pp. 173-174.
Architects of Fashion	Leopold Eidlitz	Vol. III	No. 4	Apr.-June	1894	pp. 347-353.
Architectural Treatment of Blank Walls		Vol. XXVII	No. 3	March	1910	pp. 227-233.
Architecture and the Housing Problem	C. Matlack Price	Vol. XXXIV	No. 3	September	1913	pp. 240-247.

Architecture as a Fine Art	William Nelson Black	Vol. I	No. 3	Jan.-Mar.	1892	pp. 295-307.
Architecture in Miniature	Alwyn T. Covell	Vol. XXXV	No. 3	March	1914	pp. 262-268.
Architecture of Ideas	Arthur C. David	Vol. XV	No. 4	April	1904	pp. 361-384.
Art and Life	Herbert D. Croley	Vol. I	No. 2	Oct.-Dec.	1891	pp. 219-227.
Authority in Architectural Design	John Beverley Robinson	Vol. VI	No. 1	July-Sept.	1896	pp. 71-80.
By Way of Introduction	Harry Desmond	Vol. 1	No. 1	July-Sept.	1891	pp. 3-6.
Criticism that Counts	Herbert Croly	Vol. X	No. 4	April	1901	pp. 398-405.
Decorative Art	Candace Wheeler	Vol. IV	No. 4	Apr.-June	1895	pp. 409-413.
Design, Drawing and Thinking	William R. Ware	Vol. XXVI	No. 3	September	1909	pp. 159-166.
Development of Architecture	H. W. Desmond	Vol. III	No.1	Oct.-Dec.	1893	pp. 175-185.
Do Architects Read?	Samuel Howe	Vol. XXXII	No. 6	December	1912	pp. 565-570.
Do Architects Read?, Part II	Samuel Howe	Vol. XXXIII	No. 1	January	1913	pp. 82-90.
Education of an Architect	Henry Rutgers Marshall	Vol. V	No. 1	July-Sept.	1895	pp.82-92.
Evil Effects of Competitive Bidding on Building Contracts	George C. Nimmons	Vol. XXIII	No. 1	January	1908	pp. 47-51.
Expression in Architecture	Henry Rutgers Marshall	Vol. IX	No. 3	Jan.-Mar.	1900	pp. 254-267.
History from a Garret	H. W. Desmond	Vol. IX	No. 1	July-Sept.	1899	pp. 51-64.
In the Cause of Architecture	**Frank Lloyd Wright**	**Vol. XXIII**	**No. 2**	**February**	**1908**	**pp. 155-222.**
In the Cause of Architecture	Frank Lloyd Wright	Vol. XXXV	No. 5	May	1914	pp. 405-413.
Influence of the French School on U.S. Architecture	Ernest Flagg	Vol. IV	No. 2	Oct.-Dec.	1894	pp. 211-228.
Lessons from Architectural Aberrations	John Beverley Robinson	Vol. XXVII	No. 2	February	1910	pp. 175-188.
Modern American Architecture and European Cities	**Stanley D. Adshead**	**Vol. XXIX**	**No. 2**	**February**	**1911**	**pp. 113-126.**
Modern Architecture	Montgomery Schuyler	Vol. IV	No. 1	July-Sept.	1894	pp. 1-13.
Musical Ideals of Architecture	H. Toler Booraem	Vol. IV	No. 3	Jan.-Mar.	1895	pp. 283-298.
Musical Ideals of Architecture, Part II	H. Toler Booraem	Vol. IV	No. 4	Apr.-June	1895	pp. 379-392.
New Architecture	**A. C. David**	**Vol. XXVIII**	**No. 6**	**December**	**1910**	**pp. 389-404.**
Old Wine in New Bottles	H. Toler Booraem	Vol. XXVI	No. 4	October	1910	pp. 296-300.
Orders According to Julien Mauclerc	John J. Klaber	Vol. XXXIII	No. 6	June	1913	pp. 492-500.
Our Acquired Architecture	Montgomery Schuyler	Vol. IX	No. 3	Jan.-Mar.	1900	pp. 277-314.
Outlook and Inlook Architecture	John Gaken Howard	V. XXXIV	No. 6	December	1913	pp. 531-543.
Paucity of Ideas in American Architecture	F. W. Fitzpatrick	Vol. XXIV	No. 5	November	1908	pp. 395-396.
Plea for Beauty	Alfred Hoyt Granger	Vol. XVIII	No. 2	August	1905	pp. 161-166.
Plea for Indigenous Art	George W. Maher	Vol. XXI	No. 6	June	1907	pp. 429-433.
Present System of Architectural Changes	Arne Dehli	Vol. XV	No. 6	June	1904	pp. 545-552.
Problems of National American Architecture	Robert Kerr	Vol. III	No.1	Oct.-Dec.	1893	pp. 121-132.
Professional Standing of the Architect		Vol. XXVI	No. 4	October	1910	pp. 239-242.
Relation of Sculpture to Architecture	Edward R. Smith	Vol. XIII	No. 6	June	1903	pp. 493-507.
Relation of Sculpture to Architecture, Part II	Edward R. Smith	Vol. XIV	No. 1	July	1903	pp. 29-49.
Reminiscences of Russell Sturgis	Peter B. Wright	Vol. XXVI	No. 2	August	1909	pp. 123-131.
Serio-Piffle Architecture	Ellis Parker Butler	Vol. XXVIII	No. 5	November	1910	pp. 329-334.
Shoddiness of American Building Construction	George C. Nimmons	Vol. XXIII	No. 1	January	1908	pp. 52-54.
Significance of Architectural Form	H. Toler Booraem	Vol. XXV	No. 3	March	1909	pp. 193-202.
Socialism and the Architect	Charles Henry Israels	Vol. XVII	No. 4	April	1905	pp. 329-335.
Some Handicaps of Provincial Architecture	E. C. Gardner	Vol. IX	No. 4	April	1900	pp. 405-423.
Superiority of the French-Trained Architect	Theodore Wells Pietsch	Vol. XXV	No. 2	February	1909	pp. 110-114.
The Architect	Wilfred Beach	Vol. XXXV	No. 5	May	1914	pp. 425-434.
The Architect, Part II	Wilfred Beach	Vol. XXXV	No. 6	June	1914	pp. 519-525.
The Architect, Part III	Wilfred Beach	Vol. XXXV	No. 1	July	1914	pp. 25-30.
The Architect, Part IV	Wilfred Beach	Vol. XXXV	No. 2	August	1914	pp. 143-147.
The Client	J. M. Rosé	Vol. XXX	No. 5	November	1911	pp. 441-450.
Thought and Expression in Architecture	W. L. Mowll	Vol. XXVII	No. 4	April	1910	pp. 294-298.
Value of the Curve in Street Architecture	**H. A. Caparn**	**Vol. XVII**	**No. 3**	**March**	**1905**	**pp. 231-236.**
Vicissitudes of Architecture	Leopold Eidlitz	Vol. I	No. 4	Apr.-June	1892	pp. 471-484
Vicissitudes of Architecture	Leopold Eidlitz	Vol. IV	No. 2	Oct.-Dec.	1894	pp. 147-156.
What is Architecture	Harry W. Desmond	Vol. I	No. 2	Oct.-Dec.	1891	pp. 199-218.
What is Civic Art?	Herbert Croly	Vol. XVI	No. 1	July	1904	pp.47-52.
What is Indigenious Architecture?	Herbert Croly	Vol. XXI	No. 6	June	1907	pp. 434-442.

INSTITUTIONS

American Academy in Rome	Charles Henry Cheney	Vol. XXXI	No. 3	March	1912	pp. 243-255.
Columbia University	Percy C. Stuart	Vol. X	No. 1	July	1900	pp. 1-21.
Columbia University School of Architecture	A. D. F. Hamlin	Vol. XXI	No. 5	May	1907	pp. 321-336.
Cornell University College of Architecture	Gertrude S. Martin	Vol. XXII	No. 1	July	1907	pp. 38-55.
École des Beaux Arts and its Influence on Education	A. D. F. Hamlin	Vol. XXIII	No. 4	April	1908	pp. 241-248.
École des Beaux Arts--Its Influence on our Architecture	J. Stewart Barney	Vol. XXII	No. 5	November	1907	pp. 333-342.
École des Beaux Arts--What it Means	Paul Cret	Vol. XXIII	No. 5	May	1908	pp. 367-371.
Harvard University Department of Architecture	H. Langford Warren	Vol. XXII	No. 1	August	1907	pp. 135-150.
Influence of the École des Beaux Arts in England	Francis S. Swales	Vol. XXVI	No. 6	December	1910	pp. 417-427.
L'Ecole des Beaux-Arts	Ernest Flagg	Vol. III	No.1	Jan.-Mar.	1894	pp. 302-313.
L'Ecole des Beaux-Arts, Part II	Ernest Flagg	Vol. III	No. 4	Apr.-June	1894	pp. 419-428.
L'Ecole des Beaux-Arts, Part III	Ernest Flagg	Vol. IV	No. 1	July-Sept.	1894	pp. 38-43.
La Poignée--a New Artistic Society in Paris	Pierre Calmettes	Vol. XIII	No. 6	June	1903	pp. 535-547.
MIT's School of Architecture	F. W. Chandler	Vol. XXI	No. 6	June	1907	pp. 443-458.
Student Life at the École des Beaux Arts	George S. Chappell	Vol. XXVIII	No. 1	July	1910	pp. 37-41.
Student Life at the École des Beaux Arts, Part II	George Chappell	Vol. XXVIII	No. 5	November	1910	pp. 350-355.
Student Life at the École des Beaux Arts, Part III	**George S. Chappell**	**Vol. XXIX**	**No. 2**	**February**	**1911**	**pp. 139-144.**
University of Pennsylvania	Percy C. Stuart	Vol. X	No. 3	February	1901	pp. 313-336.
Washington University School of Architecture	Louis C. Spiering	Vol. XXII	No. 5	November	1907	pp.385-396.

LANDSCAPE ARCHITECTURE

American Gardens	George F. Pentecost, Jr.	Vol. XIII	No. 5	May	1903	pp. 437-452.
Andalusian Gardens	Arthue G. Byne	Vol. XXIX	No. 5	May	1911	pp. 371-378.
Chicago parks and their landscape architecture		Vol. XXIV	No. 1	July	1908	pp. 19-30.
City Gardens	George F. Pentecost, Jr.	Vol. XIV	No. 1	July	1903	pp. 50-61.
English Pleasure Gardens	A. C. David	Vol. XIII	No. 4	April	1903	pp. 335-348.
Informal Outdoor Art	H. A. Caparn	Vol. XIII	No. 3	March	1903	pp. 259-269.
Landscape Architecture in and About Chicago	Anthony Hunt	Vol. XXXII	No. 1	July	1912	pp. 53-64.
Landscape Design and the Designer of Landscape	H. A. Caparn	Vol. XXXI	No. 5	May	1912	pp. 539--546.
Landscape Gardening	George F. Pentecost, Jr.	Vol. XXVIII	No. 1	July	1910	pp. 42-50.
Monumental Work of Landscape Architecture	Sylvester Baxter	Vol. XXV	No. 6	June	1909	pp. 389-399.
Sicilian Hill Gardens	George Porter Fernald	Vol. XXV	No. 2	February	1909	pp. 81-92.
Treatment of the Pergola	Alex E. Hoyle	Vol. XXIX	No. 4	April	1911	pp. 319-326.
Villa Garden	George F. Pentecost, Jr.	Vol. XI	No. 3	January	1902	pp. 61-68.

MATERIALS

Architectural Treatment of Concrete Structures	M. M. Sloan	Vol. XXIX	No. 5	May	1911	pp. 401-406.
Architectural Treatment of Concrete Structures, Part II	M. M. Sloan	Vol. XXX	No. 2	August	1911	pp. 165-174.
Architectural Treatment of Concrete Structures, Part III	M. M. Sloan	Vol. XXX	No. 5	November	1911	pp. 487-494.
Architectural Treatment of Concrete Structures, Part IV	M. M. Sloan	Vol. XXXI	No. 1	January	1912	pp. 69-80.
Decorative Work in Iron and Bronze	Charles de Kay	Vol. XV	No. 6	June	1904	pp. 509-530.
Glass: Its Adaptability in Building	Edgar H. Bostock	Vol. XXVII	No. 4	April	1910	pp. 350-358.
Iron Accessories in Domestic Architecture	M. Stapley	Vol. XXIX	No. 4	April	1911	pp. 301-309.
Metals in Decoration	Charles de Kay	Vol. XVI.	No. 2	August	1904	pp. 141-159.
Modern Mosaic in England	Lewis F. Day	Vol. II	No.1	July-Sept.	1892	pp. 79-88.
Modern Mosaics, Part II	Isabella de Barbieri	Vol. IV	No. 3	Jan.-Mar.	1895	pp. 277-281.
Modern Use of Bronze and Iron Decorations, Part II	Charles de Kay	Vol. XVI	No. 1	July	1904	pp. 27-45.
Mosaic as an Independent Art	Isabella de Barbieri	Vol. II	No. 3	Jan-Mar.	1893	pp. 291-301.
Ornamental Metal Work and Wire Glass	J. K. Freitag	Vol. XX	No. 2	August	1906	pp. 137-145.
Recent Brickwork in New York	A. C. David	Vol. XIII	No. 2	February	1903	pp. 144-156.
Return to Stone	W. S. Adams	Vol. IX	No. 2	Oct.-Dec.	1899	pp. 203-209.

Street Plan of a City's Business District	Charles Mulford Robinson	Vol. XIII	No. 3	March	1903	pp. 234-247.
What Paris Does for Open Air	Jean Schopfer	Vol. XIII	No. 2	February	1903	pp. 157-168.

REGION/STATE

Architecture in Southern California	Elmer Grey	Vol. XVII	No. 1	January	1905	pp. 1-17.
Architecture of the Pacific Northwest	Robert C. Sweatt	Vol. XXVI	No. 3	September	1909	pp. 167-175.
Asia Minor	Gorham P. Stevens	Vol. XXXI	No. 2	February	1912	pp. 129-138.
Colonial Architecture in the West		Vol. XX	No. 4	October	1906	pp. 341-346.
Current European Architecture		Vol. XXVII	No. 3	March	1910	pp. 241-248.
Haunt of Teutonic Knights	Charles de Kay	Vol. IX	No. 1	July-Sept.	1899	pp. 1-20.
Recent Euopean Architecture		Vol. XXVII	No. 4	April	1910	pp. 311-320.
Sicily, the Garden of the Mediterranean	Albert M. Whitman	Vol. VI	No. 3	Jan.-Mar.	1897	pp. 289-309.
Some Notes from the Rhine Valley	G. A. T. Middleton	Vol. IX	No. 4	April	1900	pp 325-332.
Suburban Residences of the Pacific Northwest		Vol. XXVIII	No. 1	July	1910	pp. 51-60.
The Old and New South	Russell F. Whitehead	Vol. XXX	No. 1	July	1911	pp. 1-56.

STYLES

Acanthus Motive and Egg-and-Dart Moulding	William H. Goodyear	Vol. IV	No. 1	July-Sept.	1894	pp. 88-116.
American Style of Architecture	Barr Ferree	Vol. I	No. 1	July-Sept.	1891	pp. 39-45.
An Architect's Opinion of L'Art Nouveau	**Hector Guimard**	**Vol. XII**	**No. 2**	**June**	**1902**	pp. 127-133.
Architecture and the "Arts and Crafts"	Elmer Grey	Vol. XXI	No. 8	February	1907	pp. 131-134.
Art Nouveau	S. Bing	Vol. XII	No. 3	August	1902	pp. 279-286.
Art Nouveau in Turin	Alfredo Melani	Vol. XII	No. 6	November	1902	pp. 585-599.
Art Nouveau at Turin, Part II	Alfredo Melani	Vol. XII	No. 7	December	1902	pp. 734-750.
Battle of Styles	Professor A. D. F. Hamlin	Vol. I	No. 3	Jan.-Mar.	1892	pp.261-275.
Battle of Styles, Part II	Professor A. D. F. Hamlin	Vol. I	No. 4	Apr.-June	1892	pp. 405-413.
Byzantine Architecture	Professor Aitchison	Vol. I	No. 1	July-Sept.	1891	pp.83-95.
Byzantium Architecture, Part II	Professor Aitchison	Vol. I	No. 2	Oct-Dec.	1891	pp. 236-239.
Byzantine Architecture, Part III	Professor Aitchison	Vol. I	No. 3	Jan.-Mar.	1892	pp. 347-362.
Byzantine Architecture, Part IV	Professor Aitchison	Vol. I	No. 4	Apr.-June	1892	pp. 485-495.
Byzantine Architecture, Part V	Professor Aitchison	Vol. II	No.1	July-Sept.	1892	pp. 93-99.
Byzantine Architecture, Part VI	Professor Aitchison	Vol. II	No. 2	Oct.-Dec.	1892	pp. 193-208.
Byzantine Architecture, Part VII	Professor Aitchison	Vol. II	No. 3	Jan.-Mar.	1893	pp. 341-350
Byzantine Architecture, Part VIII	Professor Aitchison	Vol. II	No. 4	Apr.-June	1893	pp. 493-500.
Choices in Architectural Styles	Edward A. Freeman	Vol. I	No. 4	Apr.-June	1892	pp. 391-400.
Colonial Building in New Jersey	William Nelson Black	Vol. III	No.1	Jan.-Mar.	1894	pp. 245-262.
Colonial Buildings of Rensselaerwick	Marcus T. Reynolds	Vol. IV	No. 4	Apr.-June	1895	pp. 415-438.
Conventional Patterns	William Henry Goodyear	Vol. II	No. 4	Apr.-June	1893	pp. 391-418.
Curves in Medieval Italian Architecture	William H. Goodyear	Vol. VI	No. 4	Apr.-June	1897	pp. 481-508.
Difficulties of Modern Architecture	Professor A. D. F. Hamlin	Vol. I	No. 2	Oct.-Dec.	1891	pp.134-150.
Early Byzantine Churches and French Cathedrals	William Goodyear	Vol. XVI.	No. 2	August	1904	pp. 116-140.
Early Christian Architecture of Rome	William P. P. Longfellow	Vol. IV	No. 4	Apr.-June	1895	pp. 395-403.
Early Renaissance and Sculpture	Banister Fletcher, Jr.	Vol. II	No. 4	Apr.-June	1893	pp. 419-442.
Early Renaissance Churches	Banister F. Fletcher	Vol. II	No.1	July-Sept.	1892	pp. 31-43.
Early Renaissance in France	G. A. T. Middleton	Vol. VI	No. 2	Oct.-Dec.	1896	pp. 126-133.
English Georgian Architecture	G. A. T. Middleton	Vol. IX	No. 2	Oct.-Dec.	1899	pp. 97-114
Fads in Architecture	George Keister	Vol. I	No. 1	July-Sept.	1891	pp. 49-61.
French Dining-Room of the Upper Middle-Class Type	Fernand Mazade	Vol. V	No. 1	July-Sept.	1895	pp. 35-45.
Georgian and Greek Revival Wotk in the South	J. Robie Kennedt, Jr.	Vol. XXI	No. 3	March	1907	pp. 215-221.
Georgian Work in Charleston, South Carolina	J. Robie Kennedy	Vol. XIX	No. 4	April	1906	pp. 283-294.
Good Things in Modern Architecture	Russell Sturgis	Vol. VIII	No.1	July-Sept.	1898	pp. 92-110.
Gothic Revival in New York City	Montgomery Schuyler	Vol. XXVI	No. 1	July	1909	pp. 46-54.
Grammar of the Lotus	William H. Goodyear	Vol. II	No. 2	Oct.-Dec.	1892	pp. 165-183.

Greek Horizontal Curves	William H. Goodyear	Vol. IV	No. 4	Apr.-June	1895	pp. 446-463.
Greek Revival in the Far South	J. Robie Kennedy	Vol. XVII	No. 5	May	1905	pp. 389-399.
History of Old Colonial Architecture	Montgomery Schuyler	Vol. IV	No. 3	Jan.-Mar.	1895	pp. 312-366.
Interview on Art Nouveau with Alexandre Charpentier	Gabriel Mourey	Vol. XII	No. 2	June	1902	pp. 121-125.
Lotiform Origin of the Greek Anthemion	William H. Goodyear	Vol. III	No.1	Jan.-Mar.	1894	pp. 263-290.
Lotiform Origin of the Ionic Capital	William H. Goodyear	Vol. III	No.1	Oct.-Dec.	1893	pp. 137-164.
Modern Architecture--A Conversation	Harry W. Desmond	Vol. I	No. 3	Jan.-Mar.	1892	pp. 276-280.
National Style of Architecture	J. Stewart Barney	Vol. XXIV	No. 5	November	1908	pp. 381-386.
New World and the New Art	Herbert Croly	Vol. XII	No. 2	June	1902	pp. 135-153.
Optical Refinements in Mediaeval Architecture	William H. Goodyear	Vol. VI	No. 1	July-Sept.	1896	pp. 1-16.
Refinements in Medieval Churches	Charles S Hastings	Vol. XXVI	No. 2	August	1909	pp. 132-139.
Revival of French Gothic Architecture	L. R. McCabe	Vol. XXXIV	No. 3	September	1913	pp. 202-212.
Romanesque in Spain	M. Stapley	Vol. XXXI	No. 4	April	1912	pp. 389-406.
Romanesque in Spain, Part II	M. Stapley	Vol. XXXI	No. 5	May	1912	pp. 471-484.
Romanesque Revival in America	Montgomery Schuyler	Vol. I	No. 2	Oct.-Dec.	1891	pp. 151-198.
Style in American Architecture	Ralph Adams Cram	Vol. XXXIV	No. 3	September	1913	pp. 232-239.
The Romanesque Revival in New York	Montgomery Schuyler	Vol. I	No. 1	July-Sept.	1891	pp. 8-38.
Trefoil and Palmette	A. D. F. Hamilton	Vol. VIII	No.1	July-Sept.	1898	pp. 27-47

TYPES

A Modern Cathedral	R. W. Gibson	Vol. I	No. 3	Jan.-Mar.	1892	pp. 286-294.
A Modern Cathedral, Part II	R. W. Gibson	Vol. I	No. 4	Apr.-June	1892	pp. 435-447.
American Country Estate	Herbert Croly	Vol. XVIII	No. 1	July	1905	pp. 1-7.
Apartment House	H. W. Frohne	Vol. XXVII	No. 3	March	1910	pp. 205-217.
Apartment House Interiors	Costen Fitz-Gibbon	Vol. XXXV	No. 1	January	1914	pp. 58-69.
Architects' Houses	John Beverley Robinson	Vol. III	No.1	Oct.-Dec.	1893	pp. 188-206.
Architects' Houses, Part II	John Beverley Robinson	Vol. III	No.1	Jan.-Mar.	1894	pp. 229-240.
Architects' Houses, Part III	John Beverley Robinson	Vol. III	No. 4	Apr.-June	1894	pp. 354-383.
Architects' Houses, Part IV	John Beverley Robinson	Vol. IV	No. 1	July-Sept.	1894	pp. 45-74.
Architectural Refinements in French Cathedralsl	William H. Goodyear	Vol. XVI	No. 5	November	1904	pp. 439-463.
Architectural Refinements in French Cathedrals, Part II	William H. Goodyear	Vol. XVI	No. 6	December	1904	pp. 569-590.
Architectural Refinements in French Cathedrals, Part III	William H. Goodyear	Vol. XVII	No. 1	January	1905	pp. 19-41.
Architecture and Factories	Robert Kohn	Vol. XXV	No. 2	February	1909	pp. 131-136.
Art of the High Building	**Barr Ferree**	**Vol. XV**	**No. 5**	**May**	**1904**	**pp. 445-466.**
Bank Buildings of Baltimore		Vol. XXII	No. 2	August	1907	pp. 79-101.
Bellevue-Stratford,Belvedere, & Willard Hotels	A. C. David	Vol. XVII	No. 3	March	1905	pp. 167-188.
Bridges and the New York Art Commission	Montgomery Schuyler	Vol. XXII	No. 6	December	1907	pp. 469-475.
Building a Church for a Small Congregation	Herbert Wheaton Congdon	Vol. XXVII	No. 2	February	1910	pp. 161-172.
Building a Parisian House	A. Master Mason	Vol. XIV	No. 3	September	1903	pp. 157-165.
Building the House of Moderate Cost	Robert C. Spencer. Jr.	Vol. XXXI	No. 6	June	1912	pp. 608-615.
Building the House of Moderate Cost, Part II	Robert C. Spencer	Vol. XXXII	No. 1	July	1912	pp. 37-46.
Building the House of Moderate Cost, Part III	Robert C. Spencer	Vol. XXXII	No. 2	August	1912	pp. 109-120.
Building the House of Moderate Cost, Part IV	Robert C. Spencer	Vol. XXXII	No. 3	September	1912	pp. 238-249.
Building the House of Moderate Cost, Part V	Robert C. Spence	Vol. XXXII	No. 5	November	1912	pp. 431-444.
Building the House of Moderate Cost, Part VI	Robert C. Spencer	Vol. XXXIII	No. 2	February	1913	pp. 157-162.
Building the House of Moderate Cost, Part VII	Robert C. Spencer	Vol. XXXIII	No. 4	April	1913	pp. 350-358.
Christian Altars and their Accessories	Caryl Coleman	Vol. IV	No. 3	Jan.-Mar.	1895	pp. 251-275.
Christian Altars and their Acceesories, Part II	Caryl Coleman	Vol. V	No. 3	Jan.-Mar.	1896	pp. 245-275
Clark Estate Houses--A Residence Block		Vol. XX	No. 5	November	1906	pp. 405-410.
Constructive Asymmetry in Medieval Italian Churches	William H. Goodyear	Vol. VI	No. 3	Jan.-Mar.	1897	pp. 376-405.
Contemporary Apartment Building in New York City	H. W. Frohne	Vol. XXVIII	No. 1	July	1910	pp. 61-70.
Contemporary New York Residence	Herbert Croly	Vol. XII	No. 7	December	1902	pp. 704-722.
Contemporary Suburban Residence		Vol. XI	No. 3	January	1902	pp. 69-81.
Cooperative Group Planning	David E. Tarn	Vol. XXXIV	No. 5	November	1913	pp. 467-475.
Corner Houses in Paris	P. Frantz Marcou	Vol. VI	No. 3	Jan.-Mar.	1897	pp. 310-322.
Country and Suburban Houses		Vol. XXVI	No. 5	November	1910	pp. 309-380.

Country Home	William J. Fryer, Jr.	Vol. II	No. 3	Jan.-Mar.	1893	pp. 286-290.
Country House and Garden	Clara Ruge	Vol. XXII	No. 4	October	1907	pp. 311-322.
Country House in California	Herbert Croly	Vol. XXXIV	No. 6	December	1913	pp. 483-519.
Country Houses		Vol. XXVIII	No. 4	October	1910	pp. 233-310.
Country Houses		Vol. XXX	No. 4	October	1911	pp. 305-398.
Country Houses		Vol. XXXIV	No. 4	October	1913	pp. 273-365.
Decoration of Costly residences	Russell Sturgis	Vol. XIII	No. 5	May	1903	pp. 397-422.
Decoration of the Smaller Suburban House in England	Banister Fletcher	Vol. XI	No. 2	October	1901	pp. 641-665.
Design Without Ornament--Chicago Warehouses	Peter B. Wight	Vol. XXIX	No. 2	February	1911	pp. 167-177.
Early American Churches	Aymar Embury II	Vol. XXX	No. 6	December	1911	pp. 584-596.
Early American Churches,Part II	Aymar Embury II	Vol. XXXI	No. 1	January	1912	pp. 57-68.
Early American Churches, Part III	Aymar Embury II	Vol. XXXI	No. 2	February	1912	pp. 153-164.
Early American Churches, Part IV	Aymar Embury II	Vol. XXXI	No. 3	March	1912	pp. 256-266.
Easly American Churches, Part V	Aymar Embury II	Vol. XXXI	No. 4	April	1912	pp. 417-426.
Early American Churches, Part VI	Aymar Embury II	Vol. XXXI	No. 5	May	1912	pp. 547-556.
Early American Churches, Part VII	Aymar Embury II	Vol. XXXI	No. 6	June	1912	pp. 629-638.
Early American Churches, Part VIII	Aymar Embury II	Vol. XXXII	No. 1	July	1912	pp. 81-90.
Early American Churches, Part IX	Aymar Embury II	Vol. XXXII	No. 2	August	1912	pp. 159-168.
Early American Churches, Part X	Aymar Embury II	Vol. XXXII	No. 3	September	1912	pp. 257-266.
Early American Churches, Part XI	Aymar Embury II	Vol. XXXII	No. 5	November	1912	pp. 453-464.
Early Business Buildings in San Francisco	Agnes Foster Buchanan	Vol. XX	No. 1	July	1906	pp. 15-32.
Early Dutch Houses in New Jersey	John T. Boyd, Jr.	Vol. XXXV	No. 1	July	1914	pp. 31-48.
Early Dutch Houses in New Jersey, Part II	John T. Boyd, Jr.	Vol. XXXV	No. 2	August	1914	pp. 148-158.
East Hampton, Long Island--Summer Houses	Charles De Kay	Vol. XIII	No. 1	January	1903	pp. 19-33.
Economic Development of Building Estates	George F. Pentecost, Jr.	Vol. XXV	No. 4	April	1909	pp. 275-280.
Economy of the Office Building	George Hill	Vol. XV	No. 4	April	1904	pp. 313-327.
English Farmsteads	G. A. T. Middleton	Vol. XII	No. 5	October	1902	pp. 514-536
English House Architecture	Russell Sturgis	Vol. XX	No. 2	August	1906	pp. 81-91.
English Playhouse	Hamilton Bell	Vol. XXXIII	No. 3	March	1913	pp. 262-271.
English Playhouse, Part II	Hamilton Bell	Vol. XXXIII	No. 4	April	1913	pp. 359-368.
English Roadside Cottages	Alex E. Hoyle	Vol. XXIX	No. 2	February	1911	pp. 127-138.
English Suburbs and Provences	Banister Fletcher	Vol. V	No. 4	Apr.-June	1896	pp. 321-346.
Episcopal Thrones and Pulpits	Caryl Coleman	Vol. XI	No. 1	July	1901	pp. 441-463.
Evolution of the Modern Warehouse	A. O. Elzner	Vol. XXI	No. 5	May	1907	pp. 379-384.
Evolution of the Suburban Railway Station	J. H. Phillips	Vol. XXXV	No. 2	August	1914	pp. 122-127.
Famous Roman Courtyards	M. D. Walsh	Vol. XXXI	No. 1	January	1912	pp. 81-90.
Federal Building in Cleveland	Herbert Croly	Vol. XXIX	No. 3	March	1911	pp. 193-214.
Fortress-Monasteries of the Holy Land	William G. Fitzgerald	Vol. XIX	No. 4	April	1906	pp. 275-278.
French Cathedrals	Barr Ferree	Vol. I	No.1	Oct.-Dec.	1892	pp. 125-135.
French Cathedrals, Part II	Barr Ferree	Vol II	No. 3	Jan.-Mar.	1893	pp. 302-323.
French Cathedrals, Part III	Barr Ferree	Vol. III	No.1	July-Sept.	1893	pp. 87-95
French Cathedrals, Part IV	Barr Ferree	Vol. III	No. 4	Apr.-June	1894	pp. 387-418.
French Cathedrals, Part V	Barr Ferree	Vol. V	No. 3	Jan.-Mar.	1896	pp. 276-287.
French Cathedrals, Part VI	Barr Ferree	Vol. V	No. 4	Apr.-June	1896	pp. 363-377
French Cathedrals, Part VII	Barr Ferree	Vol. VI	No. 1	July-Sept.	1896	pp. 21-28.
French Cathedrals, Part VIII	Barr Ferree	Vol. VI	No. 2	Oct.-Dec.	1896	pp. 145-162.
French Cathedrals, Part IX	Barr Ferree	Vol. VI	No. 3	Jan.-Mar.	1897	pp. 323-334.
French Cathedrals, Part X	Barr Ferree	Vol. VI	No. 4	Apr.-June	1897.	pp. 469-480.
French Cathedrals, Part XI	Barr Ferree	Vol. VII	No. 1	July-Sept.	1897	pp. 98-103.
French Cathedrals, Part XII	Barr Ferree	Vol. VII	No. 2	Oct.-Dec.	1897	pp. 125-142.
French Cathedrals, Part XIII	Barr Ferree	Vol. VII	No. 3	Jan.-Mar.	1898	pp. 333-356.
French Cathedrals, Part XV	Barr Ferree	Vol. VIII	No.1	July-Sept.	1898	pp. 49-65.
French Cathedrals, Part XVI	Barr Ferree	Vol. VIII	No. 2	Oct.-Dec.	1898	pp. 168-179.
French Farm Buildings	Anatole Girard	Vol. XIII	No. 4	April	1903	pp. 299-321.
Garden Apartments of California	E. M. Roorbach	Vol. XXXIV	No. 6	December	1913	pp. 520-530.
Greek Temple	Jean Schopfer	Vol. XVII	No. 6	June	1905	pp. 441-470.
Harvard Club, New York City	Herbert Croly	Vol. XIX	No. 3	March	1906	pp. 195-198.
Havana Tabacco Co.--the World's Finest Shop	A. C. David	Vol. XVII	No. 1	January	1905	pp. 43-49.

Hildesheim and its Churches	J. Kirke Paulding	Vol. II	No.1	July-Sept.	1892	pp. 9-29.
Historical Monuments of France	Russell Sturgis	Vol. IV	No. 3	Jan.-Mar.	1895	pp. 308-311.
How to Get a Well-Designed House	William Herbert	Vol. XXV	No. 4	April	1909	pp. 221-234.
Last Dutch Farmhouses in New York	Mildred Stapley	Vol. XXXII	No. 1	July	1912	pp. 23-36.
Making of a Museum	L. T. Gratacap	Vol. IX	No. 4	April	1900	pp. 376-402.
Modern American Residence		Vol. XVI.	No. 4	October	1904	pp. 297-406.
Modern Church Edifices	Elmer Grey	Vol. XXXIV	No. 6	December	1913	pp. 544-556.
Modern French Château	Frederic Lees	Vol. XXI	No. 7	January	1907	pp. 42-50.
Modern French Interiors	Russell Sturgis	Vol. XVIII	No. 1	July	1905	pp. 75-85.
Modern Hospitals in Europe	Alphonse de Calonne	Vol. VI	No. 1	July-Sept.	1896	pp. 29-51.
Modern House in Paris	Paul Frantz Marcou	Vol. II	No. 3	Jan.-Mar.	1893	pp. 324-331.
Modern Office Building--Some Practical Limits	George Hill	Vol. II	No. 4	Apr.-June	1893	pp. 445-468.
Monastic Architecture in Russia	Charles A. Rich	Vol. IX	No. 1	July-Sept.	1899	pp. 21-49.
Monumental Engineering	Montgomery Schuyler	Vol. XI	No. 2	October	1901	pp. 615-640.
New Bridges in New York City	Montgomery Schuyler	Vol. XVIII	No. 4	October	1905	pp. 243-262.
New New York Houses	Montgomery Schuyler	Vol. XXX	No. 5	November	1911	pp. 451-474.
New Public Buildings in Washington	Leilla Mechlin	Vol. XXIV	No. 3	September	1908	pp. 180-206.
New Theaters of New York	A. C. David	Vol. XV	No. 1	January	1904	pp. 39-54.
New Use of Old Forms--Two Houses by Pope	Herbert Croley	Vol. XVII	No. 4	April	1905	pp. 271-293.
New York Apartment Houses	Charles H. Israels	Vol. XI	No. 1	July	1901	pp. 477-508
New York Flats and French Flats	Hubert, Pirsson & Hoddick	Vol. II	No.1	July-Sept.	1892	pp. 55-64.
New York Hotels	William Hutchins	Vol. XII	No. 5	October	1902	pp. 459-471.
New York Hotels, Part II	William Hutchins	Vol. XII	No. 6	November	1902	pp. 621-635.
New York House	Montgomery Schuyler	Vol. XIX	No. 2	February	1906	pp. 83-103.
Old Church at Rockingham, Vermont	H. W. Desmond	Vol. XIV	No. 2	August	1903	pp. 93-106.
Our Four Big Bridges	Montgomery Schuyler	Vol. XXV	No. 3	March	1909	pp. 147-161.
Parisian Apartment Houses	Maurice Saglio	Vol. V	No. 4	Apr.-June	1896	pp.347-361.
Parisian Houses of Four Cardinals	Frederic Lees	Vol. XXIV	No. 1	July	1908	pp. 31-44.
Pennsylvania Farmhouses	Aymar Embury II	Vol. XXX	No. 5	November	1911	pp. 475-486.
Perspective Illusions in Midieval Italian Churches	William H. Goodyear	Vol. VI	No. 2	Oct.-Dec.	1896	pp. 163-183.
Private Residences for Banking Firms	A. C. David	Vol. XIV	No. 1	July	1903	pp. 13-27.
Properiety of Decoration in Business Places	Philip S. Tyre	Vol. XXIX	No. 5	May	1911	pp. 433-435.
Recent American Country Houses		Vol. XXXII	No. 4	October	1912	pp. 271-360.
Recent Apartment House Design	Franz K. Winkler	Vol. XI	No. 3	January	1902	pp. 98-109.
Recent Bank Buildings		Vol. XXV	No. 1	January	1909	pp. 1-66.
Recent Church Building in New York	Montgomery Schuyler	Vol. XIII	No. 6	June	1903	pp. 508-534.
Recent Railway Stations in American Cities	Harold D. Eberlein	Vol. XXXV	No. 2	August	1914	pp. 98-121.
Recent Sea Shore Residences Along the Atlantic Coast		Vol. XXVIII	No. 2	August	1910	pp. 78-138.
Renaissance in Commercial Architecture	C. Matlack Price	Vol. XXXI	No. 5	May	1912	pp. 449-470.
Rich Men and their Homes	Herbert Croly	Vol. XII	No. 1	May	1902	pp. 27-32.
School Buildings of New York	John Beverley Robinson	Vol. VII	No. 3	Jan.-Mar.	1898	pp. 359-384.
Sculpture as Applied to Paris Houses	Fernand Mazade	Vol. VI	No. 2	Oct.-Dec.	1896	pp. 134-143.
Shop Fronts From Paris		Vol. XXVI	No. 2	August	1909	pp. 113-122.
Sixteenth- and Seventeenth-Century Parisian Mansions	Frederic Lees	Vol. XXVI	No. 3	September	1909	pp. 210-230.
Sky-scraper up to Date	Montgomery Schuyler	Vol. VIII	No. 3	Jan.-Mar.	1899	pp. 231-257.
Small City House in New York	Montgomery Schuyler	Vol. VIII	No. 4	Apr.-June	1899	pp. 357-388.
Smaller Houses of the English Suburbs amd Provinces	Banister Fletcher	Vol. VI	No. 2	Oct.-Dec.	1896	pp. 114-125.
Some Apartment Houses in Chicago		Vol. XXI	No. 8	February	1907	pp. 119-130.
Some Buildings in St. Louis	William Herbert	Vol. XXIII	No. 5	May	1908	pp. 391-396.
Some California Bungalows		Vol. XVIII	No. 3	September	1905	pp. 217-224.
Some Recent Skyscrapers	Montgomery Schuyler	Vol. XXII	No. 2	September	1907	pp. 161-176.
Some Recent Warehouses	Russell Sturgis	Vol. XXIII	No. 5	May	1908	pp. 373-386.
Southern Colleges	Montgomery Schuyler	Vol. XXX	No. 1	July	1911	pp. 57-84.
Spanish-Mexican Missions of the United States	Olof Z. Cervin	Vol. XIV	No. 3	September	1903	pp. 181-204.
State Buildings at the World's Fair	Montgomery Schuyler	Vol. III	No.1	July-Sept.	1893	pp. 55-71.
Story of the Synagogue	Abram S. Isaacs	Vol. XX	No. 6	December	1906	pp. 464-480.
Suburban Architecture		Vol. XXIII	No. 6	June	1908	pp. 419-502.
Swiss Chalets	Jean Shopfer	Vol. VII	No. 1	July-Sept.	1897	pp. 33-61.

The Bungalow at its Best		Vol. XX	No. 4	October	1906	pp. 296-305.
The Duplex Apartment House		Vol. XXIX	No. 4	April	1911	pp. 327-334.
The Memorial Arch--A National Emblem of Liberty	A. L. Frothingham	Vol. XXIII	No. 1	January	1908	pp. 5-20.
The Perfect Theater	J. E. O. Pridmore	Vol. XVII	No. 2	February	1905	pp. 101-117.
Timber Churches in Norway	Olof Z. Cervin	Vol. XX	No. 2	August	1906	pp. 93-102.
To Curb the Skyscraper	Montgomery Schuyler	Vol. XXIV	No. 4	October	1908	pp. 300-302.
Trinity's Architecture	Montgomery Schuyler	Vol. XXV	No. 6	June	1909	pp. 411-425.
Two German Bridges	Montgomery Schuyler	Vol. XXVII	No. 3	March	1910	pp. 234-240.
Two New York Armories	Montgomery Schuyler	Vol. XIX	No. 4	April	1906	pp. 259-264.
Varick Street	Rawson W. Haddon	Vol. XXXV	No. 1	January	1914	pp. 49-57.
Villas All Concrete	Charles de Kay	Vol. XVII	No. 2	February	1905	pp. 85-100.
Villas of Rome	Marcus T. Reynolds	Vol. VI	No. 3	Jan.-Mar.	1897	pp. 256-288.
Villas of Rome, Part II	Marcus T. Reynolds	Vol. VII	No. 1	July-Sept.	1897	pp. 1-32.
Warehouse and Factory in Architecture	Russell Sturgis	Vol. XV	No. 1	January	1904	pp. 1-17.
Warehouse and Factory in Architecture, Part II	Russell Sturgis	Vol. XV	No. 2	February	1904	pp. 123-133.
Warehouses	Charles H. Patton	Vol. XXVII	No. 4	April	1910	pp. 334-349.
Wooden Houses in France During the Middle Ages	Jean Schopper	Vol. IX	No. 4	April	1900	pp. 333-362.
Wooden Houses in Switzerland	Jean Schopfer	Vol. VI	No. 4	Apr.-June	1897.	pp. 415-428.

TECHNICAL & TECHNOLOGY

Community of Two Great Arts	Fanny Morris Smith	Vol. XII	No. 5	October	1902	pp. 570-572.
Electric Lighting of Modern Office Buildings	William S. Monroe	Vol. VI	No. 2	Oct.-Dec.	1896	pp. 105-113.
Engineering in Architecture	H. W. Frohne	Vol. XXII	No. 1	July	1907	pp. 57-60.
Fireproof Country Homes	George E. Walsh	Vol. XVII	No. 6	June	1905	pp. 509-512.
Fireproofed and Concrete Construction		Vol. XXV	No. 5	May	1909	pp. 309-374.
Frencn Method of Cement Construction	Jean Schopfer	Vol. XII	No. 4	September	1902	pp. 375-391.
Heating of Building	George Hill	Vol. V	No. 2	Oct.-Dec.	1895	pp. 204-211.
Iron Construction in New York City	Louis De Coppet Berg	Vol. I	No. 4	Apr.-June	1892	pp. 448-469
Lineal Perspective	G. A. Middleton	Vol. IV	No. 4	Apr.-June	1895	pp. 464-472.
Linear Perspective	G. A. T. Middleton	Vol. V	No. 4	Apr.-June	1896	pp. 378-381.
Modern Vault Construction	John Beverley Robinson	Vol. VI	No. 4	Apr.-June	1897	pp. 447-459.
New French Method of Cement Construction	Jean Schopfer	Vol. XII	No. 3	August	1902	pp. 271-278.
Principles of Architectural Composition	John Beverly Robinson	Vol. VIII	No.1	July-Sept.	1898	pp. 1-26.
Principles of Architectural Composition, Part II	John Beverley Robinson	Vol. VIII	No. 2	Oct.-Dec.	1898	pp. 181-223.
Principles of Architectural Composition, Part III	John Beverly Robinson	Vol. VIII	No. 3	Jan.-Mar.	1899	pp. 297-331.
Principles of Architectural Composition, Part IV	John Beverly Robinson	Vol. VIII	No. 4	Apr.-June	1899	pp. 434-465
Problems of Design in Reinforced Concrete	H. Toler Booraem	Vol. XXIII	No. 4	April	1908	pp. 249-268.
Reenforced Concrete Construction	Governor Hill	Vol. XII	No. 4	September	1902	pp. 392-412.
Sanitation of Dwellings in England	Banister F. Fletcher	Vol. VIII	No. 4	Apr.-June	1899	pp. 407-422.
Simple Ways of Fireproofing	Russell Sturgis	Vol. XIII	No. 2	February	1903	pp. 119-133.
Skeleton Construction	**William J. Fryer, Jr.**	**Vol. I**	**No. 2**	**Oct.-Dec.**	**1891**	**pp. 228-235.**
Three-Dimensions in Architectural Drawing	Arthur G. Byne	Vol. XXXIV	No. 3	September	1913	pp. 193-201.
Thrifty Draughtsmanship	J. T. Toppy, Jr.	Vol. XXXI	No. 6	June	1912	pp. 616-620.
Unscientific Enquiry into Fireproof Building	Russell Sturgis	Vol. IX	No. 3	Jan.-Mar.	1900	pp. 229-253.
What do we know about Lighting?	F. Laurent Godinez	Vol. XXXIII	No. 3	March	1913	pp. 255-261.
What do we know about Lighting, Part II	F. Laurent Godinez	Vol. XXXIII	No. 4	April	1913	pp. 369-378.
What do we know about Lighting?, Part III	F. Laurent Godinez	Vol. XXXIII	No. 5	May	1913	pp. 457-468.
What do we know about Lighting?, Part IV	F. Laurent Godinez	Vol. XXXIII	No. 6	June	1913	pp. 574-580.
What do we Know about Lighting?, Part VII	F. Laurent Godinez	Vol. XXXV	No. 1	January	1914	pp. 80-93.
What do we know about Lighting?, Part VIII	F. Laurent Godinez	Vol. XXXV	No. 4	April	1914	pp. 375-383.
What do we know about Lighting?, Part IX	F. Laurent Godinez	Vol. XXXV	No. 5	May	1914	pp. 443-449.
What do we Know about Lighting, Part X	F. Laurent Godinez	Vol. XXXV	No. 1	July	1914	pp. 69-73.